REGIONAL SECURITY REGIMES

SUNY Series in Israeli Studies
Russell Stone, Editor

REGIONAL SECURITY REGIMES

Israel and Its Neighbors

edited by

Efraim Inbar

State University
of New York
Press

Published by
State University of New York Press, Albany

The research on this book was made possible by, and supported by, the BESA (Begin-Sadat) Center for Strategic Studies at Bar-Ilan University

Production by Susan Geraghty
Marketing by Dana Yanulavich

Printed in the United States of America

For information, address State University of New York Press, State University Plaza, Albany, N.Y., 12246

Library of Congress Cataloging-in-Publication Data

Regional security regimes : Israel and its neighbors / edited by
Efraim Inbar.
p. cm.—(SUNY series in Israeli studies)
Includes bibliographical references and index.
ISBN 0-7914-2323-9 — ISBN 0-7914-2324-7 (pbk.)
1. Israel—Foreign relations—Arab countries—Congresses. 2. Arab countries—Foreign relations—Israel—Congresses. 3. Israel—Strategic aspects—Congresses. 4. Arab countries—Strategic aspects—Congresses. 5. Israel-Arab conflicts—Congresses. 6. Security, International—Congresses. I. Inbar, Efraim, 1947–. II. Series.
DS119.8.A65R44 1995
327.569140174927—dc20 94-5046
CIP

10 9 8 7 6 5 4 3 2 1

CONTENTS

INTRODUCTION

Israel's present strategic environment is characterized by the continued existence of severe threats to its territorial integrity and population, as well as by improved chances to reach a peaceful modus vivendi with its neighbors. As Israel is gradually accepted by the Arab world, purely security considerations, rather than ideological or symbolic ones, will become that much more significant to the Arab-Israeli relationship.

This relationship is also influenced by systemic developments. Although the emergence of the new international system is having a mixed impact on the Middle East and Israel's security, it can be argued that the changes taking place inside and outside the Middle East may be conducive to the development of better relations between Israel and its Arab neighbors.

Yet peace, as understood in the West, is probably not within reach in the Middle East. Any expectation that Israel will have fundamentally different relations with the Arab states than the Arabs have among themselves is totally unrealistic. The neighboring Arab states cannot be expected to behave differently toward Israel than they behave toward their Arab brethren. Therefore, the current peace process, even if successful, cannot result in borders as peaceful as those between Canada and the United States. Such a pattern of relations as that along the American-Canadian border is nonexistent anywhere in the Middle East. Yet, the present conditions do seem conducive for the creation of a security regime—a politico-military structure more modest than peace but probably more realistic.

This volume is the product of an international conference organized by the BESA Center for Strategic Studies at Bar-Ilan University in June 1992 on Security Regimes: Israel and Its Neighbors. The planning for the conference began, immediately following the center's inauguration in May 1991. Its purpose was to discuss ways to enhance regional security in the core area of the Middle East. The developments leading to the Madrid Conference

(October 1991) and the ensuing bilateral and multilateral talks on peace and cooperation in the Middle East region made the scholarly gathering at the BESA Center particularly timely.

Despite the plethora of works on the Arab-Israeli conflict, the concept of security regime has rarely been applied to that arena. Yet, this concept is a useful analytical tool to explore the politico-military arrangements that could evolve into a more peaceful relationship between Israel and its neighbors. Especially as we remember that past experience in the area of security arrangements with Egypt, Syria, and Jordan has not been totally negative. The conceptual framework of security regimes concerns itself with the creation of international rules of behavior in situations when war and the states' individualistic pursuit of security is seen as very costly. Such regimes, once established, tend to foster moderation, cooperation and reduced chances for interstate violence. They arise under restrictive conditions, primarily with the realization by several actors of the difficulties in securing their desired outcomes unilaterally.

In the first chapter of the book, Charles Lipson helps to clarify the concept of security regime, reviewing the literature that studies the establishment of international regimes. He points out that a realistic perspective toward international relations, one that assumes the existence of an anarchic universe populated by actors pursuing their narrow interests, does not preclude the existence of cooperative security arrangements. By elaborating on two historical cases, the Concert of Europe and U.S.-Soviet relations, Lipson concludes that, despite serious obstacles, relatively equal powers can sometimes create security regimes.

Within such a theoretical framework, Yaacov Bar-Siman-Tov discusses in Chapter 2 the conditions and the learning process that led Israel, Egypt, and Jordan in the past to establish formal or informal security regimes. He argues that, in a protracted conflict such as the Arab-Israeli dispute, security regimes are a necessary, but not sufficient, condition for the shift from war to peace, which involves a learning process in which the parties redefine goals and means and even change their modes of thinking the conflict and about each other.

The next two chapters deal with important extraregional actors, as they consider the importance of systemic factors to regional security and the chances of erecting a security regime. Robert Lieber, in Chapter 3, analyzes U.S. Middle East policy in the developing international system during and after the Persian Gulf Crisis (1990–1991). He elaborates on the American commitments to this area of the world and emphasizes that the challenges to stability may be less military than political. He doubts the ability of the United States to impose its will on regional actors; however, he claims that a security regime cannot be sustained without the active engagement of the United States, because no other outside power or collective body can be a substitute for America, which has in the past provided the incentives and assurances necessary to help foster and maintain agreements. Although the new international circumstances have enhanced the American role, domestic developments may undermine American commitments.

Chapter 4 looks at the United Nations as a second extra-regional actor. Avi Beker emphsizes that a more active role for this organization is an inevitable result of the end of superpower competition. The struggle against Saddam Hussein in the Gulf War was a prime example. Although collective security can be successful only in such extreme cases, a more realistic role for the United Nations is to maintain peacekeeping operations. Such operations can be useful in the establishment of a security regime in the Arab-Israeli arena. Past experiences of troops under the U.N. flag in the Middle East and elsewhere are not entirely negative; progress in the peace process might produce greater willingness to incorporate a U.N. component into an emerging security regime.

The next four chapters of this volume deal with regional actors and regional developments. In Chapter 5 Bruce Maddy-Weitzman and Joseph Kostiner review recent thinking in the Arab world regarding a "new Arab order," both in the political and security spheres and conclude that, despite voices in the Arab world demanding greater cooperation, the legacy of past failed attempts to build viable security structures has been dominant. They analyze the attempts to translate this thinking into reality in the period after the Gulf War and look at the March 1991 "Damascus Declaration," which was intended as a blueprint for fashioning the postwar in the Middle East. Despite the ambitions of its architects the plan to establish an Arab regional security system failed. Nevertheless, the authors indicate that the marginalization of Arab radicalism and the increased American leverage in the Arab world portend well for Israel and make the Arab-Israeli conflict more "ripe" for progress toward a resolution.

Less optimistic is Aharon Klieman in Chapter 6. He turns our attention to one facet of the Arab-Israeli conflict, the Israeli-Jordanian relationship, which he terms a tacit security regime. The author reviews how this particular regime originated and how it has been maintained. He concludes that this quite effective and successful security regime is under growing strain and might soon collapse because of strains upon each actor.

In Chapter 7, Eyal Zisser turns to analyzing Syrian-Israeli relations, analyzing the new, rather careful, Syrian policy toward Israel, the changes in Syria's national security concept, and the possibilities of reaching a modus vivendi between the two rival countries in the near future. Because Syria adamantly opposes any interim agreements, the road appears to be leading to a comprehensive settlement only, although one that must incorporate security arrangements.

Arms control is one such key arrangement. In Chapter 8, Gerald Steinberg analyzes several global arms control regimes and finds them rather inadequate, considering Middle East variables and requirements. He suggests greater reliance on regional structures and enhanced verification systems, as well as linking the various arms control regimes that operate independent of each other.

Chapters 9, 10, and 11 deal with nonmilitary aspects of the security regime creation process. Chapter 9 examines psycho-cultural factors. In what he describes as a speculative essay, Adam Garfinkle argues that cultural characteristics play a major role in how questions of war and peace play out in the Middle East, while at the same time acknowledging that moving from cultural analysis to the political-military level is problematic. Yet, the author's analysis leads to several conclusions concerning the preferences and propensities of Arab leaders that are not very comforting. They aspire to acquire nonconventional weapons and have few inhibitions in using them. Deterrence is difficult to achieve because political equilibrium is seen as unnatural and undesirable, and threats necessary to establish deterrence are viewed mostly as bluffs.

Chapters 10 and 11 assess the possibilities for cooperation in areas that are not directly connected to security. Amikam Nachmani reviews the problem of water shortages in the Middle East and points out that depleted resources might become the cause of growing conflict. Cooperation among states in linking national water systems is a concept that faces formidable political obstacles. In light of such reluctance, the author suggests that desalination (a unilateral solution) is the only realistic hope for overcoming water scarcity in the Middle East.

In Chapter 11, Gil Feiler discusses the potential for scientific and technological cooperation between Israel and the Arab states in a postboycott era. Egypt is given particular attention because of its prominent economic and political role in the region and its lead in establishing relations with the Jewish state. The author concludes that political factors will continue to overshadow consideration of potential benefits in any mutual scientific and technological ventures. Therefore, this arena can hardly be expected to serve as a bridge between the parties to the conflict in the absence of political detente.

In the final chapter, Efraim Inbar and Shmuel Sandler look at Israel's strategic doctrine and identify reasons for a greater likelihood of an Israeli move away from its traditional preference for unilateral measures, toward a greater willingness to accept collaborative schemes as embodied in a security regime. Some of the effects of the change in the international system, the erosion of deterrence, a reduced ability to act effectively in a unilateral way, and the implications of the peace process—all contribute to the conditions that might cause Israel to pay greater attention to the possibility of erecting a security regime with its neighbors.

Overall, this volume investigates the chances for bringing about the establishment of a security regime between Israel and the Arabs. It assesses the chances for fostering greater restraint and cooperation (tacit or open) among the protagonists and the ways to achieve a regional climate conducive to such cooperation. Although the contributors were not chosen for their particular attitude toward the Arab-Israeli conflict, most display a rather cautious optimism about the direction the protracted conflict is taking. The analysis suggests the dominance of political factors in the emerging political equation at the expense of other considerations. The American role is considered by most authors to be very important, although the regional powers have the final say over any amelioration in relations between the parties to the conflict.

The Middle East is a very dynamic region. Policy-oriented scholarship that focuses on contemporary developments faces the problem of irrelevance by the time of publication. Ideally, the contributions to this volume will not be overtaken by events, and time (and reviewers) will judge this collection favorably.

Stuart Cohen, Shmuel Sandler, and Gerald Steinberg, who served on the organizing committee of the conference, helped to develop the conceptual flow of the intellectual enterprise and assisted in the choice of suitable participants. Special thanks are due to Sharon Harpak, my devoted assistant, who worked very hard to make the conference a success. I also wish to express my appreciation to Ben Mollov for his valuable assistance in the editing if this book.

The late Avner Yaniv, an emminent scholar on Israel's national security, had intended to deliver a lecture at the conference, but passed away two days before it convened. The conference participants, his colleagues and friends, have decided to dedicate the conference and this volume to his memory and hope their contributions match his high standards of scholarship. May his memory be for a blessing.

PART 1

Conceptual and Historical Background

CHAPTER 1

Are Security Regimes Possible? Historical Cases and Modern Issues

Charles Lipson

There are two basic and opposing views about how states should provide security for themselves. According to the dominant realist view, states should arm themselves to deter wars if possible and to fight them if necessary. They should supplement their own strength through military alliances, while recognizing that allies are necessarily impermanent because of shifting state interests. At the other extreme, idealists have argued that recurrent warfare underscores the bankruptcy of traditional diplomacy, which is premised on national self-help. Their grandest aspiration is to transcend balance-of-power politics, based on alliances, and to forge a comprehensive system of peace, based on collective security. Collective security, in this sense, is a universal alliance in which all states pledge to support any prospective victim of aggression. It is an "all for one" system rather than a standard system of counterpoised alliances.[1]

Both views, and their polar opposition, are well-known. Indeed, the modern study of international politics began with the articulation of realism by Hans Morgenthau, E. H. Carr, George Kennan, and others in the late 1940s.[2] They definitively rejected collective security as utopian legalism and supported American rearmament. They wanted to limit the tasks of new international organizations to well-defined common problems such as European reconstruction, rather than the provision of universal security. At the same time, they distanced themselves from the most popular rationale for active American involvement around the world: rabid anticommunism. They understood that the most ideological form of anticommunism was simply another kind of utopian policy, one with no inherent limits on the global tasks America should perform or the price it should pay.[3]

The realists' intellectual victory was aided mightily by the tragedies of twentieth-century European history. Woodrow Wilson's effort to abolish the old diplomacy, with its secret treaties and rival alliances, had failed to prevent Fascist expansion in the 1930s, failed to create secure borders for smaller states, and failed to overcome the narrow, self-interested diplomacy of the great powers. Italy's 1935 invasion of Abyssinia was recognized as the last, fatal moment of the League of Nations, not only because its sanctions did not deter Italy's conquest but also because it was clear that other major powers were more interested in Italy's value as a future ally than in its current invasion of Ethiopia or its direct violation of the league's covenant.[4] The league simply failed in its most basic purpose, just as it had in 1931, when Japan invaded Manchuria.[5] Once again, the old logic of national military power and alliance politics overrode vague Wilsonian hopes for collective security.

If more proof were needed that collective security was an unattainable goal and a dangerous policy, the late 1940s seemed to provide it. Plans for the United Nations, developed at Dumbarton Oaks in the midst of World War II, were less ambitious than Wilson's Fourteen Points.[6] But they did contain the core idea of collective security, memorialized in the U.N. Charter's Articles 1(1) and 2(5) and institutionalized in the U.N. Security Council.[7] In practice, however, the United Nations was unable to sustain the wartime alliance between the United States and Soviet Union. Their opposition gradually hardened into the basic bipolar structure of postwar politics. By the time the United Nations actually implemented collective security operations in the Korean peninsula, its actions only reinforced the significance of superpower opposition and military power. Indeed, the United Nations could act collectively in Korea only because the Soviets had foolishly walked out of the Security Council proceedings in protest.

These dominant historical events underlined the Realist view that states should recognize the perils of international anarchy and should therefore equip themselves for deterrence and war. Credible military threats of punishment and denial are central to this approach. What makes these observations more than banal pessimism is the idea that if each state pursues its own narrowly self-interested strategy, then no nation may succeed in providing security for itself and each may actually become more insecure. Yet none can escape: each state would be in mortal peril if it did nothing while others armed, even if *all* are worse off by pursuing these narrowly self-interested strategies instead of cooperating to limit armaments. That is the essence of the security dilemma.[8] States are trapped by systemic forces.

The dominance of Realism and the powerful logic of deterrence theory have not prevented others from exploring more cooperative efforts to provide national security—efforts that fall short of utopian collective security but recognize that conflicting national interests are often mixed with other more compatible interests and goals, which can sustain some forms of international cooperation.[9] International politics, then, is not wholly a realm of strife and confrontation, even though military conflicts are a central issue and policy mistakes can be fatal. Rather, states recognize that they often have powerful interests in cooperation and exchange.

Important joint gains are to be captured in many issues: trade, the environment, monetary affairs, arms control, and many other areas. The problem, in other words, is *not* that such social exchanges are unprofitable. The real problem is that they are often difficult to accomplish because information is poor, deception and cheating are possible, and most important, the basic rights of property and contract (and enforcement mechanisms for those rights) are simply absent at the international level.[10]

This perspective, sometimes called *neo-institutional* or *neo-liberal*, is grounded in basic Realist assumptions, particularly the anarchical character of international politics and the preeminence of nation-states as actors. But it concludes that the interaction of national interests produces a more complex terrain of cooperation and conflict.[11] One overriding problem, from this perspective, is to understand how nations can create institutions to capture the potential gains from cooperation, while minimizing the real dangers of deception and nonperformance. In the security arena, the basic aim of this approach is to understand how nations can prevent arms races, diminish the risks of surprise attack, and more generally, ameliorate the effects of the security dilemma.

Some research in this vein compares superpower cooperation in different issues and different regions.[12] These studies are valuable and suggestive even though they do not directly address larger issues of international relations theory. At the same time, other scholars have been developing middle-range theories about international cooperation between countries that are both partners and adversaries. Much of this work draws on game-theoretic ideas about strategic interaction in mixed-motive games, most recently involving games of incomplete information. But the work typically goes beyond an analysis of strategic interaction among nation-states and asks how they can institutionalize patterns of cooperation, improve information about others' preferences and choices, and protect against risks of defection.

Discussion about these institutional issues builds on earlier work dealing with the formation and maintenance of cooperative regimes in specific issues. Most of the regime literature deals with international economic issues, especially trade but also foreign investment, exchange rates, debt, communications, and other high-technology industries. In addition, there is increasing interest in the application of these regime concepts to issues where cooperation has been much more difficult to achieve, particularly security issues such as nuclear proliferation.

We will turn, then, to the starting point of this neo-institutional literature, the study of regimes, and then explore its extension from international economic issues to national security questions.

THE STUDY OF REGIMES

The study of international regimes is designed primarily to understand how cooperation is articulated and institutionalized in specific issues or regions. It focuses on the ways that states establish rules and procedures to moderate and manage the consequences of anarchy and facilitate more specific cooperative agreements.

Although this approach is obviously different from realism (including both traditional realism and neo-realism), it is also different from earlier approaches to international organization. The study of international organizations had become a kind of intellectual backwater by the 1960s. It was characterized mainly by atheoretical research on the internal operations of specific institutions, generally the United Nations and its affiliated organizations.[13] The vast growth of trade and investment in the North

Atlantic and the management of this rising economic interdependence were simply ignored. Rather, these traditional studies of international institutions continued to look at specific organizations (or suborganizations such as the U.N. Secretariat) and ask (1) how they worked and (2) what were their consequences for international politics. This work did not pose a serious challenge to the dominant realism of the day nor to its increasingly scientific specification.[14]

Later research on economic interdependence and regimes shifted that focus substantially and, in the process, redefined and revitalized the study of international organizations.[15] It examined broader patterns of cooperation in key issues and asked (1) what were their basic rules and decision-making procedures and (2) how did particular institutional processes within an issue or area help to constrain state choices and produce regularized, cooperative behavior. Specific institutions, such as the International Monetary Fund, were not ignored but rather were embedded in a broader inquiry into the creation and maintenance of international order.

This new approach was in many ways closer to earlier studies of political integration than to traditional studies of international institutions. The literature on integration, like the subsequent literature on regimes, focused on the creation and management of political order beyond the nation-state, underscoring the central importance of economic issues and nonstate actors.

There were important differences between the study of integration and the study of regimes, however. The most important one is that regime analysis dropped the basic causal dynamic of neo-functional integration theory: the idea that technical solutions to shared regional problems could produce their own, self-reinforcing logic of growing supranational institutions and pooled sovereignty.[16] This focus on technical solutions and their progressive spillover into larger projects of political integration was undermined by events that neo-functionalism could not explain. France simply blocked further integration that did not accord with its own vision of Europe and France's leading place within it.[17] In 1963, President de Gaulle vetoed Britain's entry into the European Economic Community. Later, he boycotted nearly all EEC meetings and provoked a constitutional crisis over basic differences about how the community should function.[18] These disputes, which stymied European integration for years, clearly showed that integration was still a project of nation-states and still, at heart, a matter of high politics.

Neo-functionalist theories of integration could not explain the new political limits on the EEC or the community's lethargic progress in the 1960s and 1970s. Even so, the study of regional integration had produced an important and useful analytic shift, which was later adopted in studies of regimes. The focus moved away from specific institutional procedures toward the management of common international problems.

The regime literature, like that on integration, assumed that important joint gains were to be captured from managing these problems. One difference is that integration literature maintained a clear regional focus. It concentrated on geographic areas where economic interdependence might be linked to political institutionalization.[19] The literature on regimes, by contrast, typically focused on the organization of global issues.[20] Despite this difference, both approaches recognize that many issues are inherently *transnational*. That is, they spill across national borders and cannot be managed effectively by any single nation-state.[21] Indeed, the inability of nation-states to manage such issues, and the possibility of capturing joint gains, provides incentives for both regime creation and regional integration.

These basic foci, particularly the emphasis on political cooperation to manage transnational issues, can be found from the very outset in regime studies.[22] They are linked directly to the search for international rules and convergent expectations as mechanisms for organizing interstate relations in key issues. These concerns are clearly present in Stephen Krasner's influential definition of regimes: "Regimes can be defined as sets of implicit or explicit principles, norms, rules and decision-making procedures around which actors' expectations converge in a given area of international relations. Principles are beliefs of fact, causation, and rectitude. Norms are standards of behavior defined in terms of rights and obligations. Rules are specific prescriptions or proscriptions for action. Decision-making procedures are prevailing practices for making and implementing collective choice."[23] Case studies of specific regimes have proliferated, showing how anarchy's effects can be managed and joint gains captured under diverse conditions. There are important common themes here—recurrent functions performed by successful regimes.[24] By creating an inclusive framework with well-defined norms, *regimes lower the transaction costs* of negotiating and implementing specific agreements.[25] By encouraging repeated transactions, *they lengthen the "shadow of the future."*[26] Such iteration often creates powerful incentives for states to keep their bargains in order to capture a stream of future gains, thus making some agreements self-enforcing.[27]

Regimes can make agreements more transparent by creating mechanisms and institutions to provide information otherwise unavailable or too costly to acquire. Greater transparency does not make betrayal impossible, but it lowers the gains from cheating and deception. In arms control, where cheating is a very real concern, agreements have aimed at raising transparency. There have been prohibitions against encrypting missile test data, for instance, and agreements to permit on-site inspections and surprise visits to military facilities. The real trick is to increase transparency enough to build confidence in the reliability of agreements but not so much that other military secrets are disclosed or sovereignty challenged.

Transparency is a more subtle problem in economic issues. After all, surprise is more important and potentially much more devastating in military affairs than in economic issues.[28] Economic issues are monitored by different actors as well. Private firms such as exporters have ample incentives to monitor others' compliance with economic agreements and report violations to their home government. The more usual problem is that others' noncompliance can be observed, but the reasons for that behavior are murky. This confusion about others' motives and intentions is important because some excuses for nonperformance may be perfectly acceptable and others completely unacceptable, according to the agreement. For example, we know that it is difficult for foreigners to sell products or services within the Japanese market. But is the problem basically one of nontariff barriers imposed by the Japanese government or private preferences and institutional obstacles created by Japanese firms and consumers? Most government-imposed barriers would violate trade agreements; most private barriers would not.

Finally, *regimes can provide or facilitate sanctions for rule violations* (although, in my opinion, they do this less well because sanctioning is typically costly and creates serious collective action problems). In any case, they can sanction either by threats of proscription or by retaliatory actions. The sanctions may either be centralized punishments by formal institutions or, more often, informal and decentralized punishments, principally the exclusion of violators from the future benefits of cooperation among regime participants.

Thus, regimes encourage cooperation by making it rational—by increasing the expected benefits of cooperation and raising the expected costs of noncompliance. If we assume (quite plausibly in many cases) that states are locked into relationships that resemble a Prisoners' Dilemma, then regimes may work by transforming the original PD payoffs (which encourage defection) into more tractable super-games with incentives for sustained cooperation.[29] In doing so, they perform another crucial function: *they stabilize mutual expectations* regarding future behavior and adherence to rules (because cooperation is now more profitable than defection and others understand the incentive structure and current behavior of their partners).

Considerable empirical research has been done on these issues. There are parallel and largely comparable studies of all major international economic issues and many more on important social issues such as the environment. These studies deal with

- foreign investment[30]
- exchange rates[31]
- the trading system[32]
- trade in specific sectors as textiles, autos, commodities, and air travel, among others[33]
- natural resources, the environment, and pollution[34]
- oil[35]
- debt[36]
- telecommunications and data flows[37]
- human rights[38]
- international crimes and moral issues, such as piracy, slavery, counterfeiting, drug trafficking, airplane hijacking, and the killing of endangered species (what Ethan Nadelmann calls *global prohibition regimes*).[39]

These studies typically go beyond specifying rules and norms in specific issues areas. Rather, they aim to understand the incentives and sanctions behind different rules, the logic of bargaining, and the reasons why rules and decision-making procedures develop and change. In an early critical article, Susan Strange argued that the new focus on regimes was too static, dedicated too much to the status quo, and interested too little in change, either normatively or positively.[40] In fact, virtually all regime studies have been deeply concerned with the process, causes, and consequences of international change. Some studies, in fact, are focused almost entirely on the causal mechanisms that underlie changes across regimes. Explanations range from hegemonic decline[41] to surplus production capacity[42] to changes in basic policy ideas and ideology.[43]

As regime studies have proliferated, so has the criticism of this approach.[44] Several accusations are fundamental. First, it is correctly charged that the whole approach is conceptually underdefined and imprecise in specifying key terms, such as rules and norms. In addition, there is epistemological confusion in stressing both convergent expectations (which are intersubjective and cannot be determined objectively) and objective patterns of interstate behavior (rules and procedures) and their causation, which can be investigated through the usual positivist methods. There are also serious limitations to all the general causal mechanisms that have been suggested. In particular, the idea that stable regimes require hegemonic leadership has been subjected to withering criticism on both empirical and theoretical grounds.[45] There are other gaps and problems. The regime approach concentrates on issue and areas, but there is no convincing analysis of how issue-areas are created or linked together.[46] Finally, although we now have dozens of empirical studies of specific regimes, we have no overarching theory about how international politics is fragmented into these distinct regimes, no real explanation of which issues will lack well-formed regimes (or when or why), and no real analysis of how different regimes dovetail with one another to create an overall international system. Taken together, these are serious attacks on the possibilities of creating a true "regime theory."

There is also another angle of attack. This critique points out that regime studies can never amount to a comprehensive approach to international relations, much less a theory, because the basic features of regimes are simply missing in key security issues. True, a well-specified theory of regimes could predict when and where cooperative regimes would form and where they would not, but such a theory could still say little about the character of interaction in basic security issues if they are not likely to develop rules and common expectations about behavior.[47]

This last criticism is important. It underscores the inherent limits of extending the regimes approach even if basic conceptual issues are clarified. Nevertheless, some studies of security regimes have been undertaken, particularly on issues where cooperation has been seriously attempted. Broadly speaking, these studies fall into three areas. One is arms control, where studies deal mainly with nuclear proliferation or superpower arms agreements. There are also studies of particular arms control agreements, but they go beyond the treaty's negotiation and final text to ask about the character of institutions created to deal with treaty interpretation, dispute resolution, and implementation.[48] In this sense, treaties are understood as the focal points of international institutions, often informal ones, that are needed to implement and sustain profitable agreements. Second, there are studies of the one time when multiple Great Powers cooperated for an extended period—the Concert of Europe. The question here is whether the diplomatic interactions can be fruitfully understood in terms of common expectations and rule creation, the language of regimes. Finally, the same questions about stable security cooperation have been raised about the Cold War. Although this work is usually not written as explicit "regime studies," it inquires into the same issues.

In this chapter we will concentrate on the two cases where relatively equal powers created stable forms of cooperation. We will see how regime analysis has been applied and then consider its strengths and limitations.

THE CONCERT OF EUROPE

There have been two periods in modern European history when major powers were able to manage their rivalry successfully for prolonged periods. The first—the Concert of Europe during the early nineteenth century—sustained the coalition that had defeated Napoleon and actually incorporated succeeding French governments. More recently, the United States and Soviet Union managed to set fairly clear rules of diplomatic and military conflict, not only avoiding major war but also averting any direct military engagement. In that sense, they were not only bitter rivals and adversaries but also partners with some important common understandings.

Renewed interest in the Concert of Europe is understandable. It offers a model of successful postwar planning and peaceful interaction among great powers.[49] In the aftermath of the Cold War, such a model is bound to attract attention, particularly so because it is a model of a peaceful *multipolar* world. From the beginning, the concert recognized the basic policy interests of all the great powers, even those of defeated France. Unlike the post-war plans for World War I and World War II, the Peace of Paris avoided any utopian schemes.[50]

The concert was a very deliberate scheme to create a postwar world order.[51] International order was thus deliberately constructed and was not simply the by-product of balance-of-power politics. A key part of that order was an ongoing process of diplomatic communication. Indeed, Richard Elrod defines the Concert of Europe as "the great powers meeting together at times of international crisis to maintain peace and to develop European solutions to European problems. Statesmen who had finally recognized the necessity of cooperation in the last coalition against Napoleon continued to believe in the advantages of collaboration to maintain the postwar settlement."[52]

The Treaty of Chaumont (March 1814), which established the victorious coalition, also pledged to continue that alliance after Napoleon's defeat. C. J. Bartlett, writing of British policy in the period, cites this continuity as the treaty's greatest novelty.[53] The chief aim—at Chaumont and later at the Congress of Vienna—was to prevent any French attempt to overturn the expected peace settlement. But Castlereagh, representing Britain, was disappointed in his broader hopes that the treaty would formally guarantee peace against all great powers (not merely France), settle all disputed European frontiers, and offer protection to the smaller European powers, especially the German states.[54] In other words, the concert would never become a true instrument of collective security. Its aims would be more limited, focused exclusively on the interests of Great Powers and directed against the one state that might harbor hegemonic ambitions. The Congress of Vienna, which began even before Napoleon's final defeat, ratified these basic aims and moved to establish regular, high-level communications among the powers.

These communications were sustained at repeated Europe-wide conferences with very senior representation, from foreign ministers to crowned heads. These meetings did *not* produce joint action, but they were valuable nonetheless. In particular, they allowed great powers to discuss their disputes regarding smaller countries and contested regions and, as a result, avoid threatening each other when they intervened to protect their interests. That is, they facilitated coordination and policy accommodation—a process that was doubtless encouraged by the fundamentally status quo goals of all the major powers except France.

It is also likely that the concert's sustained, high-level diplomatic communication delayed the reemergence of traditional alliance politics until mid-century. This achievement came despite potentially important cleavages among the powers, notably a basic difference between Britain and Austria over the concert's role in suppressing nationalist, democratic movements. Britain, represented by Castlereagh and later Canning, did not see how foreign intervention would contribute to its own security. It simply refused to participate in these antinationalist concert policies. Metternich, who represented an anti-democratic, multinational empire, naturally saw vital stakes in suppressing such social movements.[55] These differences split the great powers and limited their capacity for coherent action, but in spite of all that, the concert did not dissolve into rival alliances.

The absence of direct confrontation between two major powers from the Napoleonic wars until the Crimea (1853–1956) was no small achievement. It was, after all, a turbulent age when nationalist and democratic forces were emerging throughout Europe and challenging the basic principles of multinational empires (Austria, Russia, and the Ottoman Empire, which was rapidly unraveling). The social, economic, and political transformations of that period produced all too many sites for potential conflict. In the 1820s and 1830s, for instance, there were social revolts in Naples, Spain, Greece, Poland, and Belgium—all of them threatening to neighboring powers and more distant monarchies. Some Great Powers did intervene, but they did so in ways that did not threaten their peers, partly because they had communicated their intentions well in advance. Likewise, they managed to resolve several major crises (the Belgian Crisis of 1830–1832, the Near Eastern crisis of 1839–1841, the first Schleswig-Holstein crisis of 1850–1852) with little more than diplomatic maneuvering and small-scale military action.[56] There were somewhat larger conflicts after mid-century. Italian unification produced one war (1859) and German unification three (1864, 1866, 1870).[57] But after the Franco-Prussian War, the major powers did not fight each other again for nearly half a century, not until World War I. Moreover, from the Napoleonic Wars until World War I, there was no systemic war in Europe, a record that differs markedly from the eighteenth century when multipolar wars were commonplace.[58]

This stability was not simply the result of the actors' peaceful predispositions. It was, according to Paul Schroeder, the product of three new systemic arrangements:

- a system of intertwined duties and guarantees for Great Powers, including participation in concert decisions and nonintervention in each other's internal affairs;
- a network of smaller states that served as effective buffers and spheres of influence, at once separating the Great Powers and giving them common tasks to manage;
- arrangements that insulated European politics from extra-European disputes over colonies and informal empires.[59]

Schroeder's careful analysis is not explicitly framed in terms of "security regimes." But in fact he describes a well-articulated regime that combines both formal and informal institutions to produce shared normative understandings, shared rules of behavior, and common expectations about key issues. Schroeder especially underscores the importance and durability of treaty commitments throughout the nineteenth century:

> A variety of procedures and devices strengthened this network of treaty guarantees, including a system of diplomacy of conference and some general principles of a European concert. The latter protected the rights, interests, and equal status of the Great Powers above all, but they also committed these powers to the performance of certain duties connected with those rights—respect for treaties, noninterference in other states' internal affairs, willingness to participate in the Concert's decision and actions, and a general observance of legality and restraint in their international action. This system of guarantees for the rights, status, and existence of the Great Powers, though egre-

giously violated and badly strained in the mid-century wars, managed to make something of a comeback and to endure after a fashion till the turn of the century.[60]

Robert Jervis has analyzed the concert explicitly in regime terms.[61] His findings support the idea that the concert had common understandings, strong norms against efforts to change the status quo by force, and some limited institutionalization. But common understandings and rule adherence are not enough by themselves to define a regime, Jervis argues (quite properly, I think). They could arise from simple deterrence models, which rest solely on states' power capabilities.[62] So could reciprocity, which often arises outside regimes.

Jervis's own argument that the concert is best understood as a security regime is really threefold. First, behavior by Great Powers did show regularity, common understandings, and shared norms. Beyond that, they clearly recognized each other's vital interests, even if they did not always endorse them. Second, states seemed to make policy choices with an eye toward long-term benefits rather than short-term advantages. Their choices indicate that they considered the international political order relatively stable. It was an environment in which reciprocity and self-restraint could flourish because they were profitable, now and into the future. Finally, Jervis argues that, unlike balance-of-power arrangements, the concert did not always reflect the powers' underlying capabilities. Outcomes were relatively autonomous from the current distribution of power—another reflection of institutionalized rules and restraints.[63]

Why, then, did the concert collapse?[64] Jervis's answer is that memories of the destructive Napoleonic Wars slowly faded and new, unsocialized leaders came to power in the wake of the 1848 revolutions. He also observes that controlling revolutions, though a broadly shared goal, also produced conflict because Britain and France were more tolerant of domestic liberties than Russia, Austria, and Prussia. Finally, he notes that the concert, despite its informal rules, restraints, and diplomatic meetings, was not very well institutionalized.

In addition to these important observations about the sources of change, I would add two points. First, the effect of the 1848 revolutions went beyond a change of leadership. The real point was that the revolutions all failed and conservative forces quickly solidified their control over national governments. Such counter-revolution changed the logic of nineteenth international politics in two basic ways. It freed conservative governments from their obsessive concerns with domestic order and allowed them to pursue more ambitious and expansionist international policies without fearing its impact on domestic order. More important, conservatives won their victories in 1848 by presenting themselves as guardians of the nation, as nationalists. This new, ideological basis for governance made it increasingly difficult to reconcile international conflicts, many of which involved contested border regions. The biggest impact was ultimately the creation of a German empire, which not only expanded Prussian power but also eliminated the smaller German states that had served as a defensive buffer in central Europe. Second, even if one acknowledges that the concert ended at mid-century, some of the structural changes reflected in the concert lasted well beyond mid-century. Not only did great powers continue to hold conferences on major issues, they recognized duties, guarantees, and norms such as non-intervention in each other's affairs.[65] Still, the world of the late nineteenth century was a world of shifting alliances, centered on Bismarck's Germany, not a world of inclusive security regimes.

U.S.-SOVIET RELATIONS

If the world of the nineteenth century concert was unusually stable and peaceful, so was the long postwar confrontation between the United States and Soviet Union.[66] True, there were many tense moments and some close calls during the four decades after World War II, beginning with the Berlin blockade (1948–1949) and culminating with the nuclear showdown over Soviet missiles in Cuba. There were also large-scale regional wars throughout the period, many of them with direct or proxy involvement by Washington or Moscow. Several of these disputes could easily have led to larger wars, risking direct engagement between superpower armed forces.[67] Yet all were successfully managed, through a combination of diplomacy, coercive threats, and limited warfare. In the end, Soviet and American troops never met each other face to face on the field of battle. As Gordon Craig and Alexander George observe: "In retrospect, it appears remarkable that all U.S.-Soviet diplomatic confrontations and war-threatening crises—over Berlin, Korea, the Middle East, and Cuba and in South Asia—have been successfully terminated without any kind of shooting war between American and Soviet military forces. The mutual fear of igniting a fuse that could trigger thermonuclear holocaust is undoubtedly the major factor that accounts for this success."[68]

The real success of the Soviet-American relationship was not only that it averted a major war, but that it became increasingly stable over time. Writing in the late 1950s, Albert Wohlstetter could speak of a "delicate balance of terror."[69] Ten years later, the balance of terror had become durable, not delicate. It was stable enough that the nuclear terror receded into the background, even though the United States had half a million soldiers fighting Soviet-backed forces in Southeast Asia. The new, stable balance was founded on secure, second-strike deterrence. Because each side had the assured capacity to retaliate with overwhelming force *after* any nuclear attack, there was no longer a powerful incentive to launch a preemptive first strike if war threatened.[70] As a result, the danger of nuclear war declined significantly even though Cold War tensions rose and fell dramatically during the 1970s and 1980s.

Other aspects of the superpower relationship were stable as well. There were no directly contested borders in Europe after the second Berlin Crisis in 1958, when Khrushchev demanded the withdrawal of Western troops and the establishment of a "Free City of West Berlin."[71] This practical division of the continent remained tacit for decades. The United States simply refused to acknowledge any explicit spheres of influence, because that would concede Soviet control of Eastern Europe. But the division was no less fixed or clear-cut because of its informality. The U.S. did not contest it diplomatically, much less militarily. In particular, successive American presidents refused to encourage revolts within the Warsaw Pact and refused to extend aid when revolts did break out in Germany, Poland, Hungary, and Czechoslovakia.

How extensive were such cooperative arrangements in the midst of wider conflict? Did they really constitute shared rules and norms, with convergent expectations among the parties? How were they institutionalized? These questions go to the heart of whether a Soviet-American security regime really existed during the Cold War.

Broadly speaking, there are three views. One is that the United States and the Soviet Union were adversaries who deterred each other militarily, whose mutual deterrence became more stable over time, but who never produced significant broader understandings or truly shared norms. They were essentially adversaries, not partners, even if they did not go to war. In any case, there is no evidence that a security regime existed because specific political outcomes were closely tied to underlying force distributions. At the other extreme, some have argued that the superpowers developed effective ways of communicating their foreign policies and reconciling their differences, and in the process managed to construct basic "rules of the game" for international politics.[72] These rules—tacit or explicit, formal or informal—are the deliberate product of efforts to avoid common aversions, principally nuclear war. Finally, some scholars argue that *some elements* of superpower security regimes did exist but that they were limited to specific issues and regions and never became more comprehensive. Craig and George state this last position clearly. They conclude that the two superpowers "learned some fundamental 'rules of prudence' for managing their rivalry and for dealing with occasional confrontations without becoming embroiled in warfare."[73] Learning, adaptation, and appropriate behavior (including both crisis management and crisis avoidance) produced a stable peace despite sharp ideological differences. Still, according to this centrist view, it would have been "unrealistic and infeasible" to expect a "*comprehensive* U.S.-Soviet security regime, one that covered all aspects of their security relations."[74]

What is at stake here is not just different views about U.S.-Soviet interactions but different views about how international institutions can mediate international politics. These differences bear on the different ways that regimes may be understood. The strongest version is that regimes matter only if they produce outcomes different from those of underlying power capabilities.[75] A less demanding version is that regimes affect outcomes by codifying basic agreements and creating institutional settings that encourage further cooperation by reducing transaction costs and increasing transparency. In any case, underlying power resources do not yield strong "point predictions" (as its proponents acknowledge). *Institutions can thus facilitate coordination on some equilibria instead of others, encourage mutually profitable agreements by lowering the risks of cheating and deception, and encourage learning and cooperation that is (and must be) consistent with states' power and interests.*

This less demanding definition of regimes is a fruitful way to understand the nature of Soviet-American security cooperation. Cooperation was extensive despite their deep differences over basic political and economic issues and despite their global contest for power and influence. Security cooperation was grounded in the stable character of the nuclear standoff, which reassured both powers about their essential security interests and made clear how truly interdependent they were at the strategic level.

With stable second-strike capacities in place, the superpowers recognized two kinds of gains from cooperation. One was to increase the stability of nuclear deterrence at the margin: to facilitate greater communication in crises, prevent accidental launches and contain any wider consequences if they occurred, and shape nuclear force structures in ways that discouraged fears of surprise attacks. Joseph Nye has shown that this kind of nuclear cooperation and learning was extensive.[76] Indeed, Nye goes on to argue that "the two countries largely agree[d] upon broad and specific injunctions in a number of subissues within the security relationship, and one can argue that a jointly recognized regime exists in such areas."[77] Nye cites regimes that constrained short-run self-interest and reshaped ideas of long-run self-interest in several key areas: (1) destructive power in Europe, (2) prevention of nuclear accidents and control of military forces, (3) nuclear proliferation, and (4) arms-race stability (essentially the acceptance of nuclear parity and limits on offense and defense). Still, Nye notes the ambivalence that surrounded other efforts to limit conventional threats or counterforce targeting.[78]

Second, although the superpowers were often rivals in Africa, Asia, Latin America, and the Middle East, they also had mixed motives in many of those areas. As Roger Kanet and Edward Kolodziej have shown, the superpowers frequently worked together to manage regional conflicts. Their joint aims were "to prevent escalation, to staunch or cut losses, or to focus resources and priorities elsewhere."[79] Alexander George and associates have produced dozens of case studies of cooperation in specific regional security issues, from the Austrian State Treaty to Antarctica, as well as global issues such as arms control.[80] Obviously, such cooperation extended to nuclear proliferation, where both countries had overriding interests in limiting the spread of nuclear technology and delivery systems.

Thus, if regimes are understood as vehicles for learning and coordination, for lowering transaction costs and increasing information flows, and for creating settings where states can mutually restrain their pursuit of short-term gains, then the United States and Soviet Union *did* forge security regimes during the Cold War. Those regimes were not comprehensive; they did not cover all major issues or regions. Nye rightly calls them an incomplete mosaic.[81] They certainly did not imply the cessation of conflict over basic economic and political issues. Nor do they seem to have produced important outcomes divorced from the superpower military balance (although, as noted earlier, it is usually impossible to predict specific outcomes from those force configurations). What these regimes did do was encourage and institutionalize cooperative outcomes where they were supported by underlying configurations of power and interest.

CONCLUSIONS: THE POSSIBILITIES OF SECURITY REGIMES

The analysis of Soviet-American security cooperation and the Concert of Europe shows that relatively equal powers can sometimes create security regimes. These are more than simply the production of orderly patterns of behavior, which may well be precipitated by deterrence and the balance-of-power politics. Regimes must be more than that if they are to be meaningful features of world politics. They are deliberate efforts to manage international affairs to capture joint gains or prevent common losses.[82] They must be premised on some compatible configuration of preferences, reasonable information about others' choices and behavior, and some limits on the risks of cooperating. Obviously, there are serious obstacles to the creation of security regimes. If states view politics as a zero-sum struggle, if they actually desire wars of expansion, if they cannot seek joint gains for domestic political reasons, if they fail to recognize their policy choices are interdependent, if they cannot distinguish each other's offensive and defensive weapons and military deployments, if they are unwilling to reassure other states by permitting adequate verification, then the prospects for security regimes will be poor indeed.[83] Unfortunately, these are recurrent problems in security affairs. They are made more difficult because errors in judgment—including unreciprocated efforts to cooperate—may well be fatal. Therefore, cooperative and conciliatory policies in security issues carry risks that are simply not present in economic issues.[84]

Yet these obstacles are not always present and, even when some are, states can often find important areas of agreement—zones for some common management even if they are not comprehensive. Their aims are typically to avoid catastrophic losses rather than to capture potential gains. But the long peace after both the Napoleonic Wars and World War II indicates that they are well worth pursuing, while trying hard to dampen the very real risks.

NOTES

1. Charles Lipson, "Is the Future of Collective Security Like the Past?" in George Downs, ed., *Collective Security Beyond the Cold War* (Ann Arbor: University of Michigan Press, 1993); Charles A. Kupchan and Clifford A. Kupchan, "Concerts, Collective Security, and the Future of Europe," *International Security* 16 (Summer 1991): 114–61.

2. Hans J. Morgenthau, *Politics Among Nations* (1948; New York: Alfred A. Knopf, 1950); Edward Hallett Carr, *The Twenty Years' Crisis, 1919–1939* (1939; 2d ed., 1946; New York: Harper and Row, 1964); George F. Kennan, "The Sources of Soviet Conduct," *Foreign Affairs* 25 (July 1947): 566–82; John H. Herz, "Idealist Internationalism and the Security Dilemma, " *World Politics* 2 (January 1950): 157–80.

3. This limitless role for American foreign policy and its connection to anticommunism is made clear in President Truman's statement that "it must be the policy of the United States to support free peoples who are resisting attempted subjugation by armed minorities or by outside pressures," which became known as the Truman Doctrine. It is echoed in President Kennedy's inaugural speech, where he pledged America would "pay any price, bear any burden" to preserve freedom around the world." Harry S Truman, "Special Message to Congress on Greece and Turkey," March 12, 1947, in *Papers of the Presidents: Truman, 1947* (Washington, DC: Government Printing Office, 1963), pp. 176–80.

4. F. S. Northedge and M. J. Grieve, *A Hundred Years of International Relations* (London: Duckworth, 1971), pp. 140, 156; J. L. Brierly, "The League of Nations," *New Cambridge Modern History*, vol. 12: *The Shifting Balance of World Forces, 1898–1945*, ed. C. L. Mowat, 2d ed. (Cambridge: Cambridge University Press, 1968), pp. 258–60; Frank Hardie, *The Abyssinian Crisis* (Hamden, Conn.: Archon Books, 1974); Anthony P. Adamthwaite, *France and the Coming of the Second World*

War 1936–1939 (London: Cass, 1977); and George W. Baer, *Test Case: Italy, Ethiopia and the League of Nations* (Stanford, Calif.: Stanford University Press, 1976).

5. Christopher G. Thorne, *The Limits of Foreign Policy: The West, the League and the Far Eastern Crisis of 1931–33* (New York: G. P. Putnam, 1973).

6. Robert C. Hilderbrand, *Dumbarton Oaks: The Origins of the United Nations and the Search for Postwar Security* (Chapel Hill: University of North Carolina Press, 1990).

7. John F. Murphy, *The United Nations and the Control of International Violence* (Totowa, N.J.: Allanheld, Osmun, 1982); Mark W. Zacher, *International Conflicts and Collective Security Organization, 1946–77: The United Nations, the Organization of American States, the Organization for African Unity, and the Arab League* (New York: Praeger Publishing, 1979).; Mumulla Venkat Rao Naidu, *Collective Security and the United Nations: A Definition of the U.N. Security System* (New York: St. Martin's Press, 1975).

8. Robert Jervis, "Cooperation Under the Security Dilemma," *World Politics* 30 (January 1978): 167–214. The original formulation is in John H. Herz, "Idealist Internationalism and the Security Dilemma," pp. 157–80.

9. If collective security is narrowly defined to mean a universal coalition arrayed against any potential aggressor ("all for one" and all against any one violator), then it is utopian because it fails to specify a mechanism by which his coalition will form. There are potentially fatal problems of divergent interests and buck passing. For a counterargument that is optimistic about collective security, see Charles A. Kupchan and Clifford A. Kupchan, "Concerts, Collective Security, and the Future of Europe," *International Security* 16 (Summer 1991): 114–61.

10. Charles Lipson, "Why Are Some International Agreements Informal?" *International Organization* 45 (Autumn 1991): 495–538.

11. The best introduction to this work is Kenneth Oye, ed., *Cooperation Under Anarchy* (Princeton, N.J.: Princeton University Press, 1985).

12. The best works are Alexander L. George, ed., *Managing U.S.-Soviet Rivalry: Problems of Crisis Prevention* (Boulder, CO: Westview Press, 1983); Alexander L. George, Philip J. Farley, and Alexander Dallin, eds., *U.S.-Soviet Security Cooperation: Achievements, Failures, Lessons* (New York and Oxford: Oxford University Press, 1988); and Roger E. Kanet and Edward A. Kolodziej, *The Cold War as Cooperation* (London: Macmillan, 1991).

13. The intellectual history of the study of international organizations is given briefly in Friedrich Kratochwil and John Gerard Ruggie,

"IO as an Art of the State: A Regime Critique," *International Organization* 40 (Autumn 1986): 753–76.

14. Morton Kaplan, *System and Process in International Politics* (New York: John Wiley and Sons, 1964).

15. This research change was encouraged and reinforced by an editorial change in the subfield's leading journal, *International Organization*. Robert Keohane's tenure as editor came when he and Joseph Nye were publishing important work on transnational politics. The journal, which was once filled with atheoretical articles on specific international institutions, became a general forum for theories on new international issues and their management. Subsequent editors Peter Katzenstein and Stephen Krasner were protagonists in these debates and sustained the journal's focus.

16. The most important and original scholarship in this area is that of Ernst Haas. Two of Haas's works were particularly influential, *The Uniting of Europe: Political, Social and Economic Forces, 1950–1957* (Stanford, Calif.: Stanford University Press, 1958) and *Beyond the Nation State* (Stanford, Calif.: Stanford University Press, 1964). Haas's later reflections on the theoretical issues are in *The Obsolescence of Regional Integration Theory* (Berkeley, Calif.: Institute of International Studies, 1975).

17. Stanley Hoffmann, "Obstinate or Obsolete? The Fate of the Nation-State and the Case of Western Europe," *Daedalus* 95 (Summer 1966): 862–915.

18. The proximate cause of the French boycott was the operation of the community's agricultural fund. The deeper objection was to EC Commission President Hallstein's proposals to move toward majority voting (instead of unanimity) and extend the power of the central bureaucracy and Assembly at the expense of European commissioners, who were appointed by national governments.

19. The integration literature has studied political processes mainly within one geographic area, although some more ambitious studies compared integration in Europe, Africa, and Latin America. One important bridge between this regional focus and the global focus of regimes was the literature on economic interdependence, which grew out of integration theory. Efforts to define and explore the processes of economic interdependence raised questions about how trade, investment, and monetary relations were managed among trans-Atlantic partners and more broadly. This focus on the management of economic interdependence is central to studies of international regimes.

20. There are some exceptions, where the regimes literature has a regional focus (usually concentrated on a specific functional issues). See, for instance, Leah Haus, "The East European Countries and GATT: The Role of Realism, Mercantilism, and Regime Theory in Explaining East-

West Trade Negotiations," *International Organization* 45 (Spring 1991): 163–82. Similarly, Stephen Krasner and M. J. Peterson have written on the regime for managing Antarctic resources.

21. The rise of transnational relationships also has an important impact on foreign-policy decision making. In the traditional view, foreign policy decision making was highly centralized in the foreign ministry and central organs of state. The rise of multiple contacts between different states and their populations, in a wide variety of issues, means that virtually all major government ministries—from agriculture to transportation to energy and environment—have substantial foreign policy concerns. Not only is it difficult for any single nation-state to manage such issues, it is difficult for central state decision makers to control the actions of diverse ministries with powerful stakes in such issues.

22. Robert Keohane and Joseph Nye, *Power and Interdependence: World Politics in Transition* (Boston: Little, Brown and Co., 1977), pp. 19–22, and their earlier edited volume, *Transnational Relations and World Politics* (Cambridge, Mass: Harvard University Press, 1972), originally published as *International Organization* 25 (Summer 1971).

23. Stephen D. Krasner, ed., *International Regimes* (Ithaca, N.Y.: Cornell University Press, 1983), p. 2.

24. Volker Rittberger, "Editor's Introduction," in Rittberger, ed., *International Regimes in East-West Politics* (London: Pinter Publishers, 1990), p. 5.

25. Robert Keohane, "The Demand for Agreements," in Krasner, ed., *International Regimes,* pp. 141–71. There is a potentially virtuous circle here: regimes facilitate specific agreements and a rising number of specific agreements creates incentives for more comprehensive institutions that can reconcile inconsistencies among ad hoc bargains and can capture economies of scale in negotiating agreements on interdependent topics. Ibid., pp. 155–56.

26. Every model of self-enforcing contracts recognizes the importance of future payoffs and the discount parameters attached to them. The *shadow of the future* refers to this discounted payoff stream. See, for example, Robert Axelrod, *The Evolution of Cooperation* (New York: Basic Books, 1984).

27. For a path-setting study on self-enforcing agreements, see L. G. Telser, "A Theory of Self-Enforcing Agreements," *Journal of Business* 53 (January 1980): 27–44. Also, Benjamin Klein and Keith B. Leffler, "The Role of Market Forces in Assuring Contractual Performance," *Journal of Political Economy* 89 (August 1981): 615–41.

28. Charles Lipson, "International Cooperation in Economic and Security Affairs," *World Politics* 37 (October 1984): 1–23.

29. Ulrich Witt, "Evolution and Stability of Cooperation without Enforceable Contracts," *Kyklos* 39 (1986): 246.

30. Charles Lipson, *Standing Guard: Protecting Foreign Capital in the Nineteenth and Twentieth Centuries* (Berkeley: University of California Press, 1985); Kenneth A. Rodman, *Sanctity versus Sovereignty: The United States and the Nationalization of Natural Resources Investment* (New York: Columbia University Press, 1988).

31. Graham Bird, ed., *The International Financial Regime* (Toronto: Surrey University Press, in association with the Academic Press, 1990); B. Dianne Pauls, "U.S. Exchange Rate Policy: Bretton Woods to the Present," *Federal Reserve Bulletin* 76 (November 1990): 891–908.

32. Many studies, beginning with Jock A. Finlayson and Mark Zacher, "The GATT and the Regulation of Trade Barriers: Regime Dynamics and Effects," *International Organization* 35 (Autumn 1981): 561–602. One recent policy-oriented study is James M. Lutz, "GATT Reform or Regime Maintenance: Differing Solutions to World Trade Problems," *Journal of World Trade* 25 (April 1991): 107–22.

33. Vinod Aggerwal, *Liberal Protectionism* (Berkeley: University of California Press, 1985); James A. Dunn, Jr., "Automobiles in International Trade: Regime Change or Persistence?" *International Organization* 41 (Spring 1987): 225–52; Mark W. Zacher, "Trade Gaps, Analytical Gaps: Regime Analysis and International Commodity Trade Regulation," *International Organization* 41 (Spring 1987): 173–202; Jock Finlayson and Mark W. Zacher, *Managing International Markets: Developing Countries and Commodity Trade Regimes* (New York: Columbia University Press, 1988); Robert I. Rothstein, "Commodity Bargaining: The Political Economy of Regime Creation," in I. William Zartman, ed., *Positive Sum: Improving North-South Negotiations* (New Brunswick, NJ: Transaction Books, 1987), pp. 15–47; Daniel M. Kasper, *Deregulation and Globalization: Liberalizing International Trade in Air Services* (Cambridge, Mass: Ballinger for American Enterprise Institute, 1988).

34. Oran R. Young, *International Cooperation: Building Regimes for Natural Resources and the Environment* (Ithaca, NY: Cornell University Press, 1989); Peter Haas, *Saving the Mediterranean: The Politics of International Environmental Cooperation* (New York: Columbia University Press, 1990).

35. Robert O. Keohane, *After Hegemony: Cooperation and Discord in the World Political Economy* (Princeton, NJ: Princeton University Press, 1984), Chap. 10; Hans Jacob Bull-Berg and Magne Holter, *The International Oil Regime—The Conceptualization of a Non-Contractual Regime* (Polhodga, Norway: Fridjof Nansen Institute, 1983); and Bull-Berg, *American International Oil Policy: Causal Factors and Effect* (New York: St. Martin's, 1987), which also uses a regime approach.

36. Charles Lipson, "International Debt and International Institutions," in Miles Kahler, ed., *The Politics of International Debt* (Ithaca, NY: Cornell University Press, 1986), pp. 219–43; Lipson, "The International Organization of Third World Debt," *International Organization* 34, no. 4 (Autumn 1981): 603–31; and Lipson, "Bankers' Dilemmas: Private Cooperation in Rescheduling Sovereign Debts," in Kenneth Oye, ed., *Cooperation Under Anarchy*.

37. Peter F. Cowhey, "The International Telecommunications Regime: The Political Roots of Regimes for High Technology," *International Organization* 44 (Spring 1990): 169–99; Karl P. Sauvant, *International Transactions in Services: The Politics of Transborder Data Flows* (Boulder, Colo.: Westview Press, 1986).

38. Jack Donnelly, "International Human Rights Regimes," *International Organization* 40 (Summer 1986): 599–642; John Gerard Ruggie, "Human Rights and the Future International Community," *Daedalus* 112 (Fall 1983): 93–110; Nicholas G. Onuf and V. Spike Peterson, "Human Rights from an International Regimes Perspective," *Journal of International Affairs* 38 (Winter 1984): 329–42.

39. Ethan A. Nadelmann, "Global Prohibition Regimes: The Evolution of Norms in International Society," *International Organization* 44 (Autumn 1990): 479–526.

40. Susan Strange, "*Cave! hic dragones*: A Critique of Regime Analysis," in Krasner, ed., *International Regimes,* pp. 337–54.

41. The idea of hegemonic decline as a explanation of regime change has been subject to fierce and repeated criticism, showing flaws in its logic and problems in empirical explanation. It is worth remembering the conjuncture of events that once made "hegemonic decline" seem so compelling. By the early 1970s, America was clearly overstretched in its foreign policy commitments, facing the prospect of nuclear parity with the Soviet Union, and bargaining with allies that were much richer and had more powerful economies than in the 1950s and 1960s. Just as this perceived American decline set in, the international monetary system (the Bretton Woods system of pegged exchange rates) fell apart despite American objections. The problems were soon compounded by the collapse of old relationships between oil producers, international petroleum firms, and consuming states. In short, America's less dominant position came just as stable economic relationships collapsed.

42. Peter F. Cowhey and Edward Long, "Testing Theories of Regime Change: Hegemonic Decline or Surplus Capacity?" *International Organization* 37 (Spring 1983): 157–83.

43. Judith Goldstein, "Ideas, Institutions, and Trade Policy," *International Organization* 42 (Winter 1988): 179–217; Peter M. Haas, "Do

Regimes Matter? Epistemic Communities and Mediterranean Pollution Control," *International Organization* 43 (Summer 1989): 377–403.

44. The earliest and bluntest criticism came from Susan Strange, writing in Krasner's initial edited volume on regimes. Later, more reflective criticisms followed, notably that of Beth Simmons and Stephan Haggard. Strange, "*Cave! hic dragones,*" pp. 337–54; Haggard and Simmons, "Theories of International Regimes," *International Organization* 41 (Summer 1987): 491–517.

45. Keohane, *After Hegemony,* pp. 5–17, 31–64, 135–216; Duncan Snidal, "The Limits of Hegemonic Stability Theory," *International Organization* 39 (Autumn 1985): 579–614; Arthur A. Stein, "The Hegemon's Dilemma: Great Britain, the United States, and the International Economic Order," *International Organization* 38 (Spring 1984): 355–86; Bruce Russett, "The Mysterious Case of Vanishing Hegemony; or, Is Mark Twain Really Dead?" *International Organization* 39 (Spring 1985): 207–32; Timothy J. McKeown, "Hegemonic Stability Theory and Nineteenth Century Tariff Levels in Europe," *International Organization* 37 (Winter 1983): 73–91.

46. The lack of a well-defined concept of issues is important in another way. It means that there is no limit to the fractionation of issues into smaller and smaller topics. Does it make sense, for example, to speak of a "trade regime" or to analyze the myriad subissues that have their own constituencies, rules, and decision-making institutions? These analytic issues have not been resolved, even though they were posed at the very beginning of the enterprise, because the definition of *issues* here is essentially empiricist.

47. Several articles try to show how differences between economic and security issues might affect cooperation in those areas. See Jervis, "Cooperation Under the Security Dilemma," pp. 167–214; Lipson, "International Cooperation in Economic and Security Affairs," pp. 1–23; and Oye, ed., *Cooperation Under Anarchy.*

48. Abram Chayes and Antonia Handler Chayes, "Living Under a Treaty Regime: Compliance, Interpretation, and Adaption," in Antonia Handler Chayes and Paul Doty, ed., *Defending Deterrence: Managing the ABM Treaty Regime into the Tewnty-first Century* (Washington, D.C.: Pergamon-Brassey's International Defense Publishers, 1989); Chayes and Doty, ed., *Defending Deterrence.*

49. Charles Lipson, "Is the Future of Collective Security Like the Past?" in George Downs, ed., *Collective Security Beyond the Cold War* (Ann Arbor, Mich.: University of Michigan Press, 1994), pp. 105–31.

50. The first Peace of Paris (May 1814) imposed very moderate terms on France, relying on the territorial boundaries of 1792. That peace was overturned when Napoleon returned from Elba and began the Hundred Days' military campaign, ending with his defeat at Waterloo.

The Second Peace of Paris (June 1815) was less generous than the first. France lost some territory to Prussia, Bavaria, and Sardinia; was forced to pay an indemnity; and was occupied by foreign troops to ensure the indemnity was paid and fighting stopped. Even so, the peace terms were not especially harsh, and Talleyrand's effective diplomacy at the Congress of Vienna managed to return France to the ranks of Great Powers (the "pentarchy" of Austria, Britain, Russia, Prussia, and France). Edward Vose Gulick, "The Final Coalition and the Congress of Vienna, 1813–15," in *The New Cambridge Modern History*, vol. 9: *War and Peace in an Age of Upheaval 1793–1830*, ed. C. W. Crawley (Cambridge: Cambridge University Press, 1965), pp. 639–67; I. C. Nichols, *The European Pentarchy and the Congress of Verona, 1822* (Dordrecht: Martinus Nijhoff, 1971).

51. This is not meant to praise comprehensive, architectonic peace plans or to depreciate ad hoc, piecemeal arrangements. Woodrow Wilson's comprehensive plans for peace failed, as did the more ambitious plans for collective security after World War II. By contrast, the unplanned world of bipolar deterrence avoided war between the United States and the Soviet Union and proved remarkably stable.

Richard Elrod also warns us not to think that concert diplomacy itself arose fully defined or completely thought-out. Key assumptions and procedures became "customary and prescriptive through application," according to Elrod. Richard Elrod, "The Concert of Europe: A Fresh Look at an International System," *World Politics* 28 (January 1976): 161.

52. Elrod, ibid., p. 162.

53. C. J. Bartlett, *Castlereagh* (London: Macmillan, 1966), p. 131.

54. Ibid., p. 131.

55. Paul W. Schroeder, *Metternich's Diplomacy at Its Zenith* (Austin: University of Texas Press, 1962).

56. C. W. Crawley, "International Relations, 1815–30," in *The New Cambridge Modern History*, vol. 9, p. 690.

57. Gordon A. Craig and Alexander L. George, *Force and Statecraft,* 2d ed. (New York: Oxford University Press, 1990), p. 36.

58. Paul W. Schroeder, "The Nineteenth-Century International System: Changes in the Structure," *World Politics* 39 (October 1986): 4.

59. Ibid., pp. 12–26.

60. Ibid., pp. 12–13.

61. Robert Jervis, "Security Regimes," in Krasner, ed., *International Regimes,* pp. 173–94; and Jervis, "From Balance to Concert: A Study of International Security Cooperation," in Oye, ed., *Cooperation Under Anarchy,* pp. 58–79.

62. Jervis's position is not without controversy. Gordon Craig and Alexander George, scholars who understand the period well, write about

it as an "experiment" in the balance of power. Craig and George, *Force and Statecraft,* Chap. 3.

63. Jervis, "Security Regimes," pp. 178–84.

64. It should be noted that there are wild differences in dating the concert. Everyone agrees that it began with the Treaty of Chaumont, the Congress of Vienna, and the two Treaties of Paris in 1814–1815; but when did it end? For some it lasted very briefly, undermined when England refused to join the conservative powers in crushing liberal social movements on the continent. For others, it lasted until the onset of World War I, or at least until the turn of the century, because major Europe-wide conferences continued throughout the nineteenth century and attempted to manage common problems. The most common view is that the concert lasted until mid-century, when fundamental differences among the Great Powers led to war in the Crimea.

Jervis, for example, concludes that the concert "prevailed from 1815 to 1823 and, in attenuated form, until the Crimean War." By contrast, Richard Langhorne claims that "as late as 1912–13 a restricted form of the old Concert mechanism was used to control the effects of the Balkan Wars, and in the 1914 crisis itself those who strove so hard to preserve peace did so within the forms of Concert diplomacy." René Albrecht-Carrié and Felix Gilbert both support Langhorne's position. See, Richard Langhorne, *The Collapse of the Concert of Europe: International Politics, 1890–1914* (New York: St. Martin's, 1981), p. 4; Felix Gilbert, *The End of the European Era, 1890 to the Present* (New York: W. W. Norton, 1970), Chap. 3; René Albrecht-Carrié, *Concert of Europe: 1815–1914* (New York: Harper and Row, 1968); and Jervis, "Security Regimes," p. 178.

65. Schroeder, "The Nineteenth-Century International System," pp. 12–26.

66. John Lewis Gaddis, "The Long Peace: Elements of Stability in the Postwar International System," *International Security* 10 (Spring 1986): 99–142; Gaddis, *The Long Peace: Inquiries into the History of the Cold War* (New York: Oxford University Press, 1987).

67. I do not mean to minimize the seriousness of these smaller wars for the states involved and their people. I am simply noting there was no superpower war, which is both an important achievement and a historical rarity. For an empirical account of limited wars and military interventions in the period, see Herbert K. Tillema, "Foreign Overt Military Intervention in the Nuclear Age," *Journal of Peace Research* 26 (May 1989): 179–95.

68. Craig and George, *Force and Statecraft,* p. 263.

69. Albert Wohlstetter, "The Delicate Balance of Terror," *Foreign Affairs* 37 (January 1958).

70. This was the basic logic behind Mutually Assured Destruction (MAD). MAD did not solve all problems. The Americans were never sure how well it had been incorporated in Soviet military doctrine. For their part, the Americans were unwilling to give up targeting Soviet military facilities with their nuclear weapons—an unnecessary and potentially destabilizing strategy under MAD. Finally, it was recognized that nuclear targeting based solely on MAD doctrine would leave either side vulnerable to lower level attacks by conventional or nuclear forces. The side that had been attacked would be left to choose between city killing and no response.

71. The year 1958 did not mark the end of all territorial problems in Europe, only their overt manifestations. Territorial disputes simmered within the Warsaw Pact, mainly in areas where ethnic groups spilled across borders. But the Red Army's presence throughout East Europe kept them in check. They reemerged once the Soviet empire collapsed.

The last Berlin Crisis, in 1961, involved the erection of the Berlin Wall between the eastern and western portions of the city. The Wall did not contest the borders of the city; it solidified them in concrete and barbed wire. Gudrun Schwarzer discusses the successive crises over Berlin and their management in "The Berlin Regime," in Rittberger, *International Regimes in East-West Politics,* pp. 189–215.

Marc Trachtenberg has recently argued that the extended Berlin Crisis of the Eisenhower and Kennedy presidencies was prompted by the Soviet Union, which was concerned that the West Germans had gained de facto control over nuclear weapons. The Soviets provoked the crisis, according to Trachtenberg, to force the United States to retake control of the weapons. This suggests that concerns about multipolarity lurked beneath the surface of the superpower rivalry. By this view, the settlement of the Berlin Crisis in the early 1960s marked the beginning of a stable bipolar world. Trachtenberg, "A Constructed Peace? The U.S., Western Europe, and the Ending of the Cold War, 1947–1963," manuscript presented to the Program on International Politics, Economics, and Security, University of Chicago, April 29, 1993.

72. Paul Keal, *Unspoken Rules and Superpower Dominance* (London: Macmillan, 1983).

73. Craig and George, *Force and Statecraft,* p. 263.

74. Ibid., pp. 264–65.

75. Jervis makes this point in his initial article on security regimes. His argument that the Concert of Europe was a security regime is based on his judgment that it did produce outcomes that differed from those that would be predicted from underlying power. Jervis, "Security Regimes," pp. 173–94.

76. Joseph S. Nye, Jr., "Nuclear Learning and U.S.-Soviet Security Regimes," *International Organization* 41 (Summer 1987): 371–402.

77. Ibid., p. 391.

78. Ibid.

79. Edward A. Kolodziej, "The Cold War as Cooperation," in Kanet and Kolodziej, eds., *The Cold War as Cooperation,* p. 9.

80. George, Farley, and Dallin, eds., *U.S.-Soviet Security Cooperation,* and George, ed., *Managing the U.S.-Soviet Rivalry.*

81. George, Farley, and Dallin, eds., ibid.; and George, ed., ibid.

82. On regimes of common aversions, see Arthur Stein, "Coordination and Collaboration: Regimes in an Anarchic World," in Krasner, ed., *International Regimes,* pp. 115–40.

83. Janet Gross Stein, "Detection and Defection: Security Regimes and the Management of International Conflict," *International Journal* 40 (Autumn 1985): 599–617.

84. Lipson, "International Cooperation in Economic and Security Affairs," pp. 1–23.

CHAPTER 2

Security Regimes: Mediating Between War and Peace in the Arab-Israeli Conflict

Yaacov Bar-Siman-Tov

INTRODUCTION

The Arab-Israeli conflict has been described as protracted conflict in which the stakes are very high, extending over a long period of time with sporadic outbreaks of open warfare, fluctuating in frequency and intensity, and fundamentally unchanged and unresolveable.[1] However, the Arab-Israeli conflict has changed tremendously, although gradually in its nature, throughout the years since the 1948–1949 War, from a zero sum, unmanageable conflict into a more tractable kind. Not only has the Israeli-Egyptian conflict been resolved, but other important dyadic conflicts are probably moving toward conflict resolution.

This study argues that the establishment of formal and informal security regimes between Israel and its Arab neighbors (Egypt, Syria, and Jordan) was a necessary although not sufficient condition for the shift from war to peace. The failure of establishing such a regime in the Israeli-Palestinian conflict makes this conflict less tractable. The rationale for this argument is that a protracted conflict lingering over time with violent hostilities cannot be resolved without a prerequisite security arrangement that stabilizes the security and the strategic relationship between the parties of the conflict. Security regimes are institutions that control and reduce the conflict to the level where war ceases to be an attractive means to resolve the conflict and the sides are not ripe for conflict resolution. The effectiveness of the regimes may influence the sides to look for resolution, but the sides may also prefer conflict reduction to conflict resolution.

In this chapter, I would like to reassess the relevance of security regimes as a mediating tool between war and peace in the Arab-Israeli conflict; I would also like to propose that the differences in the rate and scope of learning in each of the dyadic conflicts in the Arab Israeli conflict system (Israel-Egypt, Israel-Syria, Israel-Jordan, Israel-Palestinians) influenced differently the institutionalization of each conflict that enabled the establishment of security regimes and the potential shift from war to peace.

The chapter is organized as follows. The next section discusses the theoretical relevance of security regimes as a mediating force between war and peace, by linking regime and learning theories. The third section discusses the conditions that promoted Israel, Egypt, Syria, and Jordan to establish security regimes and prevented Israel and the Palestinians from doing so. The fourth section presents the differences in the rate and scope of learning in each dyadic conflict, which enabled the resolution of the Egyptian-Israeli conflict and prevented the resolution (until now) of the Israeli-Syrian, the Israeli-Jordanian, and the Israeli-Palestinian conflicts. The last section discusses the empirical and the theoretical implications.

SECURITY REGIMES AS A MEDIATING TOOL BETWEEN WAR AND PEACE

In this section I would like to discuss first the reasons for the establishment of security regimes in regional conflicts, their functions, and the degree of their institutionalization; second, I want to discuss the roles of security regimes in facilitating conflict resolution.

Security Regimes in Regional Conflicts

Security regimes are defined here as formal and informal agreements that aim to stabilize the strategic relationships between adversaries to reduce the possibility of armed confrontation.[2] Security regimes may differ, as George suggests, in their, "scope and clarity of norms and rules, in the adequacy of procedures to implement them, in the degree of institutionalization, and in degree to which actors comply with regime normes and the extent to which they are enforced."[3]

The functions of security regimes in regional conflicts include: (1) preventing crises and arms races, (2) blocking or reducing incentives that could bring about escalation, (3) promoting and facilitating deescalatory measures, (4) establishing new patterns of behavior leading to the development of more durable norms of conflict management, and (5) encouraging expectations toward resolution of the conflict.[4] Therefore, institutionalization of conflict management, by establishing security regimes, has the potential not only to foster a better stabilization of the conflict, but also to facilitate the conditions for conflict resolution.

Institutionalization of conflict behavior is the most developed stage or technique of conflict management, because it provides the sides norms, rules, and accepted procedures of conflict management that minimize the uncertainty and make the conflict more predictable. Conflict management reaches the level of institutionalization as the norms, rules, and procedures (1) have been internalized by the sides to the conflict, (2) are expressed in traditional formal writing or some other embodiment external to the sides, and (3) are enforced by potential punishment.[5]

The establishment of security regimes in regional conflicts is an outcome of the initial or simple learning process in the conflict, in which the sides redefine their goals and means in the conflict and change their attitudes toward war. They dismiss the use of war as a legitimate political means to accomplish their incompatible objectives in a conflict.[6] Only when both sides of the conflict see "war as unattractive, with damaging and undesirable consequences, as the outcome they most wish to avoid," will the sides be ready to establish security arrangements to stabilize their strategic relationships.[7]

This initial or simple learning process is likely to develop in the aftermath of an indecisive war, which fails to achieve its minimum objectives, or when it is too costly to justify the accomplishments.[8] The limited outcomes of war make the sides realize the ineffectiveness of a military option for resolving the incompatibility of interests between them. The parties in the conflict begin to learn when the prospects for unilateral advantages in a conflict diminish tremendously and realize that only by some cooperation in conflict institutionalization and reduction is there some chance to avoid mutual damage.

The most important factors that can influence the degree of institutionalization are the balance of power between the parties (current and future power balance), the degree of shared interests, the degree of autonomy of the parties, the issues at stake in the conflict, and third party intervention.[9]

The balance of power between the parties may influence institutionalization in different ways. If the parties are relatively equal, they will be more interested in institutionalization because the prospects for unilateral attempts to attain their objectives are more costly and risky. In cases of power inequalities, the dominant party may try to improve its preferred technique of institutionalization, and the weaker side may bargain to avoid it or to manipulate its alliance or its patron-client relationship in order to reach a more favorable mode of institutionalization. The prospective power balance may also influence the degree of institutionalization. The party that expects to increase its power in the future tends to resist an unfavorable mode of institutionalization in the present, whereas the side that believes the balance will not change in its favor will prefer reaching a high degree of institutionalization in the present.[10]

The degree of shared interests is also significant in determining the level of institutionalization of conflict management. When both sides have only a common aversion to undesirable outcomes, such as a crisis or war, the degree of institutionalization will be limited to minimal military arrangements that will provide procedures to monitor behavior and reduce uncerntainty. In this case, the sides choose to cooperate not because cooperation provides substantial gains, but because it avoids losses. However, when both sides have mutual interests to extend their coordination and cooperation beyond military issues to include some political accommodation, this will increase the degree of institutionalization. In this case, leaders make cooperative choices not only to avoid losses, but also to make some substantial gains that could not be realized unilaterally.[11]

In terms of autonomy, parties that belong to a coalition or depend on external powers for their arms supply or economic assistance will prefer less autonomous forms of institutionalization than parties that are more independent. Nevertheless, external patronage may encourage a more stable institutionalization.

The types of issues involved in the conflict also affect institutionalization, because where parties are dealing with issues that they believe could require speedy and definite resolution and, therefore, pose an acute security dilemma, institutionalization is more likely to be more formalized.[12]

Third party intervention can be an important factor in determining whether institutionalization will occur. The role of a third party in influencing the degree of institutionalization depends on many factors, such as the nature of the relationship between the parties in the conflict and the third party, third party's capabilities, and its role in the international system.[13]

Security Regimes, Learning, and Conflict Resolution

Security regimes, when they are formally institutionalized, may not only prevent war, but also reduce the conflict. Effective security regimes are important vehicles that intensify the learning process in the conflict, and this allows each side to change its mode of thinking. Although the parties may have not yet redefined their fundamental beliefs and their values in the conflict, and their patterns of coordinated behavior may be limited mainly to military issues, there is a substantive transformation of their attitudes to the basic rules of management of the conflict. The parties not only realize that military means cease to be effective for accomplishing even part of their incompatible goals, they also tacitly understand that the only way to accomplish more of these goals is by conflict resolution. Moreover, the sides not only realize the need to make some concessions to advance their goals in the conflict, they also learn the rules of concession. However, much more learning is necessary to shift from the most effective stage in conflict management to conflict resolution.

Notable success in conflict reduction may create a process of further learning, to the point where the substance and the nature of the conflict may be affected and possibly even transformed. Effective security regimes may convince parties that have incompatible goals to find some peaceful solution to their conflict. When such learning happens, security regimes become not only necessary, but also sufficient for conflict resolution. However, sometimes, effective security regimes may be a serious obstacle to conflict resolution. The incentives to attempt a conflict resolution may disappear because the need for alternative political outcomes is not urgent enough and the costs of resolving the conflict may look higher than the costs of continuing it under controlled conditions, as in the security regimes.[14]

In this case, the situation that emerges is what Galtung calls negative peace; that is, the relations between the parties will be limited to conditions of maintaining and balancing power, freezing the status quo, and maintaining the security rather than seeking conflict resolution.[15] In this case, security regimes are vehicles that bring about limited learning that is necessary but not sufficient for conflict resolution.

Conflict resolution is a development process that includes not only the absence of violence, but also the removal of the sources of the conflict situation, the changing of attitudes, and the emergence of readiness to give up some of the goals in the conflict to achieve others. For negotiations to succeed in resolving a conflict, the parties much reach a stage where conflict resolution offers a potentially better alternative than a continuation of conflict management based on effective security regimes. In this situation, the parties to the conflict are motivated not only by loss avoidance, as it is the case of the establishment of security regimes, but also by expectations for relative gains, which effective conflict management could not provide. Conflict resolution is a means that not only can avoid losses, but can also secure relative gains.[16]

The specific conditions of "ripeness" for conflict resolution are (1) when the parties believe that security regimes, even if they stabilize the security and strategic relationships between them and minimize the dangers of war, lack the potential to accomplish even some of the goals in the conflict—and that the only chance to achieve these is by conflict resolution; (2) when the parties realize, due to the success of security regimes, that there are no immediate or even long-run opportunities for unilateral gain by war or more limited violence; (3) when the parties are aware that because of the success of security regimes it will be very difficult, if not impossible, to gain domestic or external legitimacy for use of military coercion to accomplish goals; (4) when there is still a concern that in the absence of progress toward resolution, the conflict may revert to its violent stage; (5) when there is a change in governmental leadership—new leaders are relatively free to undertake new initiatives, because there is some domestic expectation for that and because new leaders are less committed to their predecessors' commitments, furthermore, this change in the leadership is also likely to signal a change for the adversaries;[17] (6) when an energetic and powerful third party induces the parties to settle the conflict or coerces them to do so; (7) when a ignificant change in the international or regional system occurs (such as the resolution of another major conflict, the change in the structure of the system, the dissolution of a major ally or patron or a dramatic change in its international orientation) that forces the sides to reconsider the cost/benefit of effective conflict management to the cost/benefit of conflict resolution.[18]

THE ESTABLISHMENT OF SECURITY REGIMES IN THE ARAB-ISRAELI CONFLICT

Following the October 1973 War, for the first time, the Arab-Israeli conflict reached the era of institutionalization of its management. Egypt and Israel, and Syria and Israel, encouraged by the United States, succeeded to stabilize their strategic relationship by establishing formal security regimes. Israel and Jordan failed to formalize their security regime, and Israel and the Palestinians were far from being ripe for institutionalization. Two questions are important in this situation: How was institutionalization of conflict management possible? How did the difference in rate and scope of learning influence the degree to which institutionalization was implemented in each dyadic conflict? To answer these questions I will discuss each of the dyadic conflicts.

The Egyptian-Israeli Conflict

In the aftermath of the Ocober 1973 War, an initial simple learning process began in which Israel and Egypt decided to modify their conflict. Exhausted by three wars in six years and deadlock in a hurting stalemate, both sides were ripe to transform the means for accomplishing their incompatible objectives, although the fundamental grievances and differences between the parties remained unaltered. Both parties realized that war was no longer an effective means for achieving military and political objectives, not only because of the costs of new war, but because they calculated that the opportunity for unilateral gain was blocked.

Both sides were ripe for selecting alternative techniques of conflict management to stabilize the strategic relationship and prevent war. Both parties were motivated by the need to avoid immediate and certain losses of strategic instability, rather than looking to make relative gains. This needed some tacit or explicit cooperation. However, the mere incentive to stabilize the relationship was not enough to overcome the bitterness and the mistrust between them, especially after so costly and painful war. "A credible and energetic third party was required to transform the apparent will to collaborate into concrete initiatives."[19]

Egypt and Israel preferred the United States to help them in restructuring their security relations. Aware of the importance of solely managing and stabilizing the Arab-Israeli conflict, the United States intervened immediately to assist Egypt and Israel to stabilize the cease-fire and reduce the conflict. In a very short time two formal agreements were concluded: the Six Point Agreement (November 1973), and the Disengagement Agreement (January 1974), which both stabilized the cease-fire and institutionalized the management of the conflict.[20]

The Disengagement Agreement was the first formal agreement between Israel and an Arab state that aimed to prevent a new war. In return for Israel's withdrawal from the west side of the Suez Canal to a line west of the Mitla and Gidi Passes in the Sinai, Egypt accepted a significant thinning out of its forces in the east side of the canal. Both sides also accepted some confidence-building measures to reduce the possibility of inadvertent war: (1) a demilitarized buffer zone controlled by a U.N. force, (2) arms limitation zones in which armed forces and weapons were restricted so that neither side should deploy weapons that could reach the other side, (3) reconnaissance flights flown by the United States that would monitor the agreement, the results of which were to be made available to both sides.[21]

These confidence-building measures created a security regime, which, indeed, stabilized the conflict and tremendously reduced the danger of a miscalculated war or surprise attack. For the first time, a formal agreement was reached on some mutual cooperation and reciprocity limited mainly to military and security issues. Neverthless, some tacit understanding was also reached; accordingly, Egypt would clean and reopen the Suez Canal, rehabilitate the canal area, and permit the passage of Israeli cargo through the canal. This understanding contributed to the institutionalization of the disengagement agreement. Indeed, both sides also agreed that disengagement should not be regarded as "a final peace agreement," but that it should constitute a "first step toward final, just and durable peace."[22]

This understanding that disengagement was only the first agreement in a process of conflict reduction and, perhaps, resolution, brought about not only a high degree of institutionalization of the regime, but also high expectations as to the further development of the process.

Both sides undertook calculated risks. The territorial and military concessions made were not critically endangering their security, even if the agreement were violated. The concessions made did not disturb the underlying power balance, and they were perceived by both sides as reasonable, relative to the expected benefits. The confidence-building measures and the U.S. implicit and explicit guarantees to both sides encouraged the sides to feel protected from some of the risks that they believed their concessions entailed.

The most important lesson of this initial learning process was the mutual awareness that war could not be an effective means in managing the conflict, and that peaceful means should be tried instead.[23] However, without the third party it is doubtful if both sides could have reached the agreement. Although the initial motivation of both sides was limited to loss avoidance, rather than making relative gains (because failure to cooperate will bring loss), both sides believed that the continuation of the process of conflict reduction would also promise some relative gains. This made future cooperation even more worthwhile.

The successful implementation of this first disengagement agreement, in restructuring the security relationship of the sides in a way that did not undermine the military-strategic balance, encouraged interest in the further institutionalization and reduction of the conflict. We can, indeed, identify an incremental learning process between the Disengagement Agreement (January 1974), the achievement of the Syrian-Israeli Disengagement Agreement (May 1974), a second Israeli-Egyptian Disengagement Agreement that failed (March 1975), and its successful conclusion (September 1975).

In the twenty months between the two agreements, both sides had the opportunity to internalize the norms, rules, and procedures of their security regime, to test each others' intentions, and the third party's guarantees, and to realize the benefits of the disengagement agreement versus its costs. The failure of the sides in

May 1975 to reach a new disengagement agreement indicated that the sides failed to realize the limitations of security regimes for accomplishing far-reaching political objectives. The new learning process proved insufficient for further conflict reduction.

Israel wanted a political agreement that would include a formal termination of the state of belligerency, in return for a limited withdrawal in the Sinai that would not include the Mitla and Gidi Passes as well as the oil fields. Egypt wanted an agreement that would be essentially military and not political in nature. It called for extensive Israeli withdrawal in the Sinai, to include the passes and the Abu Rudeis oil fields.[24]

The failure in March 1975 created a new learning process, which forced the sides to learn the rules of less than peace: concessions. Security regimes are necessary for accomplishing further progress in conflict reduction, but not sufficient for conflict resolution. When concessions are limited to further institutionalization of the security regimes, one cannot expect outcomes much beyond the boundries of the security regime.

The new agreement of September 1975, indeed, reflected that new learning. Israel dropped its insistence on a formal end of the state of belligerency and accepted a withdrawal from the passes; however, those remained in the new buffer zone and were not returned to Egypt. Egypt, on its part, was ready for more political accommodation.

The agreement was modeled in part on the previous agreement. In addition to the confidence-building measures included in the first agreement, new measures were accepted by Israel and Egypt to reduce the danger of defection and improve the prospects of accurate detection. Both sides operated electronic early-warning stations on different sides of the Gidi Pass. The United States became even more involved in monitoring and verifying the implementation of the agreement, by staffing and supervising the early-warning systems in the buffer zones, in addition to undertaking aerial reconnaissance flights over the areas included in the agreement. The United States also signed four secret agreements, three with Israel and one with Egypt, that reduced the military and political risks entailed in the agreement.

The new agreement created a new strategic stability that institutionalized to a greater degree the first agreement, and gave both sides a greater sense of security. In addition to this, the agreement fostered greater political accommodation between the sides, which reflected the deepening of the learning process. Both sides committed themselves to resolving the conflict by peaceful means, and they agreed not to resort to threats or use of force; they also agreed that the mandate of the U.N. force would be extended annually. While Israel returned the oil fields at Abu Rudeis to Egypt, Egypt agreed to commit itself publicly to permitting the transit of nonmilitary cargo to or from Israel through the Suez Canal.

The agreement gave further impetus to new developments. Egypt could expect to regain sovereignty over Sinai; Israel could expect a political solution to the conflict with Egypt. The second Disengagement Agreement showed that the sides were interested not only in avoiding loss, but also in achieving relative gains; and they were ready in return to make not only more military concessions, but also economic and political ones.[25]

The Syrian-Israeli Conflict

In May 1975, Syria and Israel succeeded in reaching a disengagement agreement. This agreement was much more difficult to negotiate than the first Israeli-Egyptian disengagement, due to the history of the Syrian-Israeli conflict, which was marked with greater hostility and bitterness than the relations between Israel and Egypt, and due to the objective situation on the ground itself (the small territory that was much closer to the security interests of each side and the presence of Israeli settlements there). Three factors can explain the successful conclusion of the Syrian-Israeli disengagement: (1) the successful example of the Egyptian-Israeli agreement, (2) both sides' interests in disengagement, (3) the active intervention of the United States.

The successful conclusion of the first Israeli-Egyptian disengagement had a positive spill over effect on the Israeli-Syrian conflict. This agreement conclusively proved that disengagement is possible in the Arab-Israeli conflict, and the United States was able to convince the sides to make the necessary concessions and compensate them. Experiencing the hurting stalemate created after the 1973 War against the background of an intensified war of attrition in the front, both Israel and Syria were interested in stabilizing the cease-fire in the Golan Heights. Syria was eager to reduce the Israeli bulge toward Damascus. The Syrian concern at the military situation was even greatly heightened following the Egyptian-Israeli disengagement, which left it to face Israel alone. The Egyptian example made Syria believe that disengagement could enable it to recover the territory lost in 1973, and perhaps also a portion of the Golan Heights. Israel was also interested in disengagement, for the following reasons: to release its prisoners of war, to reach an effective cease-fire, and to moderate Syrian enmity to prevent endangering the process of conflict reduction with Egypt.

The interest of the two sides in disengagement was motivated mainly by loss avoidance, but this was not sufficient to bring about disengagement. Strong motivation from the United States was required to convince the sides to make the necessary concessions. The learning process here was much more limited than in the Egyptian-Israeli case. Both sides had not yet modified their way of thinking about the conflict, and they had not completely excluded the possibility of using war as an effective means to manage the conflict. Nevertheless, the urgent need to stabilize the strategic relationship, at least for a while, was sufficient to begin the institutionalization of the conflict management. The first Egyptian-Israeli disengagement became a model for the Syrian-Israeli disengagement; that is, Israeli territorial concessions and the same principles of confidence-building measures. Israel returned to Syria the territory that it captured in 1973 and the city of Kuneitra, which was captured in 1967. Both sides accepted a buffer zone and limited-force zones controlled and supervised by the United Nations. Nevertheless, this agreement did not include reconnaissance U.S. flights as in the Egyptian-Israeli case. These measures, coupled with Syria's tacit agreement not to permit the launching of terrorist raids from its territory and U.S. commitments to both sides that reduced the military and political risks entailed, laid the groundwork for the Israeli-Syrian agreement. Both sides realized that disengagement was only the first step toward peace.[26]

The significance of this agreement was not limited to the security aspect, but had broad psychological and political implications. It marked a major breakthrough in the Syrian-Israeli conflict. Syria, which was known as the most radical Arab state in the conflict, not only drafted a formal agreement with Israel, but implicitly recognized Israel and agreed to cooperate with it. No ideological or political obstacles prevented further negotiation between Israel and other Arab states, especially with Egypt.

Indeed, the Syrian-Israeli agreement facilitated the second Israeli-Egyptian disengagement.

The Jordanian-Israeli Conflict

The successful conclusion of the first Egyptian-Israeli disengagement and the Syrian-Israeli disengagement raised the possibility of a disengagement agreement between Jordan and Israel. However, in contradiction to the two other cases, Israel and Jordan had not shared the same interest regarding formalization of the institutionalization of their conflict. The preexistence of an informal security regime along the Jordanian-Israeli line, the absence of any hurting stalemate in this conflict, the inequality of balance of power, the lack of an energetic third party, and other Arab states' objection had prevented the formalization of the Israeli-Jordanian security regime.

Jordan itself was interested in reaching a disengagement with Israel along the same lines as the Egyptian-Israeli and the Syrian-Israeli agreements; that is, it wanted Israel to withdraw from part of the West Bank, and it wanted to establish formal confidence-building measures. Jordan's interest in such cooperation was motivated mainly by the possibility of considerable relative gains, rather than loss avoidance. However, Israel opposed any idea of territorial withdrawal from the Jordan River, preferring to restore some administrative Jordanian responsibility in the West Bank. Israel saw no relative gain in formalization of the conflict with Jordan, but only some loss avoidance, limited to warding off the PLO'S claims to the West Bank. From the Israeli point of view, military disengagement was actually less relevant in the Israeli-Jordanian front, because there had been no military engagement in the 1973 War. The tacit cooperation between Jordan and Israel developed since the Jordanian civil war in 1970 (in which Israel succeeded in halting Syria's military intervention and imposing its withdrawal from Jordan) informally institutionalized the conflict, as it, indeed, proved itself in the 1973 War, when Jordan did not join the Egyptian-Syrian coalition. Israel did not see any military or political advantage in formalizing the security relationship, when it was asked to pay for that in territorial terms.

The lack of Israeli interest and a limited U.S. interest in a disengagement with Jordan killed the Jordanian proposal. Nevertheless, the Arab world itself later rejected the so-called Jordanian option, when in its summit in Rabat in October 1974 it endorsed the PLO as the sole legitimate representative of the Palestinian people and excluded Jordan from negotiating the future of the West Bank and Gaza with Israel.[27]

The failure of formalization of the Jordanian-Israeli security regime indicates that the initial learning sufficient for the establishment of the informal security regime was insufficient for its formalization. An effective informal security regime, even with a limited degree of institutionalization, was perceived to be better than its formalization because of the territorial and political costs for one side. Only new threats to the existence of the regime itself could make Israel reconsider the issue; however, due to the inequality of the power balance, Jordan was not in a position to make such threats.

The Palestinian-Israeli Conflict

The formal institutionalization of the Egyptian-Israeli and Syrian-Israeli conflicts and the informal institutionalization of the Jordanian-Israeli conflict left the Palestinian-Israeli conflict the only uninstitutionalized conflict. Both sides still believe that conflict behavior is necessary to determine the outcomes of the conflict, and therefore, institutionalization of the conflict remains impossible. The unique characteristicts of this conflict (the state-nonstate conflict, the inequality of power, and the issues at stake) also prevented the institutionalization.

Until 1987, the Palestinian-Israeli conflict was characterized as a state-nonstate actor; that is, an Israeli-Palestinian organizations conflict, in which Israel enjoyed total military superiority. Although the Palestinian organizations believed that they could accomplish their objective—a Palestinian state instead of the state of Israel, or in addition to Israel, established by military means. Israel, on its part acted to destroy the Palestinian organizations. That kind of zero-sum conflict reached its peak in the Lebanon war, in 1982, in which Israel tried to totally destroy the PLO and its infrastructure in Lebanon, in order to eliminate the PLO as an actor that competes with Israel on the same land.[28]

The expulsion of the PLO headquarters from Lebanon, the last Arab country bordering Israel from which a direct attack was possible, suppressed the PLO's military activity against Israel, but it triggered the opening of a second front in the Israeli-Palestinian conflict—the intifada. The intifada that erupted in December 1987 in Gaza and expanded outward to the West Bank transformed the Israeli-Palestinian conflict from a state-nonstate conflict to an interethnic conflict.

The intifada, which started as a massive and popular uprising against the continuing Israeli occupation, had turned, in the last two years, to individual and small group terrorist activities. The inability of Israel to suppress the intifada made the uprising the most powerful political means available to the Palestinians.

The failure of suppression made regulation the only possible technique to manage the conflict. Regulation here differs from other dyadic conflicts in the Arab-Israeli conflict. The inequality in power (army versus civilians and even children, and recently individuals and small groups undertaking terrorist actions), the violent means used, as well as the significance of the issue at stake for both sides made regulation even more complicated. The rules of the game in the management of this conflict are based on self-restraint and domestic and external constraints (especially for Israel) rather than tacit bargaining.[29]

The potential to shift this conflict from regulation to institutionalization depends on definitive, accepted, and recognized links between institutionalization and resolution. The Palestinians are not interested in institutionalization that will freeze their conflict behavior without the promise that a resolution will end the Israeli occupation. The Israelis, on their part, are interested in institutionalization to end the intifada, but they refused to make their withdrawal from the West Bank and Gaza dependent on that. This is, indeed, very different from the other dyadic conflicts, in which institutionalization was only implicitly linked to resolution. Conditional institutionalization on a very definite resolution makes institutionalization even more complicated.

SECURITY REGIMES AND RESOLUTION IN THE ARAB-ISRAELI CONFLICT

The notable success of the security regimes in the Egyptian-Israeli case created a process of further learning in that conflict. Both sides realized that, although the security regime could stabilize the security relationship between them and reduce the danger of new war, they lacked the potential to accomplish even some of the respective goals in the conflict; and the only way to achieve these was by conflict resolution. Although it was possible to negotiate another disengagement agreement that could institutionalize the security regime even more, this could accomplish only limited gains: less than all Sinai for Egypt and less than full peace for Israel. But this did not satisfy both sides. Following the second disengagement, both sides realized that the next stage-when they were ready-should be conflict resolution. Both sides learned that this meant deescalating the conflict to the point where its substance and nature would be transformed. They realized that this involved removing the sources of the conflict situation as well as a total transformation of attitudes, even if this involved heavy military and political risks and costs.

This forced Egypt and Israel to redefine their priorities. Egypt realized that the most it could achieve was restoration of the Sinai alone, and that this could be achieved only in return for a separate peace treaty with Israel. Israel realized that the most it could accomplish was a separate peace treaty in return for the entire Sinai and deferment of any annexation of the West Bank and the Gaza Strip for at least five years. Both sides realized that they had achieved only some of their goals; however, the benefits achieved were perceived to exceed the costs of conflict resolution. Nevertheless this development was made possible by active U.S. intervention, without which the two sides alone may have failed to reach an agreement.[30]

The achievement of the peace treaty between Egypt and Israel, separately and independent of other dyadic conflicts in the Arab-Israeli conflict system, proved again, as in the establishing of security regimes, that the Arab-Israeli conflict is not a single conflict. The differences in the rate and scope of learning in every dyadic conflict proved to be even more crucial in shifting from institutionalization to resolution.

The high rate and scope of learning in the Egyptian-Israeli conflict that enabled conflict resolution is probably a result of different factors, the most important of which is the high degree of institutionalization of the security regime that was crucial for the intensification of the learning process. A realization that only political means could accomplish political objectives in the conflict and only conflict resolution could provide considerable relative gains, but not absolute gains, was the essence of the learning process. A new Israeli leadership that was ready to relinquish all the Sinai, in order to exclude Egypt from the conflict, and an energetic and powerful third party that assisted the sides to internalize the rules of concessions in peace making and compensated them in addition to benefits of the peace itself made the benefits of peace even more worthwhile.

Egypt's attempt to link its conflict resolution with Israel's resolution of other dyadic conflicts failed not only because Israel refused to accept that link, but also because the Arab states refused to shift from institutionalization to resolution. Even the formalization of a linkage between the Egyptian-Israeli agreement and the Palestinian-Israeli agreement, as Egypt reached in the Camp David accords, failed to reach positive outcomes. The Palestinians refused to be part of a treaty, not only because it was imposed on them without their consent or prior agreement, but also because there was no certainty that the autonomy would develop, in fact, into a Palestinian state. Without the participation of the Palestinians in the autonomy talks, there was no real prospect of reaching any agreement on the autonomy. The autonomy that could institutionalize the Palestinian-Israeli conflict was rejected because the rate and scope of learning in this conflict was still very low, if it existed at all. The autonomy plan, which apparently could be regarded as some learning on the Israeli side in this conflict, however, was a vehicle for facilitating the agreement with Egypt rather than a concrete move for resolution of the conflict with the Palestinians.

The initial and simple learning that facilitated the formal institutionalization of the conflict between Israel and Syria, and the informal institutionalization of the conflict between Israel and Jordan had not intensified since then. The rate and the scope of learning remained relatively low and could not enable resolution. Actually, the success of the institutionalization in both conflicts proved to be a serious obstacle to conflict resolution. Until recently, in both cases the incentives to attempt conflict resolution disappeared, because there was no immediate danger of new war and the costs of resolving the conflict were perceived to be much higher than those of continuing them under controlled conditions. Indeed, in both cases the sides preferred the benefits of conflict institutionalization and reduction to the costs of peace. Whereas Syria had ideological difficulty with the notion of negotiating a peace treaty with Israel, Jordan was prepared for such a peace treaty, but only if it entailed Israel's total return of the territories, including East Jerusalem. Israel, at any rate, was not prepared to relinquish all of the territories (or even some of them under the Likud administration) in return for a peace treaty with the two states. Thus, the situation that emerged in both cases was characterized as "negative peace." Between Jordan and Israel this developed into economic cooperation and regular secret meetings between the countries' leaders; between Israel and Syria the negative peace was limited to a military regime. Nevertheless, the existence of this regime enabled both sides to limit their clash in Lebanon in 1982 to the Lebanese territory, and it prevented it from expanding to the Golan Heights.[31]

The readiness of Syria, Jordan, Lebanon, the Palestinians, and Israel to take part in the prenegotiation stage in Madrid (1991) and Washington (1992–1993) probably indicates the first sign of a shift from institutionalization to resolution in the Syrian-Israeli and Jordanian-Israeli conflicts and from regulation to institutionalization in the Palestinian-Israeli conflict. The current prenegotiations probably indicate the emergence of some learning in these conflicts. However, it is not clear yet whether the rate and scope of this initial learning is sufficient for conflict resolution or only for prenegotiations.

The current learning is not a result of successful security regimes that intensified learning or of a hurting stalemate (excluding the Palestinians), but a result of the dramatic developments in the global and regional systems. Three factors are responsible for the prenegotiations: the Gulf War, the dissolution of the Soviet Union, and U.S. pressure. Both sides learned two things from the Gulf War. First, due to new technology and possession of unconventional weapons, any new war could be destructive, if not devastating, for both sides; and there is no guarantee that limitation can be established. Second, the international community and especially the United States delegitimized war as a means to manage the conflict; therefore, all sides concluded that the political costs of a new war may exceed its political benefits.

The dissolution of the Soviet Union also minimized the prospects of a "successful" war initiated by the Arab side. Without the Soviet patronage, war would become tremendously costly. Therefore, the only way left to accomplish some of the political objectives is conflict resolution. The U.S. pressure employed on both sides of the conflict pushed them to reconsider their options. Both sides realize that their refusal to take part in the attempt to resolve the conflict will make them face international criticism, if not punishment, and will weaken their case in the conflict.[32]

Without the internalization of these factors, it is doubtful if such factors are sufficient to make the sides change their positions and move toward their conflict resolution. The sides' agreement to attend the negotiations, though, is still motivated by loss avoidance and not by the chance to accomplish some relative gains.[33] So long as the sides are motivated only by avoidance of loss, or by looking for absolute gains, it is doubtful if the rate and scope of learning will enable conflict resolution.

CONCLUSIONS

The establishment of formal security regimes became possible in the Egyptian-Israeli and Syrian-Israeli conflicts only after the 1973 War, when the sides realized that the war ceased to be an effective means of accomplishing unilateral objectives. The informal institutionalization of the Jordanian-Israeli conflict was made even before the 1973 War, due to the strategic cooperation that saved the Jordanian regime. Formalization was not a necessary condition for reaching and maintaining security regimes. The Israeli-Jordanian regime proved to be effective. Even without formal confidence-building measures, such as buffer zones controlled by external forces, both sides succeeded in maintaining a high degree of institutionalization.

Institutionalization stabilized each dyadic conflict, and no war erupted since. The only exception was the Israeli-Syrian war in Lebanon, but it was limited to Lebanon, while the Golan Heights remained quiet. Probably the effective regime in the Golan Heights was responsible for that outcome.

Security regimes proved to be necessary but not sufficient conditions for shifting from war to peace. Actually, their achievement prevented further advancement toward resolution in the Syrian-Israeli and Jordanian-Israeli conflicts, when both sides preferred the benefits of security regimes to the costs of resolution (the territorial and political costs even prevented the formalization of the Jordanian Israeli security regime). Nevertheless, both sides to these conflicts acknowledged that institutionalization was not the last stage, but the first. The Israeli-Palestinian conflict remains the only conflict that fails to shift to institutionalization, mainly because the two sides differ as to the possible relationship between institutionalization and resolution.

The recent Israeli-Palestinian agreement on self-rule in Gaza and Jericho as a first step toward granting the Palestinians autonomy in the West Bank and Gaza is a real breakthrough and a significant change in the Israeli-Palestinian conflict. This development is, indeed, the result of an intensified learning process, in which both sides realized that only direct negotiation between the Israeli government and the PLO leadership could facilitate an agreement between Israel and the Palestinians and that an interim agreement is a necessary condition for reaching a permanent settlement. Both sides recognized that institutionalization should be a precondition for resolution. Successful implementation of the autonomy will be therefore, the real test for shifting this conflict from regulation to institutionalization and will pave the way for its resolution.

An initial learning process proved to be necessary for shifting from war to institutionalization of conflict behavior, but this was not sufficient to move from institutionalization to resolution. There was a need for a further and deeper learning process to enable conflict resolution. This happened only once, in the Egyptian-Israeli case; and active intervention of a third party proved to be necessary for internalizaing the learning process.

The fact that learning developed in each dyadic conflict, separate, independent, and different from other dyadic conflicts, enabled separate agreements, but it prevented comprehensive ones. It seems that the complexities of the Arab-Israeli conflict—many actors and different issues—hindered the development of the same rate and scope of learning in each dyadic conflict.

The establishment of security regimes as an act of cooperation in the Arab-Israeli conflict was more the result of an agent's wish to avoid loss than an opportunity to make relative gains. Nevertheless, the shift to resolution was motivated not only by loss avoidance, but also by the possibility of making some gains, and not absolute ones. The shift from loss avoidance to making relative gains is probably necessary for shifting from institutionalizaton to resolution, because not only is it a more positive way to consider the benefits of making peace, but it is also part of the learning process. This conclusion calls for further research of the factors that influence the rate and the scope of learning in shifting from institutionalization to resolution in international conflicts.

NOTES

1. Edward E. Azar, Paul Jureidini and Ronald McLaurin, "Protracted Social Conflict: Theory and Practice in the Middle East," *Journal of Palestine Studies* 8 (Autumn 1978): 41–60.

2. For definition and discussion of security regimes in general and on the global level, see, for example, Robert Jervis, "Cooperation under Security Dilemma," *World Politics* 30 (January 1978): 167–214; Robert Jervis, "Security Regimes," *International Organization* 36 (Spring 1982): 357–378; Robert Jervis, "From Balance to Concert: A Study of International Security Cooperation," in Kenneth Oye, ed., *Cooperation Under Anarchy* (Princeton, N.J.: Princeton University Press, 1985), pp. 58–79; Charles Lipson, "International Cooperation in Economic and Security Affairs," *World Politics* 37 (October 1984): 1–23; Charles Lipson, "Are Security Regimes Possible? Historical Cases and Modern Issues," Chap. 1 in this book; Alexander L. George, Philip J. Farley and Alexander Dallin, eds., *U.S.–Soviet Security Cooperation: Achievements, Failures, Lessons* (New York: Oxford University Press, 1988). For a definition and discussion of security regimes in the Arab-Israeli conflict, see for example, Yaacov Bar-Siman-Tov, "The Arab-Israeli Conflict: Learning Resolution," *Journal of Peach Research* 31 (February 1994): 75–92, Pen Osler Hampson and Brian S. Mandell, "Managing Regional Conflict: Security Co-operation and Third Party Mediators," *International Journal* 45 (Spring 1990): 191–201; Brian S. Mandell, "Anatomy of a Confidence-Building Regime: Egyptian-Israeli Security Cooperation, 1973–1979," *International Journal* 45 (Spring 1990): 202–223; Janice Gross Stein, "A Common Aversion to War: Regime Creation by Egypt and Israel as a Strategy of Conflict Management," in Gabriel Ben-Dor and David B. Dewitt, *Conflict Management in the Middle East* (Lexington Mass.: Lexington Books, 1987), pp. 59-77.

3. George et al., *U.S.-Soviet Security Cooperation*, p. 14.

4. Hampson and Mandell, "Managing Regional Conflict," p. 196.

5. Louis Kriesberg, *The Sociology of Social Conflicts* (Englewood Cliffs, N.J.: Prentice-Hall, 1973), pp. 273–276.

6. On learning in conflict, see for example, Ernst Haas, "Collective Learning: Some Theoretical Speculations" in George W. Breslauer and Philip E. Tetlock, eds., *Learning in U.S. and Soviet Foreign Policy* (Boulder, Colo.: Westview Press, 1991), pp. 62–99; Philip E. Tetlock, "Learning in U.S. and Soviet Foreign Policy: In Search of an Elusive Concept", in Breslauer and Tetlock, eds., *Learning in U.S. and Soviet Foreign Policy,* pp. 20–61; Joseph S. Nye, Jr., "Nuclear Learning and U.S.-Soviet Security Regimes," *International Organization,* 41 (Summer 1987): 371–402.

7. Stein, " A Common Aversion," p. 67.

8. Ibid.; see also, William I. Zartman, "Ripening Conflict, Ripe Moment, Formula, and Mediation," in Diane B. Bendahmane and John W. McDonald, eds., *Perspectives on Negotiation: Four Case Studies and Interpretations* (Washington, D.C.: Foreign Service Institute, U.S. Department of State, 1986), pp. 205–227; William I. Zartman, "The Middle East-The Ripe Moment?" in Ben-Dor and Dewitt, eds., *Conflict Management in the Middle East,* pp. 283–296.

9. Kriesberg, *Sociology of Social Conflicts*, p. 113; Louis Kriesberg, "Introduction: Timing Conditions, Strategies, and Errors" in Louis Kriesberg and Stuart J. Thorson eds., *Timing the De-Escalation of International Conflicts* (Syracuse, N.Y.: Syracuse University Press, 1991), pp. 5–11.

10. William I. Zartman and Johannes Aurik, "Power Strategies in De Escalation" in Kriesberg and Thorson eds., ibid., pp. 152–181.

11. Stein, "A Common Aversion," p. 63; Arthur Stein, "Coordination and Collaboration: Regimes in an Anarchic World," *International Organization*, 36 (Spring 1982): 299–324; Janice Gross Stein, "International Co-operation and Loss Avoidance: Framing the Problem," *International Journal* 47 (Spring 1992): 202–234.

12. Kriesberg, *Sociology of Social Conflicts*, p. 113; Hampson and Mandell, "Managing Regional Conflict," p. 196.

13. Brian S. Mandell and Brian W, Tomlin, "Mediation in the Development of Norms to Manage Conflict: Kissinger in the Middle East," *Journal of Peace Research* 28 (March 1991): 43–55.

14. Gabriel Ben-Dor and David B. Dewitt, "Conflict and Conflict Management in the Middle East" in Ben-Dor and Dewitt, eds., *Conflict Management in the Middle East,* pp. 298–299.

15. Johan Galtung, *Peace Research: Science or Politics in Diguise?* (Oslo: Peace Research Institute, 1967), pp. 2–3.

16. Stein, "International Co-operation," pp. 202–234.

17. Kriesberg, "Introduction," p. 5.

18. Ibid., pp. 9–10, see also, Terrence P. Hopmann, "The Changing International Environment and the Resolution of International Conflicts: Negotiations on Security and Arms Control in Europe," in Kriesberg and Thorson, *Timing the De-Escalation*, pp. 31–57.

19. Mandell, "Anatomy of a Confidence-Building Regime," p. 204.

20. Henry Kissinger, *Years of Upheaval* (Boston: Little, Brown and Co., 1982), pp. 632–646, 799–853.

21. Ibid., pp. 1250–1251; William B. Quandt, *Decade of Decisions: American Foreign Policy Toward the Arab-Israeli Conflict, 1967–1976* (Berkeley: University of California Press, 1977), p. 228.

22. Kissinger, *Years of Upheaval*, pp. 836–846, 1251.

23. Ibid., pp. 836–846; Raphael Israeli, *The Public Diary of President Sadat* (Leiden: E. J. Brill, 1979), pp. 443–469.

24. Israeli, ibid., pp. 805–896; Yitzhak Rabin, *The Rabin Memoirs* (Boston: Little, Brown and Co., 1979), pp. 234–252.

25. Quandt, *Decade of Decisions*, pp. 274–275; Rabin, ibid., pp. 253–275; Israeli, ibid., pp. 986–1089; Mahmoud Riad, *The Struggle for Peace in the Middle East* (London: Quartet Books, 1981), pp. 285–298.

26. Kissinger, *Years of Upheaval*, pp. 846–851, 935–978, 1032–1110; Moshe Dayan, *Story of My Life* (New York: William Morrow, 1976), pp. 571–580; Patrick Seale, *Asad: The Struggle for the Middle East* (Berkeley: University of California Press, 1988), pp. 226–249; Saadia Touval, *The Peace Brokers: Mediators in the Arab-Israeli Conflict, 1948–1979* (Princeton, N.J.: Princeton University Press, 1982), pp. 249–259.

27. Kissinger, ibid., pp. 847–848, 976–978, 1137–1142; Quandt, *Decade of Decisions*, pp. 229–230, 248, 255–257; Touval, *The Peace Brokers,* pp. 259–261; see also, Aharon Klieman, "The Israel Jordan Tacit Security Regime," Chapter 6 in this book.

28. Zeev Schiff and Ehud Yaari, *Israel's Lebanon War* (New York: Simon and Schuster, 1984); Rashid Khalidi, *Under Siege: PLO Decision-making During the 1982 War* (New York: Columbia University Press, 1986).

29. Robert F. Hunter, *The Palestinian Uprising: A War by Other Means* (Berkeley: University of California Press, 1991); Jamal R. Nassar and Roger Heacock, eds., *Intifada: Palestine at the Crossroads* (New York: Praeger Publishing, 1990); Arieh Shalev, *The Intifada: Causes and Effects* (Boulder, Colo.: Westview Press, 1990); Zeev Schiff and Ehud Yaari, *Intifada:The Palestinian Uprising: Israel Third Front* (New York: Simon and Schuster, 1990).

30. Moshe Dayan, *Breakthrough: A Personal Account of Egypt-Israel Peace Negotiation* (London: Weidenfeld and Nicolson, 1981); Mohamed Ibrahim Kamel, *The Camp David Accords: A Testimony* (London: KPI, 1986); Herbert C. Kelman, "Overcoming the Psychological Barrier: An Analysis of the Egyptian-Israeli Peace Process," *Negotiation Journal* 1 (July 1985): 213–234; Ezer Weizman, *The Battle for Peace* (New York: Bantam Books, 1981).

31. Yair Evron, *War and Intervention in Lebanon* (Baltimore: Johns Hopkins University Press, 1987); Itamar Rabinovich, "Controlled Conflict in the Middle East: The Syrian-Israeli Rivalry in Lebanon" in Ben-Dor and Dewitt, eds., *Conflict Management in the Middle East*, pp. 97–111.

32. Steven L. Spiegel, ed., *The Arab-Israeli Search for Peace* (Boulder, Colo.: Lynne Rinner, 1992).

33. Stein, "International Co-operation," p. 223.

PART 2

The External Actors

CHAPTER 3

The American Role in a Regional Security Regime

Robert J. Lieber

Middle East regional security is the product of a complex interplay of local actors and forces. However, it does not exist in a vacuum, and the regional environment is also shaped by the structure of the international system. It is now commonplace to observe that the wider system is itself in the throes of a profound transformation. These changes result from the end of the Cold War, the disintegration of the Soviet Union, and the unraveling of the bipolar structure that had characterized international relations from 1945 until the end of the 1980s.

The meaning of these changes for the global system remains a subject of intense debate. It is therefore not surprising that the consequences for the Middle East regional subsystem also remain in question. Some observers have suggested that with the end of the Cold War and the greatly reduced propensity of the United States and Russia to intervene, the level of regional violence is likely to decline. Moreover, the increased ability of the great powers to cooperate through the United Nations Security Council and in other ad hoc efforts may also reduce or limit conflict.

Others have argued to the contrary, that the superpowers actually exercised a certain restraining role over regional clients and that the post-Cold War environment might actually see an enhancement of regional hostilities.[1] Although a universal answer to this debate may be impossible, or is at least premature, there has been no shortage of violence in the post-Cold War world. The global picture is thus mixed, with the winding down of wars in

Angola, Afghanistan, Ethiopia, Nicaragua, and elsewhere, while bitter new conflicts have erupted in a number of areas, including portions of the former USSR and Yugoslavia. In the case of the Middle East, the evidence is also contradictory. It includes Iraq's invasion of Kuwait and the ensuing Gulf crisis and war, but also the initiation of a broad-based peace process, sponsored by the United States and involving direct Arab-Israeli negotiations.

Against that background, this chapter assesses the importance of the United States for Middle East regional stability in the aftermath of the Cold War and Gulf War. It then considers American interests and policies in the region, as well as the domestic context on which these policies rest, and it concludes with a consideration of the obstacles to an effective regional security regime. From the assessment it is evident that stability in the Middle East requires the continuation of a leading role by the United States. In part, this involves organizing and leading collective efforts, as in the Gulf War. But it also means a continuing role in providing security assistance, reassurance, and deterrence against threats to friendly states. At the same time, the United States needs to retain the capability to intervene unilaterally under certain circumstances. However, not all threats to regional security are manageable through traditional security policies. Moreover, the American domestic context places some constraints on the ability of the United States to commit resources for the maintenance of regional stability.

REGIONAL INSTABILITY: LESSONS FROM THE GULF WAR

Scholars of international relations have long been familiar with the "anarchy" problem. Its essence is that relationships among states take place in an environment where no effective overall authority exists to adjudicate the inevitable disputes that arise among them, nor to enforce internationally accepted rules, nor to defend the peace. As a consequence, states exist in a kind of "self-help" system, in which they must rely on themselves, typically by arming to protect their interests or to join alliances in pursuit of security.[2]

To be sure, the anarchy concept is a metaphor, not an iron law. It represents a propensity and is often mitigated in practice. On occasion, the existence of regional organizations such as

NATO or the European Community can alter the international environment in which states operate. To a lesser extent, so too can international organizations up to and including the United Nations. A great deal of international activity, for example, in economic and communications realms, has little to do with more traditional forms of state conflict. Moreover, security regimes can provide a degree of stability and predictability for states in otherwise conflictual arrangements. As Charles Lipson notes, the pattern of Soviet-American security cooperation during the Cold War, as well as the post-1815 Concert of Europe, illustrate not merely orderly patterns of behavior, but deliberate efforts to manage international affairs to capture joint gains or prevent common losses.[3] In the Middle East regional context, Janice Gross Stein identifies two regimes of conflict management in Arab-Israeli relations: Egypt and Israel between 1956 and 1967, and the same countries again from 1975 to 1978.[4] Finally, learning behavior can and does take place among states and their peoples, and democracies appear to have the laudable characteristic of tending not to go to war against other democracies.

Notwithstanding such mitigating factors, events that starkly reveal the underlying nature of the global landscape can still occur. In the Middle East, Saddam Hussein's August 1990 invasion of Kuwait presented just such a case. As the first great crisis of the post-Cold War period, it provided a brutal confirmation that harsh issues of war and peace—and even of survival—are an everpresent peril. Moreover, it provided graphic evidence that even in the absence of the Soviet threat, there exist major sources of regional instability.

The crisis also provided a particularly stark test of the United States' role in the post-Cold War world. A generation earlier, Washington would have been in a position to proceed with a virtually unilateral intervention. In this case, however, support from some forty other states proved crucial in a number of ways. First, without the formal request for assistance from Saudi Arabia and the use of Saudi bases and logistics, the American intervention would have been virtually impossible. Second, the change in Russian policy and behavior made possible the use of the United Nations Security Council for condemning Iraq and authorizing sanctions against it and then the use of force. Security Council resolutions provided international legitimization for the American-led effort, and the passage of Resolution 678, authorizing "all means necessary," was vital in enabling the Bush administration to obtain congressional authorization for the use of military force.[5] Provision of troops, ships and planes by a broad group of allies and even former adversaries gave the coalition a vital multinational character that was important in maintaining international support and influencing the domestic American context. Moreover, the more than $60 billion cost of the war was essentially offset by payments from Saudi Arabia, the Gulf states, Japan, and Germany, so that the war did not cause a major financial burden for the United States.

The American role was thus very much bound up with participation by other countries and the United Nations, but this international activity would have been ineffectual (indeed, much of it would not even have occurred) without American leadership. In essence, the alternative to an American-led coalition to oust Saddam from Kuwait was not some kind of global or regional effort to accomplish the same objective. By themselves, the Europeans, Japanese, Arab League, or even the United Nations could not (indeed, would not) have forced Saddam to withdraw from Kuwait nor been able to defeat him militarily. Instead, absent the American role, the alternative would have been international inaction.[6]

This is not to say that the Bush administration's role was consistently one of farsighted and effective regional leadership. Although its actions during the crisis and war were decisive and effective, its policies prior to August 2, 1990, helped to foster Saddam Hussein's strength, his regional ambitions, and his programs to acquire missiles and nuclear, chemical, and biological weapons. A basis for this orientation can be found in National Security Decision Document (NSDD) 26, an October 1989 policy directive signed by President Bush. The directive, which became available after it was partly declassified in May 1992, called for economic and political incentives to Iraq in hopes of moderating Saddam Hussein's behavior.[7] Indeed, the administration's earlier approach toward Iraq subsequently became the target of congressional inquiry. One analysis has described a "policy of appeasement," adding that "massive financial aid, comprising billions of dollars worth of loan guarantees, continued until long after it became apparent that Saddam was building an ambitious, menacing, military machine."[8]

In the aftermath of the war the administration failed again, this time in its premature cessation of hostilities, which allowed Saddam to save the Republican Guard and thereby preserve the security basis of his regime, and then in allowing Iraqi use of helicopter gunships against Kurdish and Shi'ite rebels whom the president had urged to rise up against Saddam in the first place.

Despite these serious shortcomings of administration policy, a series of revisionist objections to the American role during the crisis are unwarranted.[9] The first of these is the argument that sanctions alone would ultimately have been decisive in causing Saddam to withdraw from Kuwait. Given the Iraqi dictator's brutal treatment of his own people and his unwillingness to accept the U.N.-mandated terms for renewed oil sales after the cessation of hostilities, there is little reason for believing that sanctions would have had sufficient effect by themselves.

Second, there is the notion that military victory by the U.S.-led coalition was a foregone conclusion and that the Iraqi forces never represented a significant military challenge. This objection overlooks such facts as the Iraqis having prevailed in a grinding eight-year war against Iran, as well as their experienced army, which was the fourth largest in the world.

Third, there is the claim that the threat to oil supplies was minimal, either because no oil crisis ultimately occurred or because Saddam would have had to sell whatever oil he controlled. Such objections simply do not take into account the probable consequences had Iraq been allowed to retain control over Kuwait. With the 10 percent of the world's proven oil reserves already possessed by Iraq, an additional 10 percent from Kuwait, and the likely intimidation of Saudi Arabia and the Gulf states, Saddam would have been the dominant regional power in an area accounting for two-thirds of the world's oil reserves. The potential wealth and weaponry that these resources represented, as well as his ability to manipulate the policies of his neighbors through intimidation or the use of force, would have posed grave consequences far beyond the confines of the region.[10]

Finally, there is the argument that it not only would have been possible but desirable to avoid a war against Iraq. Here too the opposite is far more plausible. Iraq's neighbors and the entire region, as well as the United States, are fortunate that Saddam did not opt to withdraw with his forces and weapons intact and his nuclear, chemical, and missile programs all undisturbed. Had he done so, the coalition would have eventually disbanded and the United States would have found it difficult to maintain a credible presence in Saudi Arabia (for regional as well as domestic reasons). Saddam, meanwhile, after this latest demonstration to his neighbors, would have enhanced his capacity for intimidation. With Iraq so close and the United States so far, the ability and will of Gulf states to resist Saddam's domination would have been minimal.

AMERICA'S INTERESTS IN THE POST-GULF WAR MIDDLE EAST

American policies are the product of a complex interplay of factors, but they rest, initially, on a perception of national interests. For the United States, these are broadly defined, but at least four components are discernible: oil, the security of American friends and allies, regional stability, and values. First, a stable and secure supply of oil remains fundamental. The Persian Gulf accounts for two-thirds of the world's proved reserves of crude oil, whereas the United States possesses a mere 2.7 percent.[11] American oil imports now account for nearly half the country's supply, and domestic production continues a long-term decline. Two disruptive oil crises have already taken place, in 1973–1974 and 1979–1980, in addition to the threat posed by Iraq in 1990–1991. Thus, Presidents Carter and Reagan have conspicuously committed the United States to the defense of Saudi Arabia and the Gulf. In President Carter's words of January 1980, "An attempt by any outside force to gain control of the Persian Gulf region will be regarded as an assault on the vital interests of the United States of America, and such an assault will be repelled by any means necessary, including military force."[12] President Reagan in effect reiterated a comparable commitment shortly after taking office: "There is no way that we could stand by and see that taken over by anyone that would shut off that oil. Saudi Arabia we will not permit to be an Iran."[13] Previous security commitments to Saudi Arabia extend back to the administration of President Harry S Truman. Indeed, a 1947 message from Truman to King Ibn Saud states that "One of the basic policies of [the] United States in [the] Near East is unqualifiedly to support [the] territorial integrity and political independence of Saudi Arabia."[14]

Paradoxically, NSDD 26, the same Bush administration document that called for incentives to Iraq, also restated longstanding U.S. policy on Gulf oil as a vital interest: "access to Persian Gulf oil and the security of key friendly states in the area are vital to U.S. national security," and it added that "The U.S. remains committed to defend its vital interests in the region, if necessary, and appropriate, through the use of U.S. military force, against the Soviet Union and any other regional power with interests inimical to our own."[15]

Second, the United State has long supported states within the region whom it has come to regard as allies or friends. The commitment to Israel has been the most conspicuous, resting on history, shared values, strategic affinity, and long-standing agreements. Other states to which the United States has also extended some support include Jordan, Egypt after Camp David, and the moderate Gulf states. Indeed, this is explicit in the restatement of national interest in NSDD, quoted previously.

Third, and related to the first two sets of interests, is regional stability. Instability cannot only adversely affect oil and allies, it can also have adverse consequences far outside the region. To be sure, the demise of the Soviet Union has made it much less likely that the United States will be drawn into a superpower confrontation through escalation of regional conflict of the sort represented by the Yom Kippur War of October 1973. Yet, in an environment in which weapons of mass destruction have been proliferating, the likelihood that a future major regional conflict could be contained, even in the absence of the Cold War competition with the Soviets, is remote.

Fourth, and finally, there remain American values. Outsiders tend to underestimate the relevance of these to policy makers, as well as to Congress and the American public. In fact, their importance remains deepseated. For two centuries, values have been interwoven with decisions about and support for the international role of the United States. The fact that these values have sometimes been inconsistent or even contradictory, or that they have been much more important in some periods than others, is beside the point. In the present context, shared values, democratization, and a sense of commonality all have, or can have, a policy impact.

An explicit statement of overall American goals in the post-Cold War and post-Gulf War Middle East can be found in the Pentagon's revised Defense Planning Guidance for the 1994–1999 fiscal years. This confidential document, completed in May 1992 and promptly leaked to the press, sets out objectives for the region that mirror the fundamental interests already cited. Specifically,

> In the Middle East and Persian Gulf we seek to foster regional stability, deter aggression against our friends and interests in the region, protect U.S. nationals and property and safeguard our access to international air and seaways and to the region's oil. The United States is committed to the security of Israel and to maintaining the qualitative edge that is critical to Israel's security. . . . At the same time, our assistance to our Arab friends to defend themselves against aggression also strengthens security throughout the region including for Israel.[16]

Implementation of these goals rests on a combination of American capability for unilateral action and multilateral cooperation. There is a preference for "collective response" to preclude or deal with regional threats, and the revised Defense Planning Guidance puts less emphasis on unilateral action than did an original draft of the report. The document reserves the "sovereign right" of the United States for unilateral defense of its vital interests, but it describes United States military preeminence as a "catalyst" rather than an alternative to collective action.[17] The actual U.S. performance in the Gulf crisis thus appears to embody a conception of the American role that combines leadership with collective action: "Only a nation that is strong enough to act decisively can provide the leadership that is needed to encourage others to resist aggression. Collective security failed in the 1930s because no strong power was willing to provide the leadership behind which less powerful countries could rally against fascism. It worked in the Gulf because the United States was willing and able to provide that leadership."[18]

AMERICA'S POLICIES IN THE POST-GULF WAR MIDDLE EAST

In the immediate aftermath of the Gulf War, it appeared likely that the United States would attempt to fashion a security regime for the Gulf. This might have extended an American umbrella over Saudi Arabia and the moderate oil-producing Gulf states, with much of the cost absorbed locally. However, efforts to implement such measures as formal basing agreements and prepositioning of equipment tended to fall short of providing the kind of formal security regime anticipated.

Although a number of agreements were reached with Kuwait and informal cooperation continued with Saudi Arabia, the American-led regime remained largely implicit. This rested upon the historic commitment of the United States to the security of Saudi Arabia, as well as on the existence of bases and facilities that were originally "overbuilt" in the 1970s and 1980s, making it possible to accommodate a large crisis deployment of American troops and aircraft. However, other than an obscure 1977 Military Training Mission Treaty, which the two countries used as the legal framework for expanding their security cooperation,[19] there has developed neither the formal network of treaty commitments, nor integrated military command structure, nor prepositioning of tanks and other heavy equipment that characterized the long-standing American commitment to Western Europe during the Cold War.

From the Saudi perspective, this is not surprising. The regime has thus far survived the process of development and modernization while maintaining its own security and stability. In doing so, it has balanced a variety of internal and external forces, including extreme Islamic fundamentalist elements within the kingdom. An explicit, long-term, commitment to American basing, with the accompanying deployment of U.S. military personnel, could become a focal point for additional opposition to the regime, which it would otherwise prefer to avoid. Instead, Saudi leaders can point to the United States having kept its word by rapidly deploying a large force, overcoming the immediate threat from Saddam, then withdrawing over the horizon.

More important, there is the example of what the United States did to liberate Kuwait. In the absence of formal commitments, treaties, bases or prepositioned equipment, the Americans sent 541,000 troops halfway around the world to liberate a country whose importance and oil resources are considerably less than those of Saudi Arabia. Why then, from the Saudi perspective, should the kingdom incur the internal and regional liabilities posed by more extensive arrangements with the United States than already exist?

To be sure, security arrangements would be more effective with troops or heavy equipment already in place, as in the future there may not be six months for a build-up of American forces prior to the start of hostilities. Nonetheless, given the massive defeat suffered by the Iraqis, the Saudis appear to have judged that immediate threats do not pose a peril that cannot be deterred by the more distant American security guarantee. Moreover, with the demise of the Soviet Union and the defeat of Iraq, the Saudis—and others in the region—have concluded that the United States remains the world's only superpower. Other regional actors will be reluctant to incur the military wrath of the United States, even when it is visible only at long distance. To the extent the Saudis perceive the need for additional military means, they are reluctant to contemplate the presence of regional forces, such as those Egypt or Syria could provide. Even more than the Americans, the deployment of those Arab forces is seen as a potential threat to the regime. Instead, the Saudis will continue to rely on their own modest capabilities, continued additions to their air force (which appears to have performed capably during the Gulf War), and especially on informal development of security cooperation and contingency arrangements with the Americans.

A second major policy commitment by the United States, and one that has absorbed the most attention of policy makers, is to the Arab-Israeli peace process. To a degree, this has been affected by the Gulf crisis, in which the United States successfully warded off Arab introduction of the Palestinian issue. More important, the passing of both the Cold War and the Gulf War created unique opportunities. Soviet support for Arab rejectionist states and movements no longer exists. With Iraq defeated, Libya isolated, and the PLO seriously weakened after its embrace of Saddam, the conditions for pursuing the peace process became increasingly favorable.

Not only did the United States occupy a paramount position after the Gulf War, but erstwhile regional antagonists were prepared to defer to it. The fact that Syria's President Assad committed forces to the Gulf War coalition and ultimately agreed to bilateral negotiations with the Israelis owes far more to his desire to cultivate relations with Washington than to a belated embrace of moderation. Egyptian and Saudi support for the peace process was also crucial, because both countries backed a process in which the confrontation states, as well as other Arab countries, would begin negotiations based substantially on preconditions set out by the Shamir government.

In this light, beginning at Madrid in October 1991, the American-led accomplishment (with nominal cosponsorship by Russia) of face-to-face negotiations among the parties to the Arab-Israeli conflict broke a long standing taboo. Even though substantive progress in the formal negotiations was limited, and the breakthrough leading to the September 1993 agreement between Israel and the PLO occurred in secret bilateral talks separate from the established peace process, initiation of the talks represented a major achievement.

Even with the Israel-PLO agreement, significant perils remain in the peace process. One is that the September 1993 agreement may prove difficult to implement successfully. Another is that the Americans (implicitly) and Saudis (explicitly) may place exclusive emphasis on the Arab-Israeli conflict as the preponderant source of regional instability. To be sure, the Arab-Israeli conflict remains a profound source of regional instability and a possible flashpoint for a war in which missiles, chemical weapons, and even nuclear devices could be used. This logic alone is more than enough to justify a major political commitment aimed at ending the conflict. For their part, the Saudis tend to see the continuation of the conflict as the principal source of extremism in the region, and they therefore find strong reason to work toward its resolution.

Nonetheless, the Arab-Israel dimension has been irrelevant to many of the most serious upheavals in the Middle East during the past fifteen years. These include the 1979 Mecca mosque incident in Saudi Arabia, the 1978–1979 revolution in Iran and the coming to power of the Islamic fundamentalist regime of Ayatollah Khomeini, the Iran-Iraq war of 1980–1988, Iraq's August 1990 invasion of Kuwait, and Islamic fundamentalist resurgence within the Sudan, Algeria, Tunisia, Jordan and elsewhere. As a consequence, American commitment to policies that are addressed disproportionately to the Arab-Israeli dimension may not respond effectively to other significant sources of instability nor to threats to American interests.

Prior to the June 23, 1992, election victory of Yitzhak Rabin and the Labor party, the administration's confrontation with Israel over details of the peace process and especially over the Shamir-Sharon major expansion of settlements, ran the risk of conveying to Arab confrontation states that they must ultimately reach a peace agreement with the United States rather than Israel. A related problem was the investment of time by the principal figure in the Bush administration's foreign policy. Secretary of State

James Baker was forced to devote a disproportionate amount of his attention to getting the talks started. No administration has endless time available, and there is hence a risk of becoming distracted from other significant problems within the region and more widely. Moreover, American leadership in the process runs the risk of encouraging participants to believe that the United States would have the resources to pay the enormous financial costs of a regional peace. The Camp David agreements and the Egyptian-Israeli Peace Treaty created a precedent, but the United States will not have comparable resources available to underwrite the Palestinian-Israeli peace process by itself. Moreover, although the Clinton administration committed itself to a continuation of the American Middle East role, its election mandate involved greater priority for domestic policy than was the case for previous administrations.

A third major policy, closely related to the American role in fostering the peace process, has been the continuing commitment to the security of Israel and the maintenance of Israel's qualitative military edge. Here, prior to Rabin's election victory, ongoing military cooperation had taken place against the backdrop of an increasingly acrimonious political climate. Deterioration of the relationship between the Bush administration and the Shamir government began prior to the Gulf War and then accelerated sharply in its aftermath. Although the confrontation became particularly acute over the administration's refusal to support $10 billion in loan guarantees for resettlement of Soviet Jews, the problem originated earlier.

According to Secretary Baker, in October 1990, as a condition for obtaining $400 million in loan guarantees to be used in building housing for new immigrants, the Shamir government provided a letter from Foreign Minister David Levy promising to inform the United States about expenditures in the occupied territories. Moreover, in February 1991, Prime Minister Shamir's office gave private assurances to the administration that it would not increase settlement activity in the West Bank and Gaza. Specifically, some 1200 units were to be built in 1991, the same number as in the prior year. Instead, housing starts more than tripled, leading the administration to adopt a tough, even antagonistic policy toward the Shamir government on the subsequent $10 billion request.[20]

The Bush administration's stance affected a series of other issues. For example, after Israel deported twelve Palestinian activists from the West Bank, the United States voted for a January 1992 Security Council Resolution to "strongly deplore" the Israeli action—language more severe than for Iraq's invasion of Kuwait.[21] Subsequently, the State Department reaffirmed the moribund 1948 U.N. General Assembly Resolution 194, which provided for the resettlement of Palestinian refugees within Israel and called into question Israel's claim to Jerusalem. In addition, although subsequently revised, an initial draft of the Pentagon's Defense Planning Guidance offered minimal assurances to Israel; and in a particularly bitter series of leaks and unsubstantiated allegations, Israel was accused of improperly selling American weapons technology to other countries.

In the United States, a number of factors were conducive toward a recalibration of the U.S.-Israeli relationship. First, in a post-Cold War environment, and counter to the emphasis in both Washington and Jerusalem during the Reagan era, Israel was less valuable as a strategic ally against the Soviet Union and Soviet allies or proxies. Second, during the Gulf War, the administration had expended considerable effort to keep Israel out of the Gulf War coalition for fear its inclusion would jeopardize the participation of Arab forces. This was said to raise doubts about Israel's role as a strategic asset. Third, with the start of the peace process, it was argued that the United States needed to play a more evenhanded role rather than be perceived as chiefly a backer of Israel. Fourth, as a consequence of the war in Lebanon and then Israel's response to the Palestinian *intifada*, opponents of Israel increasingly sought to call into question the concept of shared values on which the U.S.-Israeli relationship was based.

In each case, a rebuttal existed: the Cold War provided only a small part of the basis for the U.S.-Israeli relationship; Iraq posed more of a threat to the region and to U.S. interests in 1990 without the USSR than in 1980 with it; Israeli retaliation against Iraqi scud missile attacks would not have caused Saudi Arabia or Syria to withdraw from the coalition; the need for American security cooperation with Israel might actually increase as American defense expenditures and capabilities declined in the post-Soviet era; the American position as intermediary in the Arab-Israeli peace process stemmed precisely from its closeness to Israel, which gave Arab states a major incentive to cultivate close relationships with Washington; and shared values and interests remained deeprooted and were reinforced by the fact that Israel continued to be the only genuinely democratic state in the region and the only one in which the United States need not fear a change of regime suddenly causing a friendly state to become hostile.

These two contradictory sets of arguments concerning the U.S.-Israeli relationship reflected opposing approaches in the American policy debate. Those critical of Israel or of long-standing American Middle East policy argued that changing circumstances dictated a major reappraisal and reorientation in policy. Those supportive of the relationship, however, continued to prevail in maintaining that American interests and commitments, as well as the stability of the region would best be served by continuing the policy of support for Israel. In any case, after taking office in January 1993, the Clinton administration emphasized its commitment to both strong support of Israel and promotion of the peace process.

Finally, beyond the policy issues of Gulf security, the peace process, and U.S.-Israeli relations, there remain security problems related to proliferation and Islamic fundamentalism—neither of which is wholly encompassed by traditional security agendas. The rapid spread of chemical weapons and ballistic missiles and the increasing number of states bent on acquiring nuclear capability pose threats of a different kind. Options for response range from unilateral attacks (as in the case of Israel's 1981 destruction of Osiraq), to regional agreements, organized restraint by suppliers, and broader international efforts aimed at restricting or halting proliferation. For American policy in the Middle East, this is a source of real or potential friction, not only in dealing with Assad's Syria or a friendly Arab state such as Saudi Arabia, but even potentially with Israel over the nuclear issue, as well as in relations with supplier countries such as Germany, Russia, China, and North Korea.

In seeking to identify and destroy Iraqi missile, chemical, and nuclear capabilities, the United States has worked through the United Nations. Washington has also become involved in multilateral efforts with existing outside suppliers of critical technologies and weapons through the Missile Technology Control Regime. However, gaining the active cooperation of North Korean or Chinese exporters of missiles, or of German manufacturers of advanced technologies, or of impoverished defense production organizations in Russia presents a difficult task. What is noteworthy about the problem of proliferation is not only its difficulty, but also the fact that many of the means for addressing it are not strictly speaking encompassed by Middle East security policy, but rather involve an international dimension that is less clearly incorporated in a regional approach. Thus the August 1992 draft agreement, negotiated under U.N. auspices, to ban the production, possession, and use of chemical weapons, can—if implemented—reduce one kind of security threat in the Middle East. However, the Chemical Weapons Convention, signed in Paris in January 1993,[22] is not something effectively understood through the concept of a Middle East security regime.

The problem of Islamic fundamentalism, at least insofar as it does not involve a discrete military challenge, also fits imperfectly within the confines of a regional security policy. The triumph of fundamentalism in Iran was largely the product of local forces, against which the extensive American program of security cooperation with the Shah was not only unhelpful but even counterproductive—particularly after May 1972 when President Nixon urged the Iranian monarch to undertake a major expansion of Iran's military forces and regional responsibilities.[23]

To be sure, the case of Iran should not be seen as prefiguring the future of Saudi Arabia. There, the regime has proven itself far better entrenched and more securely anchored in the society, and the Saudi monarchy has successfully projected itself as embodying the religious values in its society.

More broadly, however, in looking toward the challenges posed by Islamic fundamentalism across the region, in Jordan, Egypt, Lebanon, Tunisia, Algeria, the Sudan, and from the Iranian regime itself, it is not clear that an American security policy can fully address itself to a movement that might ultimately threaten U.S. regional interests. This does not mean that the United States can or should ignore the challenge or remain indifferent to it, but it does suggest the ultimate challenge may be less military than political in nature. As a consequence, response to it will depend on the capabilities and choices of local regimes and rather less on direct American actions.

The problem of Islamic fundamentalism is part of a broader, long-term crisis of modernization. As Fouad Ajami has observed, since the 1950s a series of radically different approaches have been embraced throughout the Arab world. These have been greeted as alternatives to confronting more deepseated problems stemming from the passing of traditional society ("the rupturing of the normative order"[24]) and the need for social, economic, and political adaptation. Among other alternatives, Nasserism, Pan-Arabism, reliance on oil wealth, anti-Zionism, and the leadership of Saddam Hussein have been seized upon at one time or another. Islamic fundamentalism has become the most recent and one of the most important of these challenges. However, an American security policy that seeks, in the words of the Defense Planning Guidance, "to preclude any hostile power from dominating a region critical to our interests,"[25] may be less likely to be relevant to a future challenge from Islamic fundamentalism than it was in overcoming the threat posed by Saddam Hussein.

THE DOMESTIC BASIS OF AMERICAN POLICY

American foreign policy is a product of both external challenges and the domestic political system. It reflects pulling and hauling among different domestic interests, ideas, and institutions, as well as competition among different branches of the federal government. This interplay derives from the logic of the federalists, more than two centuries ago, who bequeathed a system to the American people that is often slow in responding to problems but that also has maintained the world's oldest constitutional democracy.

In policy terms, however this means that the United States is often late in reacting to problems until it is faced with a crisis. Generally, both the broad outlines of grand strategy and the specific details of policy implementation are subject to the competing demands of various domestic constituencies. Moreover, broad consensus on the fundamentals of foreign policy, which existed from the spring of 1947 until the end of the 1980s, has now come to an end. Postwar foreign policy had coalesced around containment of the Soviet Union and Soviet communism. In consequence, the United States committed itself not only to confronting the USSR, but to global policies of security and economic cooperation with allies. This policy consensus left room for sometimes acrimonious disagreement over implementation; for example, in the case of Vietnam. Nonetheless the fundamentals were broadly shared by policy elites and the public.

With the collapse of the Soviet Union, the longtime policy consensus has also come apart. The design of a new overall foreign policy or grand strategy, as well as more specific regional policies, will be shaped in part by external events and threats, but domestic factors loom particularly large. Therefore, claims for the defense budget, aid for the transformation of the former Soviet Union, contributions to international organizations, and various forms of economic assistance to Israel and Egypt (the two largest recipients of American foreign aid) are all involved in a broader contest for resources. Competing domestic claims stem from the budget deficit, the cities, racial problems, infrastructure, education, health care (which alone consumes some 14 percent of GNP), the environment, and various types of public and private investment.

Domestic problems led, in the late 1980s, to a growing debate over American "decline." However, whatever the difficulties of the United States, the lack of immediate alternative claimants to effective global power and influence means the country has remained the paramount outside power in the Middle East. Moreover, American leadership in the Gulf crisis and war demonstrated how exaggerated some of the declinist arguments had become, and the point has been wryly characterized by Charles Krauthammer:

> Before the Gulf crisis American declinists were lamenting America's fall from its perch atop the world in—their favorite year—1950. Well, in 1950 the United States engaged in a war with North Korea. It lasted three years, cost 54,000 American lives, and ended in a draw. Forty-one years later the United States engaged in a war with Iraq, a country of comparable size. It lasted six weeks, cost 143 American lives, and ended in a rout. If the Roman empire had declined at such a rate, you would be reading this in Latin.[26]

It is thus important neither to overstate, nor to minimize, the capabilities of the United States in responding to external challenges, particularly when the country and its policymakers find themselves responding to a foreign policy crisis.

CONCLUSION: THE AMERICAN ROLE IN MIDDLE EAST SECURITY

A regional security regime in the Middle East cannot be sustained without the active engagement of the United States. None of the regional actors, individually or collectively, nor outside powers, nor collective bodies such as the European Community or United

Nations has the ability to serve in this capacity. This does not mean that the United States must always act unilaterally or commit prodigious amounts of its resources or armed forces to the region. It does require, however, that the United States remain closely engaged, both to lead collective action (as in the case of the Gulf War as well as in galvanizing the Arab-Israeli peace process) and to provide reassurance and deterrence. This is vital, not only for Israel and Saudi Arabia, but also for the purpose of affecting the behavior of regimes such as that of Assad in Syria.

Indeed, in the Arab-Israeli arena the American role has been essential for nearly every significant understanding reached among the parties. The September 1975 Sinai II agreement, the 1976 red line agreement between Israel and Syria, the 1979 Egyptian-Israeli Peace Treaty, and the sponsorship of peace talks beginning at Madrid in October 1991 are cases in point. Moreover, the stature of the United States in the post-Cold War, post-Soviet world remains unique. It is evident in the evolution of positions taken by Middle East actors that the United States has been able to shape their expectations and behavior.

More broadly, American involvement in regional security can help to contain threats to Middle East stability. Political influence, cooperation in collective security arrangements, formal and informal guarantees, deterrence, the ability to project power, contingency arrangements, security cooperation, bases, and prepositioning of equipment can be significant or even critical in preventing or responding to threats. These means may be most effective in discouraging challenges from countries such as Iran, Syria, Libya, or a resurgent Iraq (with or without Saddam), and in reducing the near-term likelihood of another Arab-Israeli war.

The effectiveness and durability of an American-backed security regime cannot, however, be taken for granted. From a domestic standpoint, although constructive engagement in the Middle East currently receives bipartisan support, the sustained commitment of political and financial resources has been called into question. Challenges to this commitment were evident in the 1992 Republican and Democratic presidential nominating contests. The candidacies of Pat Buchanan and Jerry Brown represented very different political outlooks and constituencies, but they shared isolationist language and impulses nonetheless. Although neither candidate represented the prevailing sentiment in his party, each mounted a major challenge to the party nominees, George Bush and Bill Clinton, and each appeared to speak for a substantial minority of his party's voters.

American leadership in the Gulf War thus remains an uncertain reference point. The quick and decisive military outcome produced very high—and very brief—levels of public approval for President Bush. However, authorization for the use of force passed the Senate by only a 52–47 margin. In addition, had the conflict lasted longer, the casualty toll been higher, or the financial cost more onerous, the domestic consensus underpinning the war effort might have come apart. By implication, therefore, the ability and will of the United States to sustain a long-term policy in the Middle East, particularly in the event that the financial or human costs suddenly begin to mount, is subject to potential constraints.

Development of American-led security regimes for the Arab-Israeli arena and for the Gulf region can proceed at different rates and face different obstacles. In this sense the elements of a security regime for the former may be better developed than for the latter. However, even in the case of Arab-Israeli relations, the development and stability of an emerging security regime cannot be taken for granted. Actor expectations are shaped by the anticipation of sanctions for defection and rewards for cooperation. Yet the difficulties of the Bush administration in dealing with Saddam's postwar noncompliance with U.N. resolutions and ceasefire agreements, as well as the constraints on American ability to provide significant additional resources to underwrite an Arab-Israeli peace agreement, provide indicators that expectations of reward and punishment may be exaggerated. Moreover, if the United States is unable to achieve a Gulf security regime, it is at least possible that this will adversely affect efforts in the Arab-Israeli arena.

In addition, American-led security arrangements and security regimes may not be entirely successful in coping with the proliferation of missiles and chemical, biological, and nuclear weapons, nor for addressing the internal problems of local states and peoples. Nor is the relevance of security arrangements and security regimes to the challenge from Islamic fundamentalism any more certain, let alone fostering the development of civil society and constitutional democracy without which long-term regional stability may be difficult to foresee.

Of course, significant factors are conducive to regional stability. The achievement of direct negotiations between Israel and its adversaries and the signing of the September 1993 agreement between Israel and the PLO have broken longstanding taboos and created a historic opportunity for reducing a major source of regional conflict. The collapse of the Soviet Union, the defeat of Saddam, the isolation of Libya, the weakening of the PLO, and the collapse of the Arab rejectionist front are other factors that have served to foster a climate for negotiations. Saudi Arabia has provided important political and economic strength to the moderate Arab position, and Syria has moderated its policies in response to the prevailing realities. From a Middle Eastern perspective, America stands as the one real superpower, and this has had a significant effect on the regional climate. However, regional stability over the longer term will depend not only on America's political and security commitment, but on the outcome of regional events and forces whose interplay remains highly uncertain.

NOTES

1. Kenneth Oye weighs the competing arguments and tends to conclude that "reductions in Soviet-American military competition have lowered equilibrium levels of violence in the Third World." His conclusion is based, in part, on the argument that superpower involvement in local conflicts both raised and prolonged violence. Oye does, however, acknowledge the Middle East as a major exception. See Oye, "Beyond Postwar Order and New World Order," in Oye, Robert J. Lieber and Donald Rothchild, eds., *Eagle in a New World: American Grand Strategy in the Post-Cold War Era* (New York: HarperCollins, 1992), pp. 18–19.

2. For a discussion of the resultant "security dilemma," see Glenn H. Snyder, "The Security Dilemma in Alliance Politics," *World Politics* 36 (July 1984):461. The concept originates with John H. Herz, *Political Realism and Political Idealism* (Chicago: University of Chicago Press, 1951). Also see Robert Jervis, "Cooperation Under the Security Dilemma," *World Politics* 30 (January 1978): 167–214; and the assessment in Lieber, *No Common Power: Understanding International Relations*, 3d ed. (New York: HarperCollins, 1995), pp. 246–248.

3. Charles Lipson, "Are Security Regimes Possible? Historical Cases and Modern Issues," paper presented at conference on Regional Security Regimes—Israel and its Neighbors, Bar-Ilan Center for Strategic Studies, Bar-Ilan University, June 2–3, 1992, p. 21.

4. Janice Gross Stein, "Detection and Defection: Security 'Regimes' and the Management of International Conflict," *International Journal* 40 (Autumn 1985): 599–627, at 615.

5. President Bush specifically used the "all necessary means" language of the Security Council in the resolution presented to Congress and passed by both houses on January 12, 1991. See Bob Woodward, *The Commanders* (New York: Simon and Schuster, 1991), p. 356.

6. This argument is developed in Lieber, "The United States and Europe in the Post-Cold War World," in *Eagle in a New World*, pp. 315–334.

7. Elaine Sciolino, "'89 Bush Order Says Ply Iraq with Aid," *New York Times* (29 May, 1992).

8. Mark Hosenball, "The Odd Couple: How George Bush Helped Create Saddam Hussein," *The New Republic*,((June 1, 1992), p. 27.

9. Many of these arguments were based on outdated Vietnam analogies or crudely isolationist logic. For a more sophisticated approach, which nonetheless holds that other means were available to the United States in the crisis than the use of force, see Robert W. Tucker and David C. Hendrickson, *The Imperial Temptation: The New World Order and America's Purpose* (New York: Council on Foreign Relations Press, 1992).

10. The reasons for this are developed in Lieber, "Oil and Power After the Gulf War," *International Security* 17, no. 1 (Summer 1992).

11. As of December 31, 1991, estimated proved oil reserves for the United States amounted to 26.3 billion barrels, as against a world total of 991 billion barrels. At the same time, the figure for Kuwait was 96.5, Iraq 100.0, and Saudi Arabia 260.3. Source, *Oil and Gas Journal*, December 30, 1991.

12. U.S. Department of State, Bureau of Public Affairs, "President Carter: State of the Union Address," Washington, D.C., January 23, 1980. (Current Policy No. 132.)

13. Press conference, October 1, 1981. Text in *New York Times* (October 2, 1981).

14. The message adds that if Saudi Arabia were attacked or under threat, the United States "through medium of [the] U.N. would take energetic measures to ward off such aggression." Quoted in Walter Pincus, "Secret Presidential Pledges over Years Erected U.S. Shield for Saudis," *The Washington Post* (February 9, 1992), p. A20.

15. "'89 Bush Order Says Ply Iraq with Aid," *New York Times* (May 29, 1992).

16. *New York Times* (May 24, 1992), p. 14. Additional details can be found in the *Washington Post* of the same day. Note that an earlier draft of the report, dated February 18, 1992, was leaked to both newspapers and was substantially revised in light of the ensuing controversy.

17. See Barton Gellman, "Pentagon Abandons Role of Thwarting U.S. Rivals," *The Washington Post* (May 24, 1992), pp. A1, A23.

18. Quoted, *The Washington Post* (May 24, 1992), p. A23.

19. Don Oberdorfer, "U.S., Saudis Agree to Use Old Military Pact for Expanding Cooperation," *Washington Post* (May 31, 1992), p. A10.

20. The Baker position was spelled out in a meeting with leaders of the American Jewish Committee. See Larry Yudelson, "Broken Promises: Baker Says Israel Broke Commitments and Therefore Lost Loan Guarantees," *Washington Jewish Week* (May 14, 1992).

21. See, e.g., *New York Times* (January 9, 1992).

22. As of September 9, 1993, 148 countries had signed the Chemical Weapons Convention. These included Algeria, Israel, Iran, Saudi Arabia, Tunisia, and the United Arab Emirates, but not Egypt, Iraq or Syria. However, as of that date only three countries (Mauritius, Seychelles and Sweden) had actually ratified the convention. For a definitive treatment of the convention, see *The Chemical Weapons Convention Handbook*, Edited by Amy E. Smithson (Washington, D.C.: Henry L. Stimson Center, September 1993), p. 48.

23. Nixon and his national security advisor, Henry Kissinger, had developed the Nixon Doctrine, whereby friendly regional powers would exert influence in areas where the employment of large amounts of American military power had become too costly or impractical. For an account of Nixon's meeting with the Shah in Teheran on May 30, 1972, in which he urged the Iranian to "protect me," see Gary Sick, *All Fall Down: America's Tragic Encounter With Iran* (New York: Random, 1985), p. 14.

24. Fouad Ajami, *The Arab Predicament: Arab Political Thought and Practice Since 1967* (Cambridge: Cambridge University Press, 1981), p. 6. Also, "The End of Arab Nationalism," *The New Republic* (August 12, 1991), pp. 23–27.

25. *New York Times* (May 24, 1992), p.14.

26. "The Lonely Superpower," *The New Republic* (July 29, 1991), pp. 23–27.

CHAPTER 4

The United Nations and Security Regimes: The Unfulfilled Vision

Avi Beker

The effective operation of the United Nations system during the crisis in the Gulf in 1990–1991 and the success of the United States in mobilizing an international collective security action under U.N. auspices led many to believe that the international body has undergone a major transformation and that it will play a central role in the "new international order." After so many years of paralysis during the Cold War, the Security Council of the United Nations was able to pass resolutions that gave the approval for an international military action against an aggressor. Under the mandate of these resolutions, Iraq's aggression against Kuwait was reversed and Kuwait liberated. This is exactly what Article 39, which deals with the collective security mechanism in Chapter 7 of the U.N. Charter, stipulates: "The Security Council shall determine the existence of any threat to the peace, breach of the peace, or act of aggression and shall make recommendations, or decide what measures shall be taken . . . to maintain or restore international peace and security."

In a gradual approach, as suggested by the U.N. Charter, sanctions and military actions against Iraq were unfolded. First a call and warnings to Iraq to comply (Article 40), then economic sanctions (nonmilitary acts—Article 41) and finally, "should that measures provided . . . be inadequate, it may take such action by air, sea, or land forces"(Article 42). For the believers and supporters of the U.N. this success was very revealing: "The founders of the U.N. had it right, but it took forty-five years and the end of the Cold War to prove it: given the proper international environment, the entire global community can mobilize a collective response to aggression through the U.N."[1]

Though it was not a real U.N. military force as envisaged in the charter (forces of member states made available to the Security Council—Article 43, under the responsibility of the Military Staff Committee—Article 47), the Security Council gave its blessing to the operation and in its resolutions provided the mandate to the twenty-eight nations allied with the United States to launch the war in the Gulf. Moreover, the U.N. and its agencies played a more significant role in the aftermath of the cease-fire, and they operated at the very center of international efforts meant to carry out the disarmament provisions of the agreement. Teams from the International Atomic Energy Agency (IAEA) were supervising and inspecting the dismantling of Iraq's nuclear capability and other groups from the U.N. were executing the arrangements to destroy its chemical and biological arsenals as well as its ballistic missiles and their launchers.

The destruction of Iraq's existing stocks of nonconventional weapons and ballistic missiles was authorized by resolution 687 of the Security Council. The resolution also provided for the continued monitoring of Iraq's capabilities for developing weapons of mass destruction and ballistic missiles. Resolution 715 outlines a detailed program of monitoring and spells out the prohibition of engaging in all nuclear activities (except for medical purposes). In the economic field the United Nations follows up on the international sanctions on the sales of Iraqi oil and the transfer of properties taken from Kuwait during the occupation.

Is this really the U.N. as envisiged by its founders? The collapse of the Soviet Union and other communist totalitarian regimes is undoubtedly an unprecedented situation that affects the distribution of power in international relations. What is less obvious is whether these dramatic changes have created a new order that offers more hope for world peace, security, and economic progress. Similarly, it is still early to judge to what extent are we witnessing a new United Nations with a new role in shaping the course of international relations. Despite the good showing during the Gulf War, there are many reasons to believe that without major reforms the U.N. system will not be able to cope with the new sources of conflict and tension around the world.

It should be emphasized that when President George Bush decided to go to the United Nations to receive its backing and involvement in the Gulf crisis he had in mind, first and foremost, domestic considerations. The shrewd move to internationalize the opposition to Iraq was not really an attempt to get from the U.N. military forces or, even to win the support of world public opinion. The real target was the American public and the Congress:

> While it was obvious that the United States was calling the shots, the fact that the U.N. Security Council gave its blessing to American policy each step along the way provided a stamp of international legitimacy—one that was highly influential with the American Congress and public. The fact that other members of the coalition were willing to defray the costs born by US taxpayers also made the effort much more appealing . . . by successfully mobilizing an international coalition . . . the President amassed enough authority to overwhelm all potential domestic opposition.[2]

The United Nations was regarded, as hinted by James Baker, as an important tool, for domestic policies, and its resolutions authorizing military action against Saddam Hussein made it almost "impossible for Congress to reject the use of force."[3]

The image projected by the United Nation after the Iraqi invasion of Kuwait brought to the surface many hopes that the dream of the founding fathers would seem within reach. The vision of the world collective might was perceived in an almost idealistic fashion as a just war in which the international community protected the weak against the strong, as originally intended in the U.N. Charter.

In terms of a security regime we can discuss two types of mechanism in U.N. actions: enforcement of collective security and peacekeeping. Both types were practically put into operation in the Middle East. In both cases the United Nations was using military forces which followed decisions of the Security Council. In the Iraqi case the Security Council delineated an ad hoc security regime to permit sanctions and military enforcement measures in response to the invasion of Kuwait. Indeed, according to the U.N. Charter, military forces were supposed to be provided by member states to the Security Council but these provisions were never implemented; therefore, the action taken by the Security Council against Iraq was in itself "an improvisation to permit enforcement of the council's will without the specific means provided in the Charter for that purpose."[4]

Any discussion of security regimes in the context of the U.N. system must be flexible enough to include different levels of regimes. Originally the theoretical concept of "security regime" was developed as an analytical tool for the Cold War era and areas of conflict where the rules of the game were undefined. Basically it was based on the need to develop rules of collaboration in an anarchic world.[5] In such cases, there was a need to establish "principles, norms rules and decision making procedures around which actor expectations converge in a given 'issue-area'; namely, a security regime.[6] Indeed, the notion of a security regime can be regarded as an elaboration of Thomas Schelling's theories of bargaining and communication between adversaries. Schelling envisaged "limited adversary" relationship or even "precarious partnership" between enemies despite their strategic opposition to each other.[7]

Robert Jervis underscores the potential and the limits of security regimes in a way that fits the Middle East situation. Basically the idea requires "those principles, rules, and norms that permit nations to be restrained in their behavior in the belief that others will reciprocate." This reasoning explains the successful initiatives, though limited in scope and sometimes in duration, that brought about the stationing of U.N. peacekeeping forces along the borders between Israel and its neighbors Egypt, Syria, and Lebanon. But as Jervis points out this arrangement works as long as the parties believe "that others share the value they place on mutual security and cooperation." U.N. forces failed in Sinai in 1967 precisely because of the lack of this mutuality. Also, the basic asymmetry in the Arab-Israeli conflict, where a group of states refuse to recognize and accept the legitimacy of the other, prevents a more institutionalized framework of a U.N. security regime there. As explained by Jervis: "If a State believes it is confronted by a Hitler, it will not seek a regime."[8] The progress made in the peace process between Israel, the Palestinians, and other states is changing some of these fundamental asymmetries, and providing, therefore, more measures of confidence building for a security regime.

In a regional setting the actions against Iraq can be regarded as an attempt to establish an ad hoc security regime with established rules of behavior as well as setting sanctions for rule violations. In this particular case the security regime was able to mobilize the blessing and the legitimacy of the international community and operate as a collective security force. Moreover, the follow-up, which was carried out by different teams from U.N. agencies, brought to the fore the almost unlimited potential of the notion of security regime. To evaluate this potential within the context of the United Nations and security regimes in the Middle East we shall examine two levels of analysis: collective security (enforcement) and peace keeping.

COLLECTIVE SECURITY OF FIVE POLICEMEN

As indicated by Ruth Russell, the notion of peace enforcement that appears at the center of the U.N. Charter was a convergence of President Franklin Roosevelt's ideas on postwar international order based upon the "Four Policemen" (the four major allies of World War II joined later by the fifth—China) and the more modified approach of the State Department, which was thinking more in terms of the League of Nations, the U.N. predecessor. It was clear to those involved in the preparatory work, as early as 1942, that peace enforcement would be "the most difficult problem to resolve in planning a new international institution that would be able to use force when necessary to keep the peace."[9] President Roosevelt therefore faced the task of convincing the American Congress to join an international organization that would have powers of its own and was apprehensive of the tragedy of President Woodrow Wilson's disillusioning experience with the League of Nations. President Wilson in 1920 after being personally involved in initiating the idea of the league and writing its covenant, failed to muster the two-thirds majority in the Senate to ratify the league's covenant.

President Roosevelt was really thinking in terms of a police operation. In his address to the Foreign Policy Association on October 21, 1944, he asked the American Congress and public opinion to give him the support to join the international organization and provide it with the powers to enforce peace:

> Peace, like war, can succeed only when there is a will to enforce it, and where there is available power to enforce it. The Council of the United Nations must have the power to act quickly and decisively to keep the peace by force if necessary. A policeman would not be a very effective policeman if, when he saw a felon break into a house, he had to go to the Town Hall and call a town meeting to issue a warrant before the felon could be arrested.[10]

Unlike the council of the League of Nations, the U.N. Charter is based on the assumption that a state of war among states is a reality that has to be confronted by counterforce and collective security arrangements. The charter was negotiated while the war was still raging and the major thrust of the allies was to increase their military might to win. Therefore, unlike the league's covenant, where disarmament meaures took a prominent and central role, the U.N. Charter makes a very weak and marginal reference to disarmament.[11]

The concept of collective security is the cornerstone of the charter and evidently grew out of the league's failure to contain the deterioration of international security before the outbreak of World War II.[12] The sanctions and military means of enforcement that appear in Chapter 7 grant the Security Council the right to take far-reaching measures against aggressor states, including even a permanent military force on air, land, and sea to be at its disposal. These unprecedented measures were coupled with the veto power of the major powers (the Five Policemen), thus contravening the principle of equality in the execution of the collective security concept. In this sense the veto is, as explained by Inis Claude, "a weighing device, and acknowledgment of the inequality of states."[13]

In a sense it can be argued that given its political and legal constraints, the U.N. collective security system was aimed at preventing the rise of another Hitler who would endanger world peace. Perhaps, when President Bush compared Saddam Hussein to Hitler, he might have had in his mind the sense of urgency that the world, under American leadership, must eliminate this threat. This is exactly what Inis Claude wrote in his theoretical analysis of the concept of collective security as it appears in the Charter: "The point is that collective security is not a design for organizing coalition warfare in the twentieth-century sense, but a plan for organizing international police action in an unprecedented sense.

Its aim is not to sponsor the winning team in a free-for-all, but to eliminate international brawls by forcing aggressive states to forfeit their matches before being decisively beaten."[14]

Fortunately for President Bush, he was presented with the best international environment one could dream of to proceed with his organized police action. As written by Inis Claude, more than thirty years before:

> "All this [police action] is dependent upon the existence of a power situation and the achievement of an organizational situation making the massive overpowering of potential aggressors a feasible objective. The first essential of a police force is that its power should be so considerable, and that of its opponents so negligible, that any contest will be virtually won before it has begun; otherwise, its function will be that of conducting warfare, no-matter how it be described."[15]

The Iraqi war machinery (the fourth largest army in the world) was not so "negligible" and its nonconventional components had reached alarming stages. However, the American-led "police force" was superior without any question and the euphoric celebrations of victory in America should not conceal the fact that there was no real warfare, in the classical sense, in Desert Storm. In a nutshell it was a two-stage war: six weeks of one-sided devastating air attacks and only 100 hours of ground combat with almost no real battle.

Again, it must be emphasized that Desert Storm was primarily an American military operation with the participation of few other Western allies and, with a more symbolic role, several Arab states who joined the coalition. It was not, by any means, a military or police action of a real "collective security" force. The United Nations gave its blessing and the Security Council provided auspices for the follow-up. But, as illustrated before, the United Nations played an important role in the American domestic front but not the role envisioned for it in the Charter.

PEACE KEEPING: CHAPTER SIX AND ONE-HALF

As the Cold War mounted in intensity, the United Nations became a major arena for propaganda and psychological warfare between East and West. There was a complete deadlock in the field of international security and the Security Council could not operate under the provisions of Chapter 7. In the face of the collective security stalemate, the United Nations under the leadership of an ambitious and independent secretary-general, Dag Hammarskjöld, created the innovative concept of peacekeeping forces. Instead of a join action by the big powers, military forces were recruited from lesser powers, and their goal was not to defeat aggressors but to watch or restore peace, generally without recourse to arms. Usually the operation was called at the end of a war or after the outbreak of violent hostilities with the coordination and acceptance of the exhausted host countries on whose soil the forces were stationed.[16]

Peacekeeping operations can be viewed as a component of the security regime concept. Here we witness an attempt to establish a mechanism of cooperation that will provide some confidence-building measures and stabilizing means to prevent the outbreak of violence between hostile parties.

As an improvisation aimed at bypassing the complex realities of the Cold War, U.N. peacekeeping operations fit the pattern of Chapter 6 of the Charter, which deals with peaceful settlements of disputes. Getting beyond peaceful, but stopping short of sanctions and enforcement measures (Chapter 7), U.N. peacekeeping functions have been dubbed "chapter six and one-half."[17] Although it illustrates the limits of international organization, the U.N. peacekeeping operation highlights its ability to perform on the world stage with a certain degree of independence and an effectiveness not always matched by state actors.

Peacekeeping was introduced as an idea of "preventive diplomacy" by Dag Hammarskjöld, as an instrument to help stabilize areas of conflict so that parties might be brought together. The idea was floated before by his predecessor Trygve Lie, who referred directly to the crisis in Palestine (1948) and the need for "a small guard force, as distinct from a striking force."[18] Indeed, in 1948 the U.N. authorized peace-observation missions to Palestine: the United Nations Truce Supervisory Organization (UNTSO).

The first authentic U.N. peacekeeping force was U.N. Emergency Force (UNEF), deployed in the aftermath of the Sinai war of 1956. UNEF broke fresh ground from former small groups of individual observers, "the men with the binoculars," who were sent to supervise cease-fires in border regions. UNEF was a large paramilitary "peace force" of over 5000 men, made up of homogenous national units deployed as a buffer between regular armies. Later, UNEF also served as a watchdog over freedom of navigation through the Straits of Tiran in the Red Sea. UNEF I became the prototype for U.N. peacekeeping and the paradigm by which Dag Hammarskjöld codified, already in November 1956, the guidelines for this new form of U.N. activity. In Hammarskjöld's words, the newly formed force was "para-military in nature, not a force with military objectives," and, in more specific words: "It would be more than an observer's corps, but in no way a military force temporarily controlling the territory in which it is stationed; nor, moreover, should the Force have military functions exceeding those necessary to secure peaceful conditions."[19] It was agreed that, to succeed in U.N. peacekeeping, some prior conditions should be met: consent and cooperation of the parties directly involved, voluntary participation of troop contingents by a number states other than permanent members of the Security Council, the political control of the Security Council and the consent of its permanent members, an agreed budget and willingness of individual states to pay the expenses, impartiality of the troops, and use of force only in self-defense.

It is indeed an intriguing fact that despite the dismal U.N. record in Middle East *peace making*, namely, settlement of disputes and negotiating peace, the Arab-Israeli conflict became an active laboratory for a variety of forms of U.N. peacekeeping usually adapted to new conditions and arrangements following successive wars. Because UNEF was an improvisation, the General Assembly left it to the Secretary-General to decide on the composition of the force.[20] This was confirmed in a negative way when U Thant, Hammarskjöld's successor, withdrew UNEF in May 1967 at the behest of Egyptian President Nasser. This hasty and precipitated withdrawal could only vindicate the fears of Israel, as put caustically by its foreign minister, Abba Eban: "the umbrella was removed at the precise moment when it began to rain."[21]

For "security regimes" students and proponents, the stationing of U.N. forces in Sinai is considered as a typical case for the application of the concept. Here, says Janice Gross-Stein, the regime provides the procedures for its role "as a hedge against a miscalculated accident and again as a smoke detector." At the same time, in her study of the Sinai experiences she warns against the dangers of "overexaggerating the forces of stability and undervalue the impetus to change."[22]

To the surprise of many, UNEF II returned to Sinai following the Yom Kippur War of 1973 with even greater duties. In addition to monitoring and patroling the disengagement of forces between Egypt and Israel, UNEF II also controlled the buffer zone and verified limitations of arms forces and armaments in designated areas. Similarly, as part of the disengagement agreements in the Golan Heights, the U.N. Disengagement and Observation Force (UNDOF) was deployed in 1974 to separate the forces of Israel and Syria. Finally, in 1978 the U.N. Interim Force in Lebanon (UNIFIL), was deployed in the northern border of Israel, creating virtually a circle of U.N. peacekeeping forces around Israel.

All these peacekeeping forces were meant to help the superpowers manage conflicts under the constraints of the Cold War. In 1956, the two superpowers found themselves in the middle of the Cold War, standing on the same side against Britain and France; their cooperation helped to build force, although without their active participation. In 1967 they were on opposite sides making such a force impossible. In 1973, despite their opposing camps, the policy of detente pursued by both superpowers dictated a compromise such as the reborn UNEF II and UNDOF. In 1979, because of the Arab-Soviet effort to obstruct the Camp David agreements and the Peace Treaty between Egypt and Israel, UNEF II had to leave (in 1981).

For the United Nations, which was provided with a significant role in the Peace Treaty, the establishment of a non-U.N. body—the Multinational Force and Observers (MFO)—was a bad precedent and a major blow. At the beginning, the American administration of Jimmy Carter was reluctant to establish the MFO, despite its commitments in the treaty, and only at a later stage (August 1981), the anti-Soviet administration of Ronald Reagan established and deployed the force.[23]

U.N. SECURITY REGIME

There is an interesting resemblance in the behavior of four American presidents during this century in their attempt to use international organizations on behalf of world peace and security as well as for the American national interest. Daniel Patrick Moynihan, who explores American attitudes toward international law, concludes that Wilson and Roosevelt expressed "impassioned advocacy of international law and organization . . . at moments of unsurpassed power" by the United States.[24] When American power was so clearly preeminent, these two presidents, the founders of the League of Nations and the United Nations, were ready to afford the appearance of cooperation with an international body. Later, Harry Truman in Korea (1951) and George Bush in Desert Storm tried to pursue this concept of international collective security, though in Bush's case the United Nations was used for American domestic purposes. The fascinating fact is that in Bush's days, like in the days of Wilson and Roosevelt, the vision of the so-called new world order was built on a framework that was based on Pax Americana; namely, a world without a rival superpower.

It must be emphasized that the Americans are strongly opposed to a real reform that will restructure the U.N.: "Americans only support the U.N. when it agrees with it."[25] The reassertion of U.N. authority in the Gulf crisis was to a very large extent an American gimmick. The Americans were paying lip-service to the U.N. system of collective security but the real provisions of Chapter 7 of the U.N. Charter were never invoked. In the real fighting in the deserts of the Gulf, the United Nations faded into irrelevance and was called only later to clean up the mess left by the American-led allied force. As explained elsewhere "the Kuwait crisis of 1990 led to a highly improvised application of the collective security principles in the U.N. Charter, while the Charter's provisions for U.N. enforcement of security [Military Staff Committee, U.N. troops, U.N. command] were circumvented."[26]

Events and developments that followed the Gulf War revealed the difficulties that lie ahead in any attempt to strengthen the U.N. collective security system. Most nations continue to differ on the nature and means for such operations, which may interfere with their sovereignty. The major powers, and particularly the United States, are not going to hand over their freedom of action to the Security Council of the United Nations. In various debates at the United Nations, many states expressed their apprehension about the prospects of a stronger U.N. authority with "interference" powers as well as their suspicion on the nature of a Pax Americana through the United Nations. It is clear that there will be more demands to restructure the Security Council with its five permanent members. Economic powers such as Germany and Japan, who provided substantive financial assistance to the war effort in the Gulf, are regarded as possible candidates to get veto power at the United Nations. Third World powers such as India, Brazil, and Nigeria also complain about the discriminative character of the collective security procedures in the U.N. Charter and demand permanent seats on the Security Council.

Following Desert Storm, the bloodiest international conflicts have been the conflicts in Yugoslavia and Somalia, which highlight the limits of the U.N. system. In addition to restructuring the system, there will be a difficult task of paying the bill of future U.N. security operations. The more services demanded will increase the costs of intervention in so many regional and transnational conflicts. If the United Nations undertakes collective security operations it will multiply many times the expenses of the fiscally hard-pressed organization. In Desert Storm the costs were more than ten times the budget of the United Nations with all its specialized agencies. The Bush administration succeeded in getting from its coalition partners (mainly Japan, Germany, Saudi Arabia, and Kuwait) about $60 billion. It is likely that even far lesser amounts of money will be given in the future for U.N. operations. Moreover, it seems that in future crises the big givers will ask for more "representation" for their "taxation" and will ask for more influence in the political security decision making process.

A real reform of the United Nations in the nuclear age requires restructuring that goes even further than the provisions of Chapter 7. Already in 1946, when the Americans proposed the "Baruch Plan" for international control of nuclear energy it was acknowledged that the U.N. Charter was a "preatomic" document because it was drafted and signed before the first use of atomic bombs. A *New York Times* editorial wrote: "If the United Nations cannot produce an Atomic Charter that will work then the United Nations Charter will not work, either."[27] Leonard Beaton who tries to confront the new challenges of the Atomic age rejects the notion of world government as impossible and even undesirable and suggests instead a permanent structure of world order with supranational forces, including nuclear force. According to his plan, U.N. authority will be inserted into the chain of command of nuclear weapons forces. National forces will be able to deploy "nuclear forces only after a predetermined time delay or after an international decision had been made."[28] These ideas highlight the long way the U.N. system will have to go before it will be able to engage in collective security enforcement.

SHERIFFS AND PEACEKEEPERS

With the relatively short retrospective we have available it can be argued that too much was expected of the United Nations. During 1992 and less so in 1993 it was commonplace to speak and write about the new opportunities and challenges for U.N. military operations as a result of the drastic changes in world politics. In June 1992 U.N. Secretary General Boutros Boutros-Ghali released a widely discussed report to the Security council under the title: "An Agenda for Peace." The report responded to the Council's request for a proposal to strengthen the organization's ability to resolve world conflicts. The Secretary General's report emphasized the need for a strong military force to maintain global peace and stability. The plan speaks about a de facto U.N. army, where each member state will allocate up to 1000 troops for actions to enforce peace around the world. These U.N. military missions would be conducted under the authority of the Security Council and at the command of the secretary general.

Following his report to the Security Council and U.N. members, Boutros-Ghali continued to lobby for his ideas in meetings with world leaders and appeals to world public opinion. In several articles and interviews the secretary called for expanding and reinvigorating the role of the United Nations, which suddenly stood "at the center of international efforts to deal with the unresolved problems of the past decades."[29]

Boutros-Ghali has been supported by influential writers, columnists, and editors as well as by public figures around the world.[30] Making fundamental changes in the collective security system is difficult and presents almost insurmountable problems for the international community. Thus, peacekeeping operations were viewed again as the most innovative and workable option for the United Nations. In two different editorials, the *New York Times* gave a clear reflection of the wide expectations for the "New World Cops" or the "New Blue Army." For instance, "the world can finally get serious about the most promising way to contain chaos and combat death—a new blue army. With a force capable of responding quickly, the U.N. could save lives, check massive tides of refugees and discourage warlords."[31]

It must be emphasized that the trend to resort to U.N. peacekeeping in whatever mode preceeded the complete collapse of the Soviet Union. To some extent it was a bellwether to the vacuum created by the gradual decline of the Soviet Union during the Gorbachev era. Traditionally, the Soviets rejected a U.N. role in regional conflicts, although on few occassions such a U.N. role was accepted, albeit reluctantly. To be sure, peacekeeping operations, even when approved, were systematically obstructed for decades by Moscow. Later, however, as a reflection of its growing weakness, the Soviet Union began to embrace the United Nations as the most effective conciliatory factor in Third World conflicts. In 1987–1988, the Soviet Union appeared to view the United Nations, particularly in its peacekeeping role, as an indispensable mechanism and a positive factor for regulating conflicts and enforcing peace. This sentiment was manifested most clearly in Gorbachev's speech to the U.N. General Assembly in 1988.[32]

In the field of peacekeeping operations the new circumstances and the changing attitudes were translated into a major shift of polices. Between 1948 and 1978, thirteen U.N. peacekeeping operations were established and five of them were still in place in 1993. Between 1978–1988, despite tensions and conflicts, not a single peacekeeping operation was launched. However, regardless of this deadlock, appreciation of the U.N. peacekeeping role was acknowledged in 1988 when U.N. peacekeepers were awarded the Nobel Peace Prize. Then, in four years, the United Nations dispatched peacekeeping forces to fourteen new conflict zones, five of which completed their mandates and disbanded (in Afghanistan, Pakistan-Iran, Namibia, Angola, and Central America). In the first half of 1992 the number of U.N. soldiers and police officers increased fourfold, and by 1993 it reached the figures of almost 100,000, serving in thirteen U.N. peacekeeping operations worldwide with a budget of almost $4.5 billion. In 1992 alone the debt of unpaid peace-keeping bills had soared from $816 million to $1.9 billion. In Cambodia the United Nations established the Transnational Authority in Cambodia (UNTAC), the most ambitious operation of its type ever. UNTAC was charged with the mandate to administer the country in the run-up to the election, taking over the major government ministries, monitoring the withdrawal of all foreign forces, clearing land mines, ensuring the cease-fire, and so forth.[33]

In his lobbying efforts, Boutros-Ghali has tried to develop an attractive option to meet the natural objection of states to transfer control of their armed forces. Therefore, he emphasized strongly that there is no intention "to create a U.N. standing force" something, which he descibes as "impractical and inappropriate." Instead, the plan focuses on "stand-by forces," especially trained units for peacekeeping, which governments commit to hold ready, at an agreed period of notice. Such a force could be marketed by the secretary-general as a cheap and efficient option:

> A standing United Nations force would be too expensive, wasteful and inappropriate for the organization while it is in the process of a vital restructuring exercise aimed at minimizing inefficiency and duplication. If the United Nations had the elements of a rapid deployment force at its disposal, on a stand-by basis, it would possess an enhanced capacity to deploy while not loading itself down with another layer of bureaucracy.[34]

Former U.N. Under-Secretary-General Sir Brian Urquhart, who spent much of his career developing the peacekeeping forces, was also among those who expressed hopes for a central role for the United Nations in the world order, particularly in peacekeeping. Urquhart urged others to seize the opportunities provided by the new international climate by creating a stronger structure. Instead of the previous last minute, ad hoc compromises and improvisations that have characterized peace-keeping missions, he suggested a more organized and systematic planning. He envisaged the transformation of peacekeeping from today's improvisation of a "sherrif's posse" to a more reliable and coordinated system.[35] Writing before the Gulf crisis, Urquhart provided some indications on different options that might be considered by the U.N. and its Security Council. For instance, Urquhart suggested broadening the mandate of peace-keeping operations, allowing more interference and impingement on national sovereignty. The Cambodian case serves as an example that involved an internal process, in which U.N. forces took a major role in preparing the ground for national elections. Also, in some cases the Security Council could move beyond the existing principle, understanding that the consent of all parties involved is a prerequisite for action. In other words, such a proposal injects some enforcement measures, taken from the collective security regime, into the peacekeeping security regime. This tendency may be enhanced by increasing the military strength of the forces, improving their training and assigning them new types of operations: emergency relief missions, fighting terrorism, or inspecting and monitoring arms control agreements.

Lt. General Gustav Hagglund of Finland, who served in UNEF, UNDOF, and UNIFIL, exposes the different weaknesses of existing arrangements for peacekeeping in war zones, particularly in the Arab-Israeli conflict.[36] Hagglund examines the threats and obstacles in the existing framework, which involves mainly police and inspection roles in conditions where U.N. forces are inferior in strength to the parties in conflict. However, he does not rule out *peace enforcement* by U.N. forces if it involves different forces and modes of operation. New approaches and techniques can include certain measures of disarmament and arms limitation that were applied by UNEF and UNDOF. Innovative and technologically advanced methods can be deployed in future assignments of surveillance and inspection of war activities or arms control. As agreements move toward greater mutual transparency, the notion of an Open Skies system can play an important role in a U.N. security regime. Such a system would be composed of a fleet of U.N. surveillance planes or even a U.N. satellite authority that operates satellites capable of supplying U.N. peacekeeping with up-to-date information.[37]

POST-COLD WAR DISILLUSIONS

Contrary to certain observations, the end of the Cold War did not usher in an era of global peace and security. However, one significant dividend of the dramatic improvement in relations between Washington and Moscow took place in the United Nations, which then became more relevant to the reality outside. The rhetoric and propaganda warfare that characterized the Cold War era and the days of the North-South confrontation were replaced with a more worldly and businesslike attitude, which is also reflected in Middle East debates and votes in the General Assembly. The repeal, in December 1991, of General Assembly Resolution 3379 (1975) which equated Zionism with racism, helped to restore some legitimacy to the United Nations. Prior to this, the resolution rendered the United Nations (in Israel's eyes) morally bankrupt and completely irrelevant to the peace process in the Middle East. The annual ritual around the Arab initiative to reject the credentials of the Israeli delegation came to an end in 1991, as Arab diplomats rushed to leave the General Assembly when the Israeli Foreign Minister arrived at the rostrum to deliver his statement. This process was enhanced in 1993 following the Israel-PLO (Palestine Liberation Organization) agreement and the handshake between Prime Minister Itzhak Rabin and Chairman Yasser Arafat, almost twenty years after Arafat's historic appearance at the U.N.

Following the initial euphoria and the ceremonies, it became apparent that some of the basic enmities and differences between Israel, the Palestinians, and the Arabs remain. In this context is hard to assess where the United Nations can play a constructive role. The removal of the Cold War factor from the Middle East conflict is something that may feed some hopes of a U.N. role. However, the post-Cold War nature of conflicts around the world and the United Nations' general failure to resolve them is discouraging.

The post-Cold War geopolitical situation presents us with a complicated and bewildering puzzle of threats and dangers. Instead of a clear and present danger, there is a diffusion of threats and the forces of separatism and fragmentation feed new tensions and conflicts. The demise of the Cold War has revived the old type of conflicts that were dormant for a while: civil wars, ethnic wars, wars of religion, or worse, a blend of all three, as in Bosnia. With the lack of tight control by the superpowers, sources of unrest are no longer kept in check and ethnic rivalries have reignited with even more lethal energy.

If 1992 was the year of the "U.N. optimists," the disappointments of 1993, particularly in light of the powerless U.N. peacekeepers, created the wave of the "U.N. pessimists." The United Nations record in certain conflicts during the course of 1987–1992 created unrealistic expectations and planted illusions about the United Nations possible role in the "new world order." The Iran-Iraq war, the South African presence in Namibia, the Soviet presence in Afghanistan, the Vietnamese presence in Cambodia, and the Gulf War are such examples. Perhaps the successes in these cases were a result, to a large extent, of the diminishing role of the Soviets, and superpower rivalry, in regional conflicts. However, it is wrong to conclude that the same methods or a greater United Nations' role will be effective in new emerging conflicts. The post-Cold War world is characterized by struggles involving civil war among ethnic groups, a phenomenon that is completely different from the interstate conflicts the U.N. Charter discusses and its peacekeepers have dealt with. Lofty principles such as "the right of intervention for humanitarian purposes" lost their attractiveness as soon as political support by public opinion in the West, particularly in the United States, began to evaporate.

The *New York Times,* which in a 1992 editorial urged the U.N. world cops "to contain chaos . . . and discourage warlords," presented a contrasting opinion in October 1993 in light of the difficulties in Somalia. Under the title "Bring Them Home Now" the editorial asserted: "Americans need feel no shame in withdrawing. The mission to Somalia was undertaken as a humanitarian gesture, to get food to starving people. The American public did not sign on to armed intervention in the clan politics of a chaotic country that poses no international threat."[38]

The shifting attitudes of American public opinion and opinion makers is remarkable. In September 1992 the *New York Times* regarded the U.N. forces mandate as fitting "to contain chaos . . . and discourage warlords." A year later it found it appalling to intervene "in the clan politics of a chaotic country." More revealing, and perhaps testifying to world public opinion's acceptance of ethnic bloodshed, is the refusal to intervene in countries "that pose no international threat." Therefore the yardstick is no longer humanitarian but rather security oriented, that is, self-interest. In the case of former Yugoslavia the same record of shifting attitudes can be detected. The future of the 24,000 blue-helmeted U.N. troops there is uncertain. U.N. presence in Bosnia has done nothing to stop the fighting and little to relieve the suffering. The troops there are watching how peace is deteriorating. The United Nations saddled itself with a series of tasks that were beyond the reach of its mission and traditional peacekeeping. The forces were not there just as a buffer, but were trying to set up interethnic law and order in a disintegrating society with hostile communities. Some of the temporary achievements of the U.N. forces and the positive role of their presence is overshadowed by the bloodshed, atrocities and human suffering that continues in the proximity of U.N. "peacekeeping."

The peace process in the Middle East and the evolution of an independent Palestinian autonomous entity may revive old ideas of a U.N. role in the territories. This was always supported by the Arabs in their efforts to force Israeli withdrawal from the territories. Also, for a while, in the post-Soviet world many suggestions were made that the United Nations engage in "nation building" and foster development and democratization (as suggested in Boutros-Ghali's agenda for peace).

The operation in Cambodia may be offered as a relevant model. The U.N. Transitional Authority in Cambodia has spent $2 billion, in essence to run the country until elections were held in May 1993. The 20,000 U.N. personnel, however, can claim only partial success. The conduct of the voting was a remarkable success but it is still questionable whether this will bring lasting peace to Cambodia. In the Middle East, even in the Palestinian context, it is hard to conceive a similar role of a "poll watcher" for the United Nation. The Israel-PLO agreement did not even mention a U.N. role and showed a clear preference for the bilateral committees between the parties. American involvement is likely to continue but U.N. failures elsewhere will not encourage the parties to bring in the blue helmets.

As explained by Henry Kissinger, statements that cite Cambodia as a model of a successful U.N.-led "political solution" are deceiving. In fact he says, Cambodia proves the opposite. After twenty years of warfare all the parties in Cambodia were completely exhausted: "The 'political solution' reflected the military situation; it was not a substitute for it. The United Nations provided the forum in which the exhausted parties could talk."[39]

The conflict in Somalia and the failures in Yugoslavia are case studies in understanding the limits of U.N. peacekeeping in the new conflicts of the post Cold War era. The headlines in the American press tell it all: "Somalia, the Making of a Fiasco" or "Anatomy of a Disaster," just to quote few.[40] The prospects for future operations are pessimistic, and as *Time* magazine explains, the attempt to broaden U.N. intervention powers seemed to fail in Somalia. The intent was that the American-initiated "Operation Restore Hope" in Somalia would serve as a forerunner for a new kind of U.N. intervention. That is not just "to monitor a peace but to establish one" without the traditional need to get the consent of the host country. Somalia instead had set a very different precedent: "of extreme US reluctance to mount or join any peacekeeping operation except one that poses little or no risk of casualties."[41] The lessons of more recent U.N. peacekeeping operations are still being absorbed and digested. The most fundamental lesson of the post-Cold War order is that there are too many Bosnias, and Somalias but not enough political will to do anything about them.

The war in the Gulf was regarded as a prototype of the conflicts where a U.N. army would fight and materialize the concept of "collective internationalism." It seems today that such conflicts in which the leading superpower has so many vital stakes (oil) and the aggressor is clearly identifiable are the likely exceptions in the world system. The more fitting model of U.N. operations is the messy U.N. intervention in the Belgian Congo (now Zaire), which lasted from 1960 to 1964, involving a total of over 93,000 troops from thirty-four countries, cost $411 million, and ultimately proved disastrous. In this case, it is widely argued, the U.N. intervention internationalized and prolonged a local conflict that could have been dealt with quickly.[42]

A U.N. stand-by force would not help because the major powers are not willing to risk their soldiers or finance operations in areas that do not affect their immediate security. Moreover, the U.N. Charter itself has designated peace enforcement in those instances that pose threats to "international peace and security" and in the post-Cold War this is a questionable concept. Tragic civil wars and horrible ethnic killings are heartrending to any observer but they are very complex to settle and do not appear to justify further loss of life by outside peace enforcers. If Europeans or Africans lack the political will to counter aggression and slaughter on their own continents, it is inconceivable to expect the United States, which no longer looks at the world through the bipolar prism, to police every interethnic dispute. The American behavior under the Clinton administration shows a clear retreat from activism in international affairs. Peacekeeping in complex situations is less suited for a superpower in the post-Cold War. Superpowers are well equipped for total wars and in a bipolar competition they do not allow unchecked escalations in regional conflicts. Unipolar worlds are inherently unstable and the parties in the Middle East will have to find most of the components for confidence building within their own region.

NOTES

1. Edward C. Luck and Toby Trister Gati, "Whose Collective Security?" *The Washington Quarterly* (Spring 1992): 43. The authors are president and senior vice-president for policy studies, respectively, of the United Nations Association of the USA.

2. David Gergen, "America's Missed Opportunities," *Foreign Affairs, America and the World* (1991): 5.

3. Ibid., p.10.

4. Bruce Russett and James S. Sutterlin, "The UN in a New World Order," *Foreign Affairs* (Spring 1991): 69.

5. Arthur Stein, "Coordination and Collaboration: Regimes in an Arachic World," *International Organization* 36, no. 2 (Spring 1982): 99–324.

6. Stephen Krasner "Structural Causes and Regime Consequences," *International Organization* 36, no. 2 (Spring 1982) 185.

7. Thomas Schelling, *The Strategy of Conflict* (New York: Oxford University Press 1963).

8. Robert Jervis "Security Regimes," *International Organizations* 36, no. 2 (Spring 1982): 361.

9. Ruth B. Russell, *A History of the United Nations Charter—The Role of the United States: 1940–1945* (Washington, D.C.: Brooking Institution, 1958), p. 227.

10. Franklin D. Roosevelt "Peace Like War, Can Succeed Only Where There Is Will to Enforce It, and Where There Is Available Power to Enforce It." Radio address at the Foreign Association, New York City, October 21, 1944, in *Public Papers of Franklin D. Roosevelt*, ed. Samuel Rosenman, 1944–45 (New York: Harper and Brothers, 1950), p. 350.

11. For further analysis see Avi Beker, *Disarmament Without Order—The Politics of Disarmament at the United Nations* (Westport, Conn.: Greenwood Press, 1985), pp. 8–14.

12. Ruth B. Russell, *The United Nations and United States Security Policy* (Washington D.C.: Brookings Institution, 1968) p. 51.

13. Inis L. Claude, *Swords into Plowshares* (New York: Random House, 1971), p. 153.

14. Ibid., p. 258.

15. Ibid.

16. For a general discussion of U.N. peacekeeping forces and their operation in the Arab-Israeli conflict, see Avi Beker, *The United Nations and Israel—From Recognition to Reprehension* (Lexington, Mass.: Lexington Books, 1988), chapter 9: Peacekeeping and Peace-unmaking.

17. A. Leroy Bennet, *International Organizations*, (Engelwood Cliffs, N.J.: Prentice-Hl, 1980), p. 180.

18. *Public Papers of the Secretaries-General of the United Nations.* Vol. 1: *Trygve Lie, 1946–1953,* ed. Andrew W. Cordiers and Vilder Foote (New York: Columbia University Press, 1969), p. 131.

19. Introduction to the Annual Report of the Secretary-General on the Work of the Organization, 16 June 1959–15 June 1960.

GAOR, 15th Session Supplement No. 1A (A/4390/Add.1)

20. R. Higgins, *United Nations Peacekeeping 1946–1967: Documents and Commentary*, Vol. 1: *The Middle East* (London: Oxford University Press, 1969) p. 300.

21. John G. Stoessinger, *The United Nations and the Superpowers* (New York: Random House, 1977) p. 100.

22. Janice Gross-Stein, "Detection and Defection: Security 'Regimes' and the Management of International Conflict," *International Journal* 40 (Autumn 1985): 625.

23. See Beker, *The United Nations and Israel*, pp. 109–115.

24. Daniel Patrick Moynihan, *On the Law of Nations* (Cambridge, Mass.: Harvard University Press, 1990), p. 176.

25. Keith Hindell "Reform of the United Nations," *The World Today* (February 1992), p. 32.

26. Luck and Gati, "Whose Collective Security," p. 48.

27. *New York Times* (June 14, 1946). For further analysis, see Beker, *Disarmament Without Order*, chap. 2: "The Pre-Atomic Charter: Security, Disarmament and the Nuclear Factor."

28. Leonard Beaton, *The Reform of Power* (New York: Viking Press, 1972), pp. 201–211.

29. Boutros Boutros-Ghali "Empowering the United Nations," *Foreign Affairs* (Winter 1992–1993), p. 89. The original document appeared also as a 1992 U.N. booklet, "An Agenda for Peace: Preventive Diplomacy, Peace-Making and Peacekeeping," U.N. Doc. A/47/277, 17 June 1992.

30. For a critical review and listings of some of these see Jeffrey R. Gerlach "A UN Army," *Orbis* (Spring 1993), pp. 223–236.

31. "The New Blue Army," *New York Times* (September 20, 1992); "The New World Cops," *New York Times* (June 28, 1992).

32. On the changes in the 1980's, see: Augustus R. Norton and Thomas G. Weiss, "Superpowers and Peacekeepers," *Survival*, (May–June 1990), pp. 212–220.

33. Boutros-Ghali, "Empowering the United Nations," and in Thomas G. Weiss "New Challenges for UN Military Operations: Implementing an Agenda for Peace," *The Washington Quarterly* (Winter 1993): 52–66 and *Newsweek* (October 11, 1993).

34. Boutros Boutros-Ghali "UN Peacekeeping in a New Era: A New Chance for Peace," *The World Today* (April 1993), p. 69.

35. Brian Urquhart "Beyond the 'Sheriff's Posse'," *Survival*, 32, no. 3 (May–June 1990), pp. 196–205.

36. Gustav Hagglund, "Peacekeeping in a Modern War Zone," *Survival*, 32, no. 3 (May–June 1990), pp. 233–240.

37. See Michael Krepon and Jeffrey P.Tracey, "Open Skies and UN Peacekeeping," pp. 253–263, and Johan Jurgen Holst, "Enhancing Peacekeeping Operations," pp. 264–275, both in *Survival* 32, no. 3 (May–June 1990).

38. *New York Times* (October 9, 1993).

39. Henry Kissinger, "Foreign Policy Is About the National Interest," *International Herald Tribune* (October 25, 1993).

40. "The Making of a Fiasco," *Newsweek* (October 18, 1993); "Anatomy of a Disaster," *Time* (October 18, 1993).

41. *Time*, ibid., p. 50.

42. See Geralch, "A UN Army," p. 231; and Ensest W. Lefever, "The Limits of UN Intervention," *Foreign Affairs* (Summer 1993), p. 19.

PART 3

Regional Interactions

CHAPTER 5

The Damascus Declaration: An Arab Attempt At Regional Security

Bruce Maddy-Weitzman and Joseph Kostiner

Iraq's invasion of Kuwait on August 2, 1990, triggered the international system's first post-Cold War crisis. Although Mikhail Gorbachev's support for the American-sponsored anti-Saddam coalition wavered at times, the Soviet Union ultimately stood aside while its longtime ally Iraq had its armed forces pulverized. In essence, the crisis signaled the definitive end of forty-five years of a bipolar international system and its replacement by a unipolar, American-dominated system.

The change, characterized by the oversimplified concept of a "new world order" (and its companion concept, Fukuyama's widely but often unfairly discussed "end of history"), was correctly understood in the Arab world as being of the profoundest significance for the Middle East region.[1] Moreover, the trauma of the Gulf crisis, the worst inter-Arab conflict in the history of the Arab League, was itself a cause for acute soul-searching among Arab practitioners and thinkers regarding the preferred future directions of Arab politics, encapsulated by the declared search for a "new Arab order." The failure of the previous *ad hoc* arrangements for Gulf security was sobering for the Arab world. Moreover, Iraq's neutralization provided new opportunities for the Arab members of the anti-Saddam coalition—Egypt, Syria, and the six Gulf Cooperation Council (GCC) monarchies, led by Saudi Arabia—to translate their "common aversions" to aspiring hegemons in the Gulf into concrete action. Therefore, the guns had barely fallen silent when the so-called six-plus-two group issued, on March 6, 1991, the "Damascus Declaration," intended as a blueprint for fashioning the postwar era in the Middle East, particularly in the security realm but also in the political and economic spheres. Despite the ambitions of its architects, however, the plan to establish an Arab regional security system for the Gulf was stillborn.

A brief examination of the historical legacy of attempts to attain regional security may be instructive in understanding the dynamics that shaped both the issuing of the declaration and the failure to implement its provisions.

THE HISTORICAL LEGACY[2]

The structure and underlying patterns of interaction of both the Middle East and Arab state systems were established during the late 1940s and early 1950s and have remained remarkably durable despite the massive political and socio-economic upheavals that have buffeted the region over the past forty-seven years.[3] In theoretical terms, the Arab state system has been sui generis in a number of important respects. Inter-Arab relations have been characterized by a unique combination of jealous protection of particular interests, mutual suspicions, and intense competition, on the one hand, and a high degree of cultural, religious, and linguistic unity and adherence to a common, highly emotive set of general political principles, on the other. An intricate balance of power evolved; as a result, no one state has ever been able to gain hegemony over the others. But this equilibrium was not maintained according to strict "realist" principles.[4] To be sure, although inter-Arab relations were conducted gingerly within a threat environment with occasional resort to force—most notably Egypt's involvement in Yemen during the mid-1960s—it was not until the end of the 1980s that the threat became primarily military in nature. In general, Arab states did not deter their Arab rivals by maintaining credible military threats of punishment and denial. Rather, other factors combined to maintain regional equilibrium: the growing capabilities of states to assert particularist interests and deflect pan-Arab appeals and to mobilize both Arab and non-Arab support to maintain their independence when necessary; the limited capabilities of those states aspiring to hegemony; and deeply held notions of Arab solidarity and commonality that, however much ignored, still dictated the resolution of disputes by peaceful means and thus denied overly ambitious rulers much-need system legitimacy.

The neo-liberal approach expounded in international relations literature, in which states minimize risks by creating functioning cooperative institutions, is similarly unhelpful in explaining inter-Arab historical patterns. The record of sustained multilateral Arab cooperation is very poor: proposals for an Arab common market are almost as old as the Arab League; subregional organizations established during the 1980s with great fanfare—the GCC, the Arab Maghrib Union (AMU) and the now-defunct Arab Cooperation Council (ACC)—produced little in the way of economic development or overall policy integration.

The legacy of attempts to build viable security structures is similarly dismal. The Arab League's 1945 founding charter included provisions obligating the league council to mediate in situations that threatened to lead to war between member states or between a member and a nonmember. But the Arab states were not prone to submitting bilateral disputes to collective forums, and Arab mediation efforts, although incessant, hinged upon the partisan efforts of one or more states and were nearly always ad hoc.

In 1950, Arab League members agreed on a joint defense and economic cooperation treaty in which they attempted to institutionalize their oft-expressed adherence to collective security norms. Armed aggression against one member state was to be considered directed against all and to obligate an immediate response. A joint defense council and a permanent military commission were to be established to prepare appropriate collective responses.[5] However, inter-Arab divisions blocked their implementation. Similarly, efforts to establish a united Arab command along the eastern front against Israel, as mandated by the January 1964 Cairo Arab Summit Conference, foundered and then lapsed. Jordan's placement of its armed forces under Egyptian command on the eve of the June 1967 Arab-Israeli war was done out of peculiar circumstances having little or nothing to do with Arab collective security and was, in any case, an unmitigated disaster for Jordan.[6]

The natural result of the contradiction between particular state interests and all-Arab concerns during the last quarter-century was that inter-Arab politics were characterized by ad hoc, albeit sometimes durable, military and political-economic alliances designed for specific purposes: the formation of war coalitions against Israel in 1967 and 1973 and their subsequent dismantling; the anti-Sadat coalition of the late 1970s and early 1980s; the ebbs and flows of the Egyptian-Saudi, Egyptian-Iraqi, and Syrian-Jordanian relationships; the gradual coalescence of Arab support for Iraq against Iran; the stationing of Jordanian and Moroccan units in the various Gulf states; and the Egyptian commitment during the latter stages of the Iraq-Iran war to help defend the GCC states against Iran are some examples. No lasting alliances, based on ideology or regional contingüity, have ever emerged.

The 1980s witnessed renewed efforts to promote collective security schemes. The six-member GCC, made up of Saudi Arabia, Kuwait, the United Arab Emirates, Bahrain, Qatar, and Oman was formed in 1981. As originally conceived, the GGC was designed to strengthen economic cooperation and assert the members' independence and nonalignment vis-à-vis both revolutionary Islamic Iran and radical Ba'thi Iraq, and to counter the attempts of both to foment subversion.[7] Military cooperation among them began in the mid-1980s, albeit hesitantly at first, owing to the fear among the five smaller states of Saudi domination. To that end, the GCC states established "Peninsula Shield," an experimental 10,000-man multilateral force, conceived as an expression of common policy and purpose and as a symbolic tripwire to deter Iran (which by that time held the upper hand in its eight-year war with Iraq). "Peninsula Shield" was never tested during the Iran-Iraq war, and as the Iraqis demonstrated in August 1990, it had no deterrent value whatsoever.

As for the other two multilateral Arab groupings (both of which were established in 1989), Iraq and Jordan wanted the ACC, a quadripartite body that also included Egypt and Yemen, to have a security component, but the idea was resisted by Egypt, which was loathe to antagonize the Saudis and suspicious about the whole idea. Egyptian leaders saw it, ex post facto, as part of an Iraqi strategy to entrap Egypt and prepare the ground for adventurism in Gulf. The AMU was underpinned by a Moroccan-Algerian rapprochement that included a substantial Algerian disengagement from the Polisario movement's struggle against Morocco for the Western Sahara. The AMU framework was visibly promoted by its five members, but produced little in the way of concrete results, and the continued political turmoil in Algeria between 1990–1992 placed its activities on indefinite hold.[8]

FASHIONING THE POSTWAR ORDER

Iraq's crushing defeat in January–February 1991 at the hands of the U.S.-led international coalition resulted in the restoration of Kuwait as a sovereign entity, the removal of the Iraqi "revisionist" threat against Saudi Arabia, and the resanctification of the principle of territorial inviolability within the international system. Paradoxically, at the same time, the end of the Gulf War immediately raised the prospect of Iraq's disintegration into Kurdish, Shi'ite, and Sunni statelets and, with it, the potential of Turkish and Iranian intervention, with inevitable but unpredictable ruptures in the regional balance of power. The prospect was anathema: "we must say it loud and clear," declared Mubarak. "No to the dismemberment of Iraq. The territorial integrity of Iraq is sacred."[9] To be sure, the anti-Saddam Arab forces were convinced that no stable Arab order was possible as long as Saddam remained in power, but they preferred that Saddam be overthrown by members of the Sunni ruling elite, not by Shi'ites likely, in their view, to be dominanted by Iran. The failure of an anti-Saddam coup to materialize was disappointing to Saddam's Arab foes, and the Saudis were even driven to open a dialogue with Iraq's Shi'ite opposition to explore alternative means of removing him from the scene.[10] But there were no tangible results. As of this writing (October 1993), Saddam's grip on the reins of power remained remarkably firm, and some of his Arab adversaries seemed to be seeking ways to ease Iraq's isolation.

While anxiously watching Saddam struggle to survive at home during the immediate aftermath of the Gulf War, Egypt, Syria, and the six GCC states moved to institutionalize their wartime alliance by establishing a regional security system that would be able to meet future challenges of the type posed by Iraq's invasion of Kuwait. On March 6, 1991, their foreign ministers spelled out their vision of the postwar Arab and regional order in the Damascus Declaration. Not surprising, it was to be based on the principles embodied in the U.N. and Arab League charters, with special emphasis on respecting every state's sovereignty and territorial integrity, "the inadmissability of seizing territories by force, nonintervention in domestic affairs and a commitment to settle disputes by peaceful means" (although this clause was directed at Iraq, it also contains an implicit pledge by Egypt and Syria not to interfere in the internal affairs of the Gulf states). Economically, the signatories pledged to establish an "Arab economic grouping" that would be able to respond to the challenges posed by the establishment of regional economic groupings elsewhere (the imminent economic union among the EC countries was uppermost in their minds). More immediately, it would establish a framework by which Egypt and Syria would receive generous financial support from the GCC states in return for providing vital military services, an important tradeoff between resource-poor and rentier states and encompassing two different subregions of the Arab world (the Egyptian-Syrian "core" and the Gulf). However, the parties did not reach firm agreement on the specifics of the tradeoff.

Most significant was the security component of the declaration. The participation of Egyptian and Syrian forces in the anti-Saddam military coalition was not characterized as a one-time event. Rather, the declaration defined their troops as constituting "a nucleus for an Arab peace force" that would safeguard the security of the Arab states in the Gulf as well as serve as "an example that would guarantee the effectiveness of the comprehensive Arab defense order." Egypt and Syria, it was envisioned, would supply sufficient ground forces—infantry and armored units—to obviate any further need for a large-scale foreign, non-Muslim military presence. To be sure, Iraq's crushing defeat had removed the immediate threat to the Gulf Arab regimes. But, however tardily, their overall threat perception had been heightened. This, together with concurrent new thinking on security matters among both Arab officials and thinkers,[11] lay behind the declaration's security and defense component.

Like so many previous inter-Arab coalitions, the declaration's signators proclaimed their intention to formalize their alliance, through periodic meetings of foreign ministers, to be followed by a "contractual formula." It would be open to all Arab states that subscribed to the declaration's principles, a traditional stipulation designed to defend the group against charges of having formed a divisive axis within the Arab system.[12]

Four days after issuing the declaration, the foreign ministers of the "six-plus-two" group met with U.S. Secretary of State James

Baker, who implicitly endorsed the declaration's principles. Their willingness to advertise their pro-American tilt was unprecedented in modern Arab history and seemed to indicate their determination to go forward with the establishment of a regional security structure consisting of cooperation among a new core group of Arab states, which would in turn be intimately linked to the new unipolar international system. For the United States, association with the Damascus Declaration was a manifestation of the notion of extended deterrence; namely, an effort to ensure that its vital interests in the Gulf region were protected via the deterrence of covetous, ambitious regimes by local allies (a variation on the theme articulated by the Nixon administration back in the 1970s of promoting "regional influentials").

It quickly became obvious, however, that there would not be a multilateral Arab military force. Indication to that effect was given by Mubarak's announcement on May 8, 1991, of a phased withdrawal of Egyptian forces from the Gulf, declaring their mission to have been accomplished. The Syrians followed suit in June. Underpinning Mubarak's act was widespread anger with what Egyptians perceived to be Kuwaiti and Saudi ingratitude for Egypt's contribution to defeating Saddam. To be sure, the decision was congruent with the Egyptian public's longstanding reluctance to deploy troops beyond its borders (stemming mainly from Egyptian involvement in the Yemeni civil war during the 1960s, but also from the debacle inflicted on Egypt's expeditionary force in 1948 during the first Arab-Israeli war). In spite of this ingrained tendency, however, the Egyptians were in fact quite ready and willing to station troops in the Gulf if the Kuwaitis and Saudis were to request them. The accompanying economic and strategic benefits that rendered Egypt willing would have been considerable: ongoing large-scale financial transfers and the fashioning of an Egyptian-guided pro-Western regional order, whose two pillars would be a stable Gulf and the Egyptian-Israeli peace treaty. However, the necessary request from the Gulf states was not forthcoming.

Mubarak may have hoped that his announcement would force the pace, stimulate the "Damascus eight's" ongoing contacts and lead to results. But it was not to be, and the projected Egyptian role became increasingly marginal. In June 1991, press reports did speak of an agreement to establish a multilateral "tripwire" force of 26,000 along Iraqi-Kuwaiti border, in which Egyptian and Syrian contributions would be mainly symbolic.[13] The Gulf states, as explained later, preferred no non-GCC presence at all, favoring instead the establishment of a regional Rapid Deployment Force. Standing concentrations of (non-GCC) troops, declared Bahrain's crown prince, would have "many negative aspects."[14] Thus, the "tripwire" notion, which combined the concepts of political deterrence and a temporary blunting of the initial thrust of an invading force, was discarded in favor of a more amorphous combination of political and military arrangements. On July 16, the foreign ministers of the "six-plus-two" group issued a revised version of the Damascus Declaration. It heaped praise on Egypt and Syria, but pointedly deleted the previous characterization of their armed forces as constituting a "nucleus for an Arab peace force."

What had happened? Why the failure to translate principles into agreement? The reasons for the swift emasculation of the Damascus Declaration are manifold. The Egyptians, as referred to previously, had some hesitation about a permanent deployment; and the Syrians, who had even less of a history of power projection beyond their immediate "Greater Syrian" environs, must have been concerned over the likely negative reaction of their Iranian ally to Syrian participation in an exclusively Arab defense arrangement in the Gulf that would, by definition, exclude Iran, and even be implicitly directed against its supposed hegemonic ambitions there. More important, the GCC states were reluctant to rely militarily on Syrian and Egyptian forces, whose performances during the war to liberate Kuwait were far from impressive, paling beside those of the Western contingents. More important still was that the Kuwaitis and Saudis, pegged to host the Syrian and Egyptian units, feared the introduction of "foreign" Arab units that would potentially serve as a fifth column to subvert Gulf regimes, particularly in the event of regime changes in Syria and Egypt. The legacy of such attempts by radical Egyptian and Syrian governments during the 1960s was still remembered. In addition, Gulf rulers were also reluctant to grant Egypt and Syria the considerable remuneration being demanded (according to Western sources, c. $10 billion) The Kuwaitis and Saudis easily convinced the other GCC states to toe the line on this matter. Thus, intermittent discussions with Egypt and Syria during the remainder of 1991 and 1992 exposed the GCC's reluctance to institutionalize the Damascus Declaration's projected security and economic framework.[15] The GCC states were desirous of Syrian and Egyptian troops coming to the Gulf states' aid in time of need, as they had in 1990–1991, but they refused to countenance their presence on a permanent basis, favoring only *ad hoc* arrangements underpinned by "Arab solidarity" (not by ongoing grants of Gulf oil revenues), which would end after the danger had passed. Hence, the GCC states did not want a long-term binding arrangement that would entail an open-ended commitment to Egypt's and Syria's economic well-being and expose them to Syrian and Egyptian wrath in the event of disagreements.

The establishment of a viable security regime in the Gulf also hinged upon effective arrangments between the GCC states and the two most likely "revisionist" regional powers, Iran and Iraq. In principle, the GCC states had gained an opportunity to embark on their time-honored strategy of playing off Iran and Iraq against each other and thus increasing their own security. But in practice, they were embroiled with both states. The Iranians had objected in 1991 to being left out of the budding security arrangements, and to the possibility of a non-Gulf Arab military presence. As the prospect of a standing Egyptian and Syrian presence faded, GCC-Iranian relations seemed for a time to be developing satisfactorily. GCC leaders complimented Iran for its neutral role during the war, including its observance (even if less than 100 percent) of the blockade against Iraq and its nonreturn of Iraqi war planes that had flown to Iran to escape coalition bombing. They stressed their interest in establishing an understanding with Iran based on good-neighborliness and noninterference in each other's internal affairs.[16] Broadly speaking, GCC states were comfortable with Tehran acting out of its own interests as a balancer against Iraq (as it had done during the Gulf War) but not as part of a regional agreement: its active, practical participation in a regional security framework was deemed out of the question. For GCC leaders (and their American patrons), this would be akin to letting the fox into the chicken coop.

As had been the case with Egypt and Syria, the GCC's position toward Iran fell, not unexpectedly, short of Tehran's expectations. For under the leadership of President Hashemi-Rafsanjani, Iranian ambitions included playing the role of a top-ranking regional power, competing for influence in the newly independent Muslim republics in Central Asia and in the Gulf basin itself, as well as projecting its power further afield in support of Muslim radical movements. Iran therefore objected to what it considered the Gulf states' policy to rely on "foreign powers" for their defense. Moreover, the Iranian leadership wanted the GCC states to give concrete acknowledgment that, just as during the days of the Shah, Iran would play a dominant role in Gulf waters. To drive home their determination, Iranian forces extended, beginning in April 1992, their rule over the entire island of Abu Musa, unilaterally abrogating the power-sharing arrangement with the UAE that existed since 1971 and expelling UAE citizens from the island.[17] By incorporating Abu Musa, Iran could oversee the entrance to the Straits of Hormuz.

The move evoked a wave of anger among GCC leaders: the UAE even referred its claim over Abu Musa to the International Court of Justice at the Hague, but to no avail. Even more threatening to the GCC states was Iran's purchase of three Russianmade submarines for usage in Gulf waters. The Egyptians, for their part, wasted no time in condemning Iran for its brazeness. Already angry with Iran for pressuring the GCC states to distance themselves from the Damascus Declaration and for providing sustenance and succor to radical Islamic movements in Sudan, North Africa, and Egypt itself, Cairo sought to drive home to the GCC states the dangers of Iranian actions for the entire Middle East and the need for closer relations with Egypt to maintain their own security. Cairo therefore tendered a number of proposals designed to implement the Damascus Declaration principles, including those related to regional security. But its efforts were rebuffed. Following a September 1993 meeting of the "six-plus-two" foreign ministers in Doha, in the wake of further Iranian action on Abu Musa, Egypt's Foreign Minister `Amr Musa told an interviewer that the conferees had agreed that security relations be established on a bilateral, rather than a collective basis. Egypt was fully satisfied with that outcome, he said, emphasizing the importance of continued dialogue and cooperation among the "six-plus-two" to build the Arab order.[18] But an Egyptian columnist in *al-Akhbar* expressed another view, no doubt widely felt in Egypt: "Is it not better for us . . . for our dignity, prestige, and good relations with others . . . to wash our hands of this declaration and treat it as something that never existed? This way we can avoid reluctance and embarrassment and can be realistic and understand that the Gulf brothers have reasons preventing them from implementing the agreement."[19]

GCC states' relations with Iraq remained extremely tense. The U.N. commission charged with fixing the demarcation of the Iraqi-Kuwaiti border released its findings on July 21, 1992. They were heavily weighted toward Kuwait, alloting it small patches of what had previously been Iraqi territory, notably part of the port of Umm Qasr, which served as Iraq's primary outlet to Gulf waters. Iraq responded by repeating its previous declarations that Kuwait itself was merely a usurped part of Iraqi territory. This and other concurrent Iraqi measures against the Shi'ites in the south led the United States and its allies to declare a no-fly zone in southern Iraq south of the 32nd parallel.[20]

The GCC states themselves failed to demonstrate a united front in the war's aftermath. Traditional border disputes and suspicions of each others desires for territorial expansion continued to impede strategic cooperation. In fact, in late September 1992, an exchange of fire occurred between Saudi Arabian and Qatari units over a disputed border area. Fearing Saudi expansion, Qatar temporarily suspended its participation in GCC activities until December 1992,[21] thus effectively halting the "GCC march" for several months.

In the security sphere, Oman's Sultan Qabus proposed in late 1991 the establishment of an all-GCC defense force of 100,000 to supplant the existing GCC "Peninsula Shield" of 10,000, a body that had existed since the mid-1980s but was militarily meaningless. The December 1991 GCC summit had postponed discussion of the proposal, Secretary-General Bishara stated, because it was such a "sensitive matter."[22] The smaller GCC states feared that the creation of a united army would entail the loss of power and influence to the others, particularly to Saudi Arabia, which would undoubtedly make the largest contribution to the force and thus be in a position to dominate the rest.[23] The matter was raised intermittently throughout 1992. According to Saudi Arabia's King Fahd, "Peninsula Shield" would serve as the nucleus for a unified army. What remained to be agreed upon, he declared, were the specifics, for example, the coordination of arms supplies, unified training exercises, and the joint command of armies under the umbrella of the GCC General Secretariat.[24] GCC defense ministers, meeting in Kuwait on November 14–15, 1992, reportedly prepared recommendations for the upcoming GCC December summit regarding the linking of command and control procedures in the proposed joint command of the "Peninsula Shield" force.[25]

The absence of Qatar's defense minister from the meeting, because of Qatar's concurrent dispute with Saudi Arabia, cast a temporary shadow over the validity of the recommendations, but following the resolution of the dispute, they were ratified by GCC heads of state.[26] Still, their implementation seemed far off.

For all of the talk of a new institutional framework, GCC ruling elites concluded early on that the only viable means of security available to them was to rely on a series of bilateral agreements with Western powers. Therefore, Kuwait concluded defense agreements with the United States (in September 1991) and with Britain and France, (in February, 1992), whose provisions included training for the newly revitalized Kuwaiti army and immediate intervention in the event of aggression against Kuwait. The Saudis discussed similar arrangments with the United States but stopped short of signing new agreements, owing to differences with Washington over the prepositioning of U.S. personnel and weapons, and over the purchase of sophisticated weaponry, which the U.S. Congress refused to endorse.[27]

Overall, GCC leaders were far less shy or embarrassed about their ties with the West than during the heyday of militant Arab nationalist rhetoric and tradition. Another quote from the GCC Secretary-General is instructive: "We are not harmed or worried by the fact that Western countries have interests in our region. . . . We see no shame in cooperating with the West at this stage to achieve security and stability until our preparations for Gulf security arrangements are completed. . . . All of Europe and Japan rely on the U.S. role. International security is interlinked and consequently, it does not disgrace us and we should not be annoyed by these facts."[28] Iran's continued muscle flexing in the Gulf during 1992, including taking full control of Abu Musa and purchasing three Soviet submarines, further reminded the Gulf states of the difficulty in placating Iran and their need to link themselves as tightly as possible with the West. From another angle, however, the contrast between the Saudi reluctance to formalize a defense relationship with the Western powers and the eagerness of some of the other GCC states to do so pointed to the continuing lack of a unified strategy toward implementing their commonly held defense conceptions.

In sum, the GCC states could not establish a collective security arrangment in the Gulf region. Their inherent vulnerability and internal division rendered them incapable of bridging the inherent contradictions among the various proposed security options and effectively "managing" the competing interests in the Gulf of Egypt and Iran. The GCC states also had difficulties in distinguishing between friends and foes in this case: Iraq had been their guardian against Iran during much of the 1980s, only to turn into their arch-foe. Therefore, they feared, perhaps subconsciously, what the role of Egypt and Syria, their Arab shield during the Gulf War and self-styled linchpin of the proposed Gulf security regime, might be in the future. Consequently, the GCC states chose to stick to what they considered to be the most realistic and logical option—reliance on Western forces.

IMPLICATIONS FOR ARAB-ISRAELI RELATIONS

No new Arab order emerged from the Gulf crisis, at least not in any institutionalized sense. Regional Arab politics continued to be a "mixed game," governed by both competitive and cooperative interests dictated by the exigencies of the moment. What changed was that a new inter-Arab alignment had congealed, based on the marginalization of Arab radicalism, the near monopoly of U.S. diplomatic leverage and the utter absence of countervailing Soviet power. This is the real underpinning of the Damascus Declaration. Insofar as the Damascus Declaration continues to be the basis for Egyptian, GCC, and even Syrian foreign policies, the implications for Arab-Israeli relations are salutary. A dominant pro-Western Arab alliance that augurs for orderly behavior and interstate cooperation strengthens the hands of both Arabs and Israelis bent on achieving a diplomatic resoultion of their conflict. Moreover, there exist a broader confluence of interests between the two sides: Israel and the dominant Arab bloc shared a common aversion (although acknowledgments to that effect from the Arab side were only rarely forthcoming) to the power of radical or adventurist forces in the region, embodied by Iraq, Iran, and Islamic fundamentalists everywhere.

In addition, the failure to implement the declaration's military aspects has even a limited positive impact on the Arab-Israeli sphere, for it deepens the conviction that each state must look out for itself, mainly by forging bilateral ties with the United States. On the other hand, one must also note that the underlying divisions preventing the Arab states from coalescing even minimally in the defense and security sphere may make it more difficult in the long run for Israel to make peace with an Arab world at odds with itself than with one that exhibits at least a degree of harmony and likemindedness on core issues.

With specific regard to the peace process, the circumstances in the region were never so propitious for productive Arab-Israeli diplomacy. For the first time ever, no single Arab country or group of countries was willing or capable of derailing, or even negatively influencing, the Arab-Israeli peace process. Iraq has been neutralized; Libya has always been peripheral and is now even more limited by bilateral interests with Egypt and U.N. sanctions; Algeria has imploded; Syria, traditionally Israel's most difficult interlocutor, has decided that it can best protect its interests by participating in the peace process. The change of government in Israel in June 1992 led to concrete progress in the Syrian-Israeli sphere, suggesting that the two countries were closer than at any time in their history to concluding a peace agreement.[29] Iran, a non-Arab country, has of late been active in leading the regional opposition, but its capabilities remain limited for the time being and the Gulf is its primary area of interest. All of these developments helped to set the stage for the breakthrough in the Israeli-Palestinian track during August–September 1993.

The structure of the Arab world is also relevant to the foregoing analysis. The Arab world is multipolar:[30] The actions of each state are closely watched by the others. The Arab state system's competitive aspects have not been supplanted by cooperative ones. The primary challenge for Arab ruling elites is to juggle the conflicting pressures imposed by internal, regional, and international demands to ensure their continued survival, achieve a modicum of progress for their populations, and check the influence of Muslim fundamentalist opposition. In this light, the ruling elites of most Arab countries—Egypt, the GCC states, Jordan, and Morocco—understand that there is no alternative to the current, American-sponsored peace process. The Saudis were quite enthusiastic about the peace process up until late 1991, but distanced themselves somewhat from active support of the peace process, partly as a result of increased friction with Egypt and Syria over the Damascus Declaration and partly because of the government's need to avoid giving its own Islamic opposition groups further political ammunition. Saudi pique with PLO executive committee chairman Yasir 'Arafat over the latter's support for Saddam

Husyan during the Gulf crisis contributed (albeit probably in an unintended fashion) to the PLO's financial crisis during 1993, which in turn helped to catalyze the Israeli-PLO agreement on a Declaration of Principles and mutual recognition. Thus do the patterns of historical dynamics work in unforseen ways.

In addition to the near-unanimous acceptance of the peace process by Arab states, a certain degree of Arab-Israeli normalization has already taken place. For example, the levels of Israeli exports to the Arab world reportedly exceed $1 billion. Israeli tourism to Morocco has already reached considerable proportions. The participation of most Arab states in the multilateral talks also bears witness to the evolution of Arab thinking regarding future relations with Israel.

It is worth noting that Jordan, among the so-called neutrals in the Gulf War, was the most eager of all Arab states to see the peace process resumed. Moreover, from the Jordanian perspective, the fall from power of the Likud-led coalition in Israel rendered the regional environment considerably safer. However, Jordan's "nervous quotient" reached new heights with the Israeli-PLO agreement and was not completely assuaged by Israel's reassurances. Whether or not the traditional Jordanian-Israeli tacit alliance would reassert itself during the implementation of Palestinian-Israeli interim arrangements and the negotiations over the final status of the West Bank and Gaza remains to be seen.[31]

From another angle, it is too early to speak about overt, above-board military cooperation between Israel and particular Arab states, but the kind of partial military arrangements that developed in the Egyptian-Israeli sphere will be studied closely during the course of Israel's negotiations with Syria, Jordan, and the Palestinians. In spite of some hints from both Egypt and the Gulf states during the spring of 1991 of the need to strive to achieve a single, integrated political and security regime in the Middle East, including Israel, nothing happened, and so the Arab-Israeli and Gulf-centered arenas remained largely distinct from one another.

To be sure, there are countervailing trends in the region. The continuing strength of Islamic fundamentalism, although it does not seem to be an imminent threat to existing Arab regimes, promises to be a permanent feature of Middle Eastern politics for the forseeable future. The pressures in many Arab states for greater democratization, or at least for the widening of the bases of political participation (e.g., Jordan, Egypt, Morocco), are far from being an unmixed blessing and could pose considerable danger for both regional and domestic political stability. Algeria's failure to make the transition from a one-party state and command economy to a pluralistic order has been particularly instructive. The likely proliferation of nonconventional weapons in the region is most sobering. Iran's efforts in this regard, and its support for fundamentalist groups in Sudan, Algeria, Lebanon, and Egypt, in particular, are generating increasing concern among both Arab states and in the West.

In conclusion, the collapse of the Soviet Union and the overwhelming assertion of American and Western power during the Gulf crisis profoundly influenced inter-Arab affairs, occasioned much soul-searching by Arab officials and thinkers alike, and compelled Arab leaders to attempt to refashion an Arab regional security regime. As in the past, ideals for a stable Arab order clashed with inherent structural constraints, resulting in the failure to institutionalize the Damascus Declaration's blueprint for collective security and regional economic cooperation. At the same time, the growing power of both Iran and Turkey promise to pose, albeit in very different ways, new challenges to the Arab state system. On the other hand, the emergence of a unipolar international system had a stablizing impact on Middle Eastern, and particularly Arab-Israeli affairs. In the Arab-Israeli sphere, at least, the resulting changes in inter-Arab and global configurations have made the Arab-Israeli conflict more "ripe" for a diplomatic resolution, to be accompanied—presumably—by an American-centered security regime for the Arab-Israeli arena.

NOTES

Thanks to the Israel Foundations Trustees for helping to finance our data collection.

1. Even prior to the collapse of the Soviet Union, the internal changes underway there during the second half of the 1980s, and Moscow's resulting shift away from unstinting support for the Arab cause against Israel, was acutely felt throughout the Arab world. Syria's President Hafiz al-Assad described that period thus: "all the previous world changes that emerged in the aftermath of World War II . . . seemed of little significance, in terms of reprecussions on the Arab homeland when compared to the upcoming far-reaching changes." (Radio Damascus,

March 12—Foreign Broadcast Information Service [FBIS], Near East and South Asia, *Daily Report*, March 13, 1992.)

2. Some of the material presented in this and parts of the following sections draws on Maddy-Weitzman's "A New Arab Order? Regional Security After the Gulf War," *Orient*, no. 2 (1993).

3. Louis Cantori and Steven Spiegel, *The International Politics of Regions* (Englewood Cliffs, N.J.: Prentice-Hall, 1970); Leonard Binder, "The Middle East as a Subordinate International System, *World Politics* 10, no. 3 (April 1958); Yair Evron, *The Middle East: Nations, Superpowers and War* (London: Elek, 1973); Bruce Maddy-Weitzman, *The Crystallization of the Arab State System* (Syracuse, N.Y.: Syracuse University Press, 1993).

4. For stable security arrangements in accordance with a "realist" outlook, see Charles Lipson's chapter in this book.

5. For the texts of the league charter and joint defense pact, see Muhammad Khalil, *The Arab States and the Arab League*, vol. 2 (Beirut, Khayats, 1962), pp. 56–61, 101–105.

6. Samir A. Mutawi, *Jordan in the 1967 War* (Cambridge: Cambridge University Press, 1987), pp. 85–162.

7. For the origins of the GCC, see Esther Webman, "The Gulf States," in *Middle East Contemporary Survey (MECS)*, Vol. 5, 1980–81 (New York: Holmes and Meier, 1982), pp. 458–462.

8. For the establishment of the ACC and the AMU, see Bruce Maddy-Weitzman, "Inter-Arab Relations," in *MECS*, Vol. 8, 1989 (Boulder, Colo., and London: Westview Press, 1991), pp. 122–128, 144–147.

9. Radio Cairo, March 16—FBIS, March 18, 1991.

10. In March 1992, the head of the Supreme Assembly of the Islamic Revolution in Iraq (SAIRI), Shiite Ayatollah Muhammad Baqr al-Hakim, made a high-profile visit to Riyadh, where he conferred with the Saudi leader and other Iraqi opposition figures.

11. See Maddy-Weitzman, "A New Arab Order: Regional Security After the Gulf War," *Orient* 2 (1993).

12. For the text of the declaration, see Radio Damascus, March 6-FBIS, March 7, 1991.

13. *Financial Times* (June 16, 1991); *New York Times* (July 8, 1991).

14. Interview in *al-Sharq al-Awsat* and *al-Ayyam*, quoted in *Ha'aretz*, (June 27, 1991).

15. *Al-Sha`b* (Cairo) (June 23, 1992).

16. Bishara's interview in *al-Musawwar* (February 28, 1992); Kuwaiti News Agency (KUNA) (May 3, 1992).

17. *Al-Hayat* (April 9, 1992); *Middle East Economic Survey* (April 20, 1992).

18. *Al-Hayat*, (October 1)—FBIS, October 6, 1992.
19. *Al-Akhbar*, (July 13)—FBIS, July 22, 1992.
20. KUNA, August 27—FBIS, August 28, 1992.
21. AFP, October 1—FBIS, October 1, 1992.
22. *Al-Ahram al-Masa'i* (January 7)—FBIS, January 14, 1992.
23. Saudi Arabia's ground forces consist of a 40,000-man army and an approximately 25,000-man national guard. An additional 30–35,000 members of the national guard are charged with internal security functions. Of the eight army brigades, three are deployed facing southern Jordan and Israel, two facing Yemen, and two facing Iraq and the Gulf. The Saudi air force numbers 273 combat aircraft, about 110 training craft, 5 AWACS planes, and approximately 150 helicopters. The Saudi navy is considered to be of high quality, even superior to that of Iran. The Saudis long-term goal is to double the size of the armed forces. The size of the armed forces (the bulk of which are army units) of the other GCC members is as follows: Oman, appoximately, 27,000; Kuwait, 21,000 (this appears to be a pre-Gulf War figure, which the Kuwaitis aim to reestablish); Bahrain, 6,000; Qatar, 8,200; United Arab Emirates, approximately, 48,000. With the exception of a small number of Kuwaiti units and UAE aircraft, none of the smaller GCC forces were tested during the Gulf War. The Saudis of course were involved, in land, air, and sea operations: The performances of their forces varied, but both Western and Saudi analysts agreed that there was much room for improvement. (*The Middle East Military Balance, 1992–1993*, ed. Shlomo Gazit, Zeev Eytan, Amos Gilboa (published for the Jaffee Center for Strategic Studies by Jerusalem and Boulder, Colo.: The *Jerusalem Post* and Westview Press, 1993.)
24. SPA, March 28—FBIS, March 30, 1992.
25. KUNA, November 15—FBIS, November 16, 1992.
26. GNA, December 23—FBIS, December 23, 1992.
27. See, for example, *Jerusalem Post* (August 6, 1991).
28. *Al-Musawwar* (February 28)—FBIS, March 3, 1992.
29. Israel's chief negotiator in the negotiations with Syria, Prof. Itamar Rabinovich, told an interviewer at the very end of 1992 that he believed that the talks had attained a "critical mass" from which it would be difficult to withdraw and expressed the hope that a peace agreement could be signed by the end of 1993. *Ha'aretz* (December 31, 1992).
30. In this sense, recent trends toward a more multipolar international system are imitating earlier similar trends in the Arab world. Ironically, in many Arab eyes, the trend in international politics has been primarily toward a unipolar system, with the United States possessing an overwhelming preponderance of power.
31. Jordan's long-standing fear was that the Likud, committed to the ideology of the whole Land of Israel, from the Jordan River to the

Mediterranean, would seek to solve the Palestinian problem at Jordan's expense. The promotion of a large-scale exodus of Palestinians from the West Bank was viewed by the Jordanians as a likely scenario, which would inevitably lead to destabilization of the East Bank, the downfall of the Hashemite monarchy, and its replacement by a Palestinian government. The Labor party, by contrast, has always been committed to a peace settlement involving territorial compromise on the West Bank and the reassertion of Jordanian rule in those parts evacuated by Israel. Despite the fundamental gaps between Labor's views and Jordan's insistence on total withdrawal, both sides have long recognized their common interests in taming radical Palestinian Arab nationalism.

CHAPTER 6

The Israel-Jordan Tacit Security Regime

Aharon Klieman

In today's international relations there is singular importance to Ernst Haas's challenge to explore how "islands of order can form in an ocean of disorder."[1] And nowhere more so than in the "uncommon" and polarized Middle East.

I argue that the relationship between the Jewish state of Israel and the Hashemite kingdom of Jordan qualifies as a full-fledged bilateral security regime. But in defending this thesis—and before outlining how this unique regime originated in the past, the manner in which it functions at present, and its future prospects—a brief prefatory critical comment is warranted.

When the study of international regimes emerged in the early 1980s as a distinct and exciting new subfield of inquiry, signaled by the special 1982 issue of *International Organization*,[2] it was presented as an unorthodox counter to the traditionally normative, legalistic-formalistic and institutional focus on treaty alliances, the United Nations, and multilateral organizations. This refreshing openness is best captured in Stephen Krasner's widely-accepted initial definition of *regimes* as consisting of shared "principles, norms, rules and decision-making procedures around which actor expectations converge."[3] Efforts since then at introducing greater refinement in usage of the term reinforce the real-world emphasis of regime study by adding for good measure that they may be formal or *informal*, explicit or *tacit*.[4]

Yet, judging from the literature, the emphasis once again has become rather narrow and restricted, focusing almost exclusively on the formal and the explicit. In addition, the recent work on regimes suggests a preoccupation with

- the purely theoretical or historical (Jervis's "Concert of Europe" as a regime[5]);
- nonpolitical issue areas (economics, resources, welfare, technology, communications and, environmentalism)[6] rather than *security* regimes;
- even in those few instances of security-related studies, the emphasis is on superpowers and hegemons, on strategic and nuclear arms control regimes, and as Oran Young notes,[7] only those that are highly coherent and internally consistent constructs.

The results can be seen in Roger K. Smith's at once too demanding and too categorical 1987 statement: "There is little security regime analysis because there are currently no security regimes."[8]

I beg to differ. There are many more security alignments than meet the naked eye. We must simply concentrate our attention on less formal institutional arrangements and collective decision-making procedures that are unregularized and merely implicit.

This need for greater conceptual and analytical flexibility is admirably expressed in Alexander George's notion of a "partial" security regime, because "There are recognizable variations in the scope and clarity of norms and rules, in the adequacy of procedures to implement them, in the degree of institutionalization, and in the degree to which actors comply with regime norms and rules and the extent to which they are enforced."[9]

Nowhere are real-world regimes as typically unsystematic and ambiguous as in the Middle East. Even still, what little work that has been done on security relationships in this region is confined really to only the two instances: Egypt-Israel, 1956–1967; 1975–1978;[10] and Syria-Israel.[11]

Remarkably neglected is arguably the single most durable, insightful, complex and successful—indeed, most obvious—illustration of Middle East security regime dynamics; namely, the longstanding one between Israel and Jordan.

Security regime theory is indispensable in helping decode the nature of these ties, separating fact from propaganda and fiction. Just as, by the same token, the Amman-Jerusalem axis helps us in buttressing theoretical concepts with actual case material. To the best of my knowledge, this chapter will be the first attempt at systematically connecting Israel and Jordan to the literature on security regimes in seeking to explain a friendly relationship between obvious enemies.

Nor is this an isolated instance of what I will refer to as a limited or "tacit" international security regime. Indeed, it may serve as a paradigm for nonsuperpower, nonhegemonic, nonWestern, noncontractual and noninstitutionalized cooperation. It falls somewhere between: Although neither explicit nor institutionalized, nevertheless, it is far from chaotic or inchoate. As such it may be indicative of such other tacit security dyads as South Africa and each of the black African border states, the PRC and Taiwan, or North and South Korea, as well as conceivably Israel and Saudi Arabia.

Israel and Jordan, if properly understood as a tacit security regime, help us to distinguish "adversaries" from implacable "enemies"; to appreciate the capacity of warring states for what Puchala and Hopkins refer to as "discernably patterned behavior"[12] and Janice Stein describes as "creative conflict management,"[13] incorporating informal understandings and arrangements that in turn enable orderly, predictable behavior to take place in a setting of interdependence. And this between opponents still legally and officially in a state of war after more than four decades![14]

Earlier I called Israel and Jordan the most obvious expression of a security regime in the Mideast region. Use of the term *obvious* is of course slightly mischievous, because the most salient feature about the regime is the absence of salience! Indeed, its tacitness is what makes it so distinctive. It is also one of several attributes helpful in defining the special nature of the relationship.

To begin with, while perhaps falling short of Karl Deutsch's "amalgamated security community,"[15] the Zionist-Hashemite alignment does bear close resemblance to Robert Jervis's less rigorous "security regime,"[16] Barry Buzan's "security complex"[17] and Charles Lipson's "bounded cooperation."[18] Second, the Israeli-Jordanian connection qualifies as a security regime based upon Oran Young's three requisites for all regimes: (1) a substantive element, consisting of defined guides to action; (2) a procedural component, "recognized arrangements" for resolving situations requiring collective choice; (3) implementation, by means of "compliance mechanisms."[19] Third, this "grouping of the willing" is functional, meaning that it is based on rational choice, and is less than comprehensive. Enhanced security may be primary but it is not the sole collective good. Fourth, this particular regime is mixed adversarial. Reminiscent of Thomas Schelling's "mixed motive" game[20] and Robert Keohane and Joseph Nye's "complex interdependence,"[21] the historical record of the secret bilateral relationship shows evidence of both collaboration and conflict, simultaneous cooperation in one area, say security, and competition in another, political, area. So, too, does it feature an admixture of promises with threats.[22]

But fifth, and above all, this particular regime is tacit. I prefer the term to, for example, Ned Lebow and Janice Stein's 1987 coining of the term "*limited* security regime"[23] because that wording leaves us uncertain as to whether the regime is limited to security, or perhaps, alternatively, that the security function is only partially achieved.

The term *tacit*, on the other hand, conveys the idea that the Israel-Jordan regime, although not entirely "unspoken or wordless," does arise and operate without any "express contract." The regime does possess the requisite collection of rights and rules, however, these are unwritten and uncodified. Taking place through Robert Keohane's "decentralized enforcement" of understandings,[24] it is therefore less visible. Signals and subtleties are exchanged more often than not behind the scenes, between the lines, and under the table, via back channels involving indirect but also direct communication.[25] Official government statements, planted items in each country's state-controlled press, the opening of a Jordanian branch bank in Hebron or Nablus, beefed-up Jordanian border patrols, a message transmitted by an unofficial third party intermediary visiting both capitals, face-to-face meetings between middle-level bureaucrats or technical experts—these are but a few examples.

Precisely this shadowy feature permits "plausible denial" even though the tacit Israel-Jordan regime's by-now "transparency" makes it the best-kept "open secret" in Middle Eastern politics, even if not as yet in the academic literature.[26]

I suggest that despite this veil of secrecy and tacitness or, rather because of it, the two countries have moved in time from wary antagonists to silent but quite active, informed, responsible partners enjoying enhanced security and sustaining a climate of cooperation. Built up incrementally and regularized by these unspoken rules and "gentlemen's" agreements, the Israel-Jordan "mutual security zone" has widened, especially in the last twenty-two to twenty-five years, extending now beyond security into other functional areas that reflect a "configuration of interests."

Young distinguishes three stages of "regime dynamics": formation, or regime building; maintenance; transformation.[27] Accordingly, some remarks are needed about how this particular security regime originated, how it operates, and last, which general scenario possibly awaits it—perpetuation (open-ended), dissolution, or consummation.

THE EARLY FOUNDATIONS

The origins of the Jordan River regime actually predate the achievement of sovereign status by either Israel or Jordan. The general outlines precede their political independence by at least a decade, going as far back as 1937, and certainly once the 1947–1949 events left them as copartitionists of British-mandated Palestine.[28] Since then such basic considerations as geographic proximity, accessibility, overlapping interests and symmetry have acted as reinforcements. Both symmetry and the time factor are terribly important, and merit further comment.

Conventional wisdom emphasizes the obvious disparity in the correlates of *military* power between Israel and Jordan (Table 6.1). Nevertheless, in other key ways they are essentially equals. The epitome of David Dewitt's "prisoners of insecurity,"[29] they deserve to be seen as two small, vulnerable, defensive, conservative status-quo oriented actors, with shared fears and common aversions—to the Palestinian national movement; to radicalism, whether ideological, political or religious; to Arab unity. Consequently, both are prudent and cautious; neither is a risk taker. As "egoists," each acts out of self-interest. Motivated by Schelling's "conscious calculation of advantages,"[30] each carefully weighs costs, benefits, and risks. Having along the way discovered congruent, parallel core interests, as well as complementary anxieties and capabilities, they now epitomize Kenneth Waltz's classic "self-help system."[31] Theirs is a *common* rather than a *single* policy, but nevertheless has produced joint gains. And in compensating for their respective weaknesses they represent in effect each

Table 6.1
The Israel-Jordan Military Balance (1990)

	Israel	*Jordan*
Armed Forces Personnel		
Army	498,000*	170,000
Airforce	86,000	9,700
Navy	20,000	300
Total	604,000	180,000
Tanks	3,860	1,115
Artillery	1,300	600
Combat Aircraft	638	107
Helicopters	218	68

*figure includes reservists.
Source: Joseph Alpher, ed., *The Middle East Military Balance, 1989–1990* (Boulder: Westview Press, 1990); International Institute for Strategic Studies, *The Military Balance, 1989–1990* (London: Brassey's, 1989).

other's "force multiplier." Israel's declaratory policy defining the invasion or stationing of Arab armies inside Jordan as a casus belli has reinforced Jordan's security, much as Jordan's policing of the Jordan River frontier and effective control over the East Bank has provided Israel with the closest thing possible to security in depth, however imperfect. What I would symbolize as the Israeli sword and Jordanian shield has proven itself especially since the 1970 Jordanian crisis.[32]

1970—"BLACK SEPTEMBER"

The chronology of the 1970 Jordanian crisis is treated extensively in other works; their focus, however, tends to be either the internal struggle between Hussein and the PLO around Amman, or the role played by American foreign policy. The contribution rendered by Israel in the preservation of the Hashemite kingdom, while touched upon, is largely understated by comparison. Perhaps that is as it should be in a tacit relationship. Nevertheless, precisely because of the insight it offers into the utility and actual workings of the Israel-Jordan security alliance, the 1970 case deserves to be singled out for separate treatment here.

The 1970 Middle East crisis lasted from September 6–27. The following main events are relevant:

Sept. 6	Airfields in Jordan are used by PLO terrorists for holding hostage three civilian airliners and their passengers.
Sept. 15	Hussein, rather than see Jordan compromised, places the country under martial law and gives the army full power to put down resistance.
Sept. 17	A full-scale civil war erupts.
Sept. 18	Syrian armored probe is on the Jordanian border; the Soviet Union warns against all outside interference.
Sept. 19–20	Syrian tanks push deep into Jordan in what the United States denounces as an invasion; Irbid falls to Syrian and Palestinian forces; Hussein appeals for help.
Sept. 21	The United States and Israel discuss plan of action; the Jordanian air force and army launch an air and ground counter attack.
Sept. 22	Syrian forces begin withdrawal.
Sept. 27	Hussein and Arafat sign fourteen-point agreement in Cairo ending the civil war.

The crisis was the most acute in the history of Jordan and of Hussein's troubled reign. In the past the monarch and his loyalists had to contend with either a domestic or an external challenge; here there were two simultaneous threat sources: PLO defiance of the throne and an attempt at seizure of power as part of the organization's strategy for the liberation "in stages" of Palestine; outside intervention by Syria. The kingdom threatened to fall apart under this combined assault, as portended by the capture of Irbid; and this explains the desperate call for assistance by Hussein on September 19–20. Which leads to Israel's role at the peak of the crisis.

Consistent with its traditional doctrine of casus belli, Israel feared Jordan's collapse whether from within or through external pressure. As to the former, however, in the instance of 1970 none of the accounts indicate that Israel had prepared to intervene on Hussein's behalf in the struggle against the PLO. This was a domestic conflict. It was unclear how Israel might be of assistance. A few voices expressed the unconventional opinion that the downfall of the Hashemites and their replacement by a Palestinian regime in Amman possibly might offer a breakthrough in the enduring conflict. But, above all, by 1970 Israeli leaders had high regard for Hussein who, after all, had weathered each of the previous storms. In the early stages Israel's only apprehension was that Hussein might not act or else act too late in suppressing the PLO challenge.

Instead, the primary concern from the outset was the situation on Jordan's northern borders. And not so much at the prospect of Syrian intervention as with the threat posed by the presence of some 18,000 Iraqi troops already stationed inside Jordan. In the event, Iraq did not become implicated, whether because of Soviet caution, self-restraint or realization of the improbability that Israel would permit the most radical Arab state to move forces closer to its borders. Nevertheless, menacing gestures by Baghdad had sufficed to put both the United States and Israel on alert since the beginning of the month, making it equally clear that Israel, for its part, was both aware of Syrian troop movements and prepared not to tolerate any type of similar intervention by Damascus. Therefore, Syria became Israel's chief concern.

Amman made no known direct appeals for assistance to Jerusalem during the crisis, or if it did, Israeli diplomats have been too discreet to disclose them. A number of indirect messages and appeals did exchange hands, however, especially as Hussein's predicament worsened. Both the United States and Israel agreed on the strategic imperative making the survival of Jordan and Hussein essential. They saw eye to eye on the need for action should Syria or Iraq enter the conflict. Where they differed, however, was on how to proceed at the tactical level.

Three possibilities existed:

- that the United States act alone,
- that Israel act on its own,
- that, as Washington warned Moscow on the September 19, both Israel and the United States might be forced to intervene unless the Syrians pulled back.

Here, accounts differ as to who advocated what at any given moment. At one extreme, there is a view of the American administration relying heavily upon Israel. Kissinger, for his part, opposed a joint U.S.-Israel operation and advocated that America's role be limited to "holding the ring," which could mean only some sort of unilateral action by Israel. In the end, because the

United States preferred not to get involved, Israel provided that intermediate third option so sought after by decision makers between the United States doing nothing or else acting directly.

Even then, the U.S. administration could not make up its mind as to the precise nature of the desired Israeli response in trying to steer among Jordanian, American, and Israeli constraints.

If, indeed, official Washington was deeply concerned lest Israel react to the Jordan crisis in too rash a manner and through "precipitate military moves," these worries appear largely unfounded. Instead, the image of Israel is one of circumspection. What Israeli leaders carefully sought after was a balance between restraint—relying on the one hand upon Hussein, and on the other upon the United States—and respecting its own security commitment through symbolic support for Jordan and deterrence of Syria. Consequently, even Kissinger later praised Israel for having showed "remarkable caution" in 1970.

Israeli contingencies included

- air strikes; either in Jordan itself or within Syria;
- a diversionary armored strike through the Golan Heights toward Damascus, forcing Syra to redeploy against this new front;
- crossing of the Jordan River to confront the Syrian tank force near Irbid and to eliminate PLO bases in the border area.

Hussein's preference was for ground action inside Syria, not Jordan; whereas, because of the risks this entailed, the Israeli government favored an attack by the air force followed by the sending of an armored force into Jordan, and only if this proved insufficient, a drive into Syria as well. As late as September 22, Kissinger records being informed by Israel that its ground action, if it took place, would be confined to Jordan and would not include attacking Syria. The goal, as always, remained preserving Jordan as a neutralized buffer zone. But at that critical moment for decision Israel, like the United States, was spared the need to choose by Syria, which elected to withdraw rather than escalate, and by Jordanian resolve. The shield held firm, thereby alleviating resort to the Israeli sword.

In retrospect, during the crisis, Israel did take a number of specific yet measured steps: of sharing intelligence, reconnaissance flights over the combat zone in northern Jordan, concentrating armored units on the Golan Heights for the possibility of a breakthrough into Syria, moving troops to the Jordan border opposite Irbid, maintaining its air force at a state of high preparedness. Admittedly these actions did not constitute in any way armed intervention and suggest relatively low levels of power increments and commitment. They were largely symbolic force demonstrations and signals of intent that are, to be sure, the components of effective deterrence. And the point is that in the case of the 1970 crisis they proved adequate. Other functions performed by Israel need to be added, two in particular. Jerusalem provided critical support—moral, political, and indirect military—for both the United States (at a time when European allies like Britain abstained) and for Jordan at a critical moment in its history. Second, signs of tangible commitment not to allow Jordan to collapse surely had to have had a sobering effect upon Syria as well as the Soviet Union, but also upon Iraq at the outset of the crisis.

For its efforts Israel was informed by the conveyor of messages throughout the crisis, Henry Kissinger: "The president will never forget Israel's role in preventing the deterioration in Jordan and in blocking the attempt to overturn the regime there." Nixon noted further that "the United States is fortunate in having an ally like Israel in the Middle East. These events will be taken into account in all future developments." New U.S. esteem for a strong Israel as a friend in the Middle East was but one of the benefits accruing from the successful handling of the Jordan crisis and its termination. In retrospect 1970 could easily have proven disastrous because of the ambivalence and hesitancy shown by Jordan, its superpower, and regional allies: Hussein, in wavering over whether to encourage overt Israeli aid; the United States, in leaning for support upon Israel yet uncomfortable at such an intimate association; Israel, in weighing the possible implications of actually having to exercise its professed commitment to the defense of the Hashemite kingdom.

Only in the postcrisis stage, when the dust had settled, was it possible to clarify some of these fundamental dilemmas. Of the three actors, Hussein would appear to have achieved the greatest clarity—and this represents the other of the major benefits from 1970. By reasserting his authority over the Palestinians on the East Bank, Hussein brought about the stabilization of Jordan, itself a gain for Israel. Convinced of Israel's strategic commitment, the king, for his part, reaffirmed his respect for the rules of the game with Israel. It is upon these foundations of stability and trust between Jerusalem and Amman that Israeli-Jordanian relations were able to push beyond minimal security concerns into other areas of mutual interest.

A MUTUAL LEARNING EXPERIENCE

Our second variable—the time factor—offers a number of further lessons. The mere longevity of the security relationship has enabled an incremental learning experience. Ties and trust have evolved piecemeal and on a contingent basis. By reiteration, trial, and error leaders on each side have had a chance to test the other's trustworthiness in something akin to Robert Axelrod's "tit-for-tat" strategy.[34] The long time-frame suggests that the regime has been forged by situations of adversity and acute crisis as well as under routine conditions approximating normalcy. Similarly, the relationship is an organic one, mirroring ups and downs, success and failure. Last, only a time perspective can help us appreciate the regime's remarkable durability despite the tremendous obstacles in its way.

The transformation in both the nature and purpose of the relationship over the course of time has been profound. It has gone from conflictual at the start (witness the 1948 fighting in Jerusalem between the Haganah and the Arab Legion) to at least a "mixed adversarial" one. From a "self-help" system, each going about its business without getting in the other's way, we can now sense a certain "jointness" that is guided by rules of active engagement on behalf of mutual or common interests. Having long since advanced from rudimentary policy coordination to policy cooperation, the two actors have likewise progressed from tactical steps designed to neutralize or subvert each other to the strategic level, enlisting and even relying on each other, albeit guardedly and on a case-by-case, issue-by-issue basis. Even so, the pattern has broadened from a single specific issue—security—to a diffusion and multiplicity of shared interests in the economic, commercial and cultural sphere.

Focusing narrowly on the security end of the spectrum, we note the accent on the positive. In the span of four decades the thrust has shifted from what might be termed *negative* security to *positive* security: instead of expending their energies on conflict avoidance and reducing uncertainty, tension, misunderstanding and risks, the two sides have long since moved on to increasing certainty, enhancing confidence, promoting cooperation and greater understanding while also distributing positive gains. In the process, a system of disincentives has converted into positive incentives, just as early compliance mechanisms, such as Israel's policy of reprisals in the 1950s, yielded to more sophisticated avenues of persuasion, so that deterrence and compellance have been replaced by reassurance. In sum, the dynamic change in the Israel-Jordan equation points to Charles Osgood's "GRIT" tension-reducing measures[35] leading to confidence-building ones.

The turning point came comparatively early in the historic relationship—and in all likelihood not in a single moment, decision, or event—when both parties came to appreciate (1) that "by sacrificing some ability to harm the other, the state can increase the chances of mutually beneficial cooperation";[36] (2) that the costs of self-reliance were excessive; (3) that their national securities could not realistically be considered apart from one another; and (4) that, as a result, facts on the ground dictate a single security zone.

Today the signposts of this Israel-Jordan tacit mutual security zone—with *security* defined in its broader sense of political stability and economic viability as well as physical well-being—include the following:

- a relatively quiet border, with armed incursions or rockets from Jordan into Israel the rare exceptions rather than the rule;
- effective border patrols and "good faith" surveillance measures;
- reported exchanges of information and intelligence data;
- conventions worked out to regulate aerial maneuvers, civilian flight patterns, and maritime commerce to and from the twin-sister ports of Aqaba and Eilat.

One cautionary sign, to be sure, was evidenced in the 1990–1991 Gulf crisis, when Israeli concerns at the fragility of the "sword and shield" conception were heightened by Iraqi-Jordanian steps aimed at closer military coordination, such as Iraqi stockpiles inside Jordan, aerial reconnaissance close to Israel's border and talk of a joint military command, not to mention Amman's complicity in providing an alternative resupply route to Baghdad, demonstrations of mass support for Saddam and even references to positioning of scud missile batteries by Iraq on Jordanian territory.[37]

Still, the point here is not that the security relationship is foolproof or that such tensions are impossible—of course, they have happened often in the past—but, rather, that the danger of misunderstanding, miscalculation, or surprise is reduced almost to the minimum thanks to the discreet lines of communication in place between Amman and Jerusalem. Certainly the exploratory summit meetings and direct dialogue maintained between King Hussein personally or his top emissaries and Israeli leaders, whether Labor or Likud, has been instrumental in safeguarding mutual security needs. Probably the two high points came during the 1970 "Black September" Jordanian crisis and, again, during the 1973 Yom Kippur war when even Hussein's token gesture of military support for Egypt and Syria, placement of a symbolic tank unit on the Golan Heights, took place with Israeli cognizance.[38]

On the other hand, contrary instances when the security system came closest to backfiring occurred on at least two notable occasions: the king's defection in June 1967 (which can be explained away as taking place when the "rules of the game" were as yet poorly defined) and, again, in the Kuwait crisis when Jordan's position became tenuous and its pro-Iraqi tilt might easily have gotten completely out of Hussein's control. A third instance, one little cited and taking place fairly early in the relationship, happened in 1966 when a retaliatory raid by the Israeli army against the Jordanian village of Samu'a led to an explosion of pent-up grievances against the monarchy that nearly led to the young king's downfall.[39] The military operation, in keeping with the strategic doctrine of active reprisal, was certainly not intended to weaken Hussein. Yet, in exposing the kingdom's weakness, overnight a wave of West Bank demonstrations against the regime calling for its overthrow threatened to get out of control, fanned by Syrian, Nasserist, and PLO agitation; Hussein was forced to call in the army to put down the protest and restore order.

BEYOND SECURITY

From this early perspective, and these exceptions aside, the relationship has progressed from meeting minimal security needs such as physical survival to providing enhanced security. In this maturation process, sheer restraint led to coexistence, and from coexistence to accommodation. Through spillover, the fruits of accommodation are now to be seen perhaps even more overtly in the nonmilitary sector. Take, for example, expressions of tacit cooperation in peaceful farming on both sides of the Jordan valley; understandings worked out in direct talks over Jordan River water allocation; development of Aqaba and Eilat as popular tourist sites; the "open bridges" policy permitting the flow of agricultural produce, goods, tourists, Muslim and Christian pilgrims, and family visitors to and from the East Bank. Surely this policy is the most concrete proof of the robustness of the regime and the mutual endorsement for "peace in parts."

Less readily apparent is the acquiescence of the Israeli authorities administering the West Bank territories ever since 1967 in Jordan's "most favored nation" status. It is reflected inter alia by retention of the Jordanian dinar as legal tender; a judicial system based on Jordanian law and precedents; approval by the Ministry of Education in Amman for textbWest Bankooks, classroom materials, and matriculation exams used in West Bank schools; consent for the local chambers of commerce acting as representatives for Hashemite interests, just as the Jordan-controlled Muslim *waqf* in east Jerusalem serves to funnel religious funds. Clearly, this Jordanian "presence" could not exist or be felt in the daily life and commerce of the Arab residents without Israel's tacit consent. Implicit admission of the pivotal role allocated to Jordan in governing, in implementing any interim form of administrative and autonomous self-rule, in policing the disputed area, and in the negotiating process is best mirrored by the 1978 Camp David framework accords—and this by no less a hardliner than the late Prime Minister Menahem Begin.[40] Nothing better refutes the official Jordanian propaganda strategy of portraying Israel as hell-bent upon destabilizing the Hashemite regime and displacing King Hussein in favor of a "Jordan is Palestine" endgame.

Truth be told; there is no stronger pillar of security support for Jordan than its most proximate neighbor to the west and none more than Israel with a vital interest in Jordanian stability. For the central reigning perception of the Hashemite kingdom remains as powerful a national consensus in Israel as it has always been. Not only is King Hussein the lesser of the evils (e.g., the Palestinians, the PLO, Yasir Arafat), but Jordan as presently constituted approximates the ideal: powerful enough to implement the basic mutual security zone by ensuring law and order on Israel's long eastern front, yet too weak by itself to pose a direct military threat to Israel.

Surveying the relationship at present, several outstanding overall features are worthy of mention. First, that tacitness has been turned into a definite plus by Israeli and Jordanian interlocutors. Second, the regime has developed a set of complex linkages, with errant as well as good behavior by one or other of the two parties on a particular issue either being sanctioned or rewarded in a different sphere through a unique system of interlocking prizes and penalties—but never going to either extreme of genuine peace or a total severing of contacts. Third, and related, the balance sheet in the aggregate most decidedly shows a favorable balance for each party of advantages over liabilities. Fourth, the regime shows an extraordinary degree of both flexibility and resilience. For these reasons the Israeli-Hashemite special brand of international regime deserves to be cited more prominently by way of replying to the general question posed some time ago by Haas: "How can there be international collaboration despite the persistence of conflict, and of differentials in the power of actors?"[41] This particular regime suggests such cooperation is possible—and in the most sensitive field of national security; while also providing a virtual guidebook on practical measures for pursuing this goal.

DOES THE REGIME POSSESS REAL STAYING POWER?

In concluding by hazarding an opinion upon the tacit security regime's future prospects, a fifth feature, however, must be added. For all of the psychological and tangible gains realized through it, the regime is locked in at the narrow lower half of the functional spectrum. It serves, as it was meant to serve, both Israeli and Jordanian military and security goals rather than ultimate political strategies; there are few aspirations about the longer term. Similarly, the alignment's raison d'être is defense, not peace. It focuses on conflict management—a sub-optimal outcome—rather than on conflict resolution. The distinction is crucial. Thus, it is doubtful in the extreme whether the Jordanian royal family, for example, any longer retains any illusion that *its* "Israeli option" is likely to result in a return of all the territories including Jerusalem to Hashemite control. As one might expect, the picture on the Israeli side is less monochromatic, with the Likud essentially relating to Jordan as a convenient and necessary security partner. Within Labor party circles, however, there are those who still perceive of Jordan as a peace partner—with or without a Palestinian component—and of the "Jordanian option" *cum* "territorial compromise" formula as the key to ultimate resolution of the core Arab-Israel dispute.[42]

A note of guarded pessimism needs to be sounded concerning both scenarios: the former, that the existing limited regime simply perpetuate itself; the latter, that the tacit security-centered alignment be pursued to its logical end and become converted into an open, explicit, contractual peace as part of a comprehensive settlement.

Regarding the first, it is entirely conceivable in theory and in principle that the present regime be self-sustaining, continuing indefinitely. Yet, in international and Middle East politics there is no standing still. If nothing else, the initiative for change is left to actors less committed, and even hostile, to the existing regime and the status quo it is meant to serve. Tacit regimes in particular find it difficult in the extreme to safeguard against incremental decay and erosion. Despite their best efforts, they become increasingly subject to either detection or defection.

As regards moving forward to culminate in an outright bilateral peace structure, although not impossible, there are any number of objective as well as subjective constraints. Perhaps foremost are the reasons governing traditional insistence by the Jordanians on secret ties; namely, their fear of the consequences of an open peace with Israel both domestically and for Jordan's inter-Arab relations.

Even this obstacle aside, I, for one, am not sure any Israeli government can convince King Hussein to abandon his noncommittal position of straddling the political fences or can offer him "minimax" terms for a territorial and political compromise that he can accept that are less than complete withdrawal by Israel from the West Bank, including Jerusalem. And even should these conditions be possible, it is even less probable that the Hashemites have both the will and the capacity to recross the Jordan River and to enforce the settlement terms vis-à-vis an overwhelming Palestinian majority in the East Bank, let alone on the West Bank, too.[43]

I am therefore drawn to the conclusion that the regime already may have reached the peak of its performance and that, of the three alternative courses: steady state, full peace, or regression—the last seems the most likely, with the major turning point probably taking place before the close of the decade.

The grounds for this assessment are theoretical as well as case specific. In general, we find regime change or demise occurring because of miscalculation, third-party interference or initiative, new preferences or expectations by at least one of the partners, a reordering of goals as circumstances change or perhaps a significant redistribution of power capabilities making the regime redundant and obsolete, or by simple neglect and insensitivity.

Applied to the Israeli-Jordanian context, the very effectiveness and success of the tacit functional arrangement could become its undoing. What I would call the *dynamic* of the going concern creates a false sense of security and encourages complacency. Moreover, it is a disincentive to diplomacy, because neither party feels any particular urgency in pressing for a clear-cut, binding peace pact, especially given the risks it would entail for each.

Second, continuation of the existing network of understandings assumes predictability in a part of the world that enjoys a well-deserved reputation for unpredictability. As mentioned before, making do with an essentially static strategy and frozen bilateral situation plays into the hands of other outside Middle East actors. Sworn opponents of an Israeli-Arab rapprochement, and of the Hashemite-Zionist entente in particular, thus are left the initiative to alter the larger security environment and create sudden desert storms.

Third, the entire elaborate superstructure of Israeli-Jordanian cooperation is premised upon (1) Jordan's stability and (2) Israel's credibility. As we approach mid-decade, both premises are questionable. The assumption of continued stability in the East Bank kingdom either ignores or takes a benign view of deep, structural economic, social and demographic problems that may be insurmountable in the long run, any one of which has the potential for destabilizing the domestic regime and monarchy. Even should Hashemite rule be maintained, it must be emphasized that so much of the relationship with Israel, like everything else about Jordanian life and policies over the past forty years, is personalized and traceable to the incumbent monarch. Jordan faces a grave and uncertain succession problem. Quite simply, the country without King Hussein will be different than with him on the throne. Nor is it clear how strong a personal commitment his successor will have to a complex relationship so carefully crafted by the king and his grandfather, the Amir Abdullah, before him.

So, too, are there reservations about Israel's credibility and commitment. We may leave aside those in Israel who unlike in 1970 might view with favor the establishment in trans-Jordan of a Palestinian national home. The fact is that in the wake of the 1982 Lebanese entanglement Israeli strategists fear entrapment arising from Jordanian weakness. Surely there will be precious little Israeli public enthusiasm for any direct military intervention by Israel inside Jordan on Hussein's behalf in honoring the "sword and shield" strategy.

In consequence, fourth, the possibility always exists of defection by either one of the participants to the tacit regime through the many escape hatches so loose an arrangement provides, as Jordan did in 1967 and came very close to repeating in the Gulf crisis.[44] The relationship, to be sure, does contain a record of disappointment and recrimination by each side toward the other. Charges of "bad faith"—ranging from misinterpretation of assumed understandings through noncompliance and nonperformance of obligations all the way to words of regret at uncompensated gestures and trust—have been exchanged, often in private, between Amman and Jerusalem.

In short, the two central pillars of trust and certainty are shaky in the instance of Israel and Jordan. Far more serious than the periodic lapses in communication may be either of two extremes: that the mutual security blanket's lulling effect reduces each other's expectations or, alternatively, that both sides expect more from each other than they can possibly deliver. Nor would it necessarily take long for so decentralized a self-compliance security regime to unravel, whether because of a sudden and stressful Middle East crisis situation or under the debilitating impact of confidence-reducing measures, intentional or not. Only then, belatedly, will we have a ringing confirmation of the fact that, yes, regimes do matter.[45]

Written in mid-1992, the chapter ended by questioning the future staying power of the limited Israel-Jordan regime as constituted for the last two decades. Its cautionary warning that the essentially defensive and anti-Palestinian bilateral pact could unravel was confirmed most dramatically in September 1993, with the opening of an official Israel-Palestinian axis—something King Hussein had confidently come to regard all these years as unthinkable. In the undiplomatic language of strategists and games theorists, this amounts to "defection" by the Peres-Rabin government from the unratified understandings that have made up the "Jordanian option."

A direct, unbrokered deal with the PLO—no matter how delicately phrased to placate the bruised feelings in Amman—has the effect of relegating Jordan to the status of a subordinate actor in the negotiating process. And should the dialogue with the PLO climax (as already seems inevitable) in an independent state, whether that "Palestine" is federated, confederated or unaffiliated with Hussein's Jordan it can have only the most profound consequences for the Hashemites, their security, and regime.

NOTES

1. Ernst B. Haas, "Why Collaborate? Issue-Linkage and International Regimes," *World Politics* 32, no. 3 (April 1980): 385.

2. The Spring 1982 issue of *International Organization* was devoted to the subject of international regimes. Edited by Stephen D. Krasner, the collection of essays was then published in book form by Cornell University Press in 1983. Both publications gave the topic of regimes in world politics greater saliency as well as recognition as a distinctive subfield within the discipline.

3. Stephen D. Krasner, "Structural Causes and Regime Consequences: Regimes as Intervening Variables," *International Organization*, 36, no. 2 (Spring 1982): 185.

4. This awareness of the need for greater flexibility in defining and then identifying regimes is reflected in Krasner's own early thinking. For in truth he offers two variant definitions. In his introduction to the special issue, Krasner presented a consensual definition and one that to this day serves as the basis for any analysis of regimes. However, on the very next page he defines them in less restricted terms as "sets of *implicit* or explicit principles, norms, rules and decision-making procedures. . . ." It remains unclear why he opted for the more exclusive definition in the first instance and, second, why it has entered the literature as the more accepted standard. See pp. 185–186.

5. Robert Jervis, "Security Regimes," in Stephen D. Krasner, ed., *International Regimes* (Ithaca, N.Y., and London: Cornell University Press, 1983), pp. 173–194.

6. Nye, for example, presents international regimes as dealing with monetary issues, international trade, management of natural resources, cooperation against terrorism, control of armaments, environmental pollution, and the management of particular geographic areas. Joseph S. Nye, Jr., *Bound to Lead* (New York: Basic Books, 1990). Mark W. Zacher stresses the utility of regimes in a single issue or area: economic welfare. "Toward a Theory of International Regimes," *Journal of International Affairs* 44, no. 1 (Spring–Summer 1990): 139–157. See also Ethan A. Nadelmann, "Global Prohibition Regimes: The Evolution of Norms in International Society," *International Organization* 44, No. 4 (Autumn 1990): 479–526.

7. Oran R. Young, "International Regimes: Problems of Concept Formation," *World Politics* 32, no. 3 (April 1980): 341.

8. Roger K. Smith, "Explaining the Non-Proliferation Regime: Anomalies for Contemporary International Relations Theory," *International Organization* 41, no. 2 (Spring 1987): 253.

9. Alexander L. George, Philip J. Farley, and Alexander Dallin (eds.), *U.S.-Soviet Security Cooperation* (New York and Oxford: Oxford University Press, 1988), p. 14.

10. See, for example, Janice Gross Stein, "A Common Aversion to War: Regime Creation by Egypt and Israel as a Strategy of Conflict Management," in Gabriel Ben-Dor and David B. Dewitt, eds., *Conflict Management in the Middle East* (Lexington, Mass.: Lexington Books, 1987), pp. 59–78.

11. Common to the following works by Israeli scholars is a sensitivity for the possible "red lines" of tacit understanding between Damascus and Jerusalem: Avner Yaniv, *Dilemmas of Security* (New York: Oxford University Press, 1987); Yair Evron, *War and Intervention in Lebanon: The Israeli-Syrian Deterrence Dialogue* (Baltimore: Johns Hopkins University Press, 1987); Itamar Rabinovich, "Controlled Conflict in the Middle East: The Syrian-Israeli Rivalry in Lebanon," in Ben-Dor and Dewitt (eds.), *ibid.*, pp. 97–112.

12. Donald J. Puchala and Raymond F. Hopkins, "International Regimes: Lessons from Inductive Analysis," in Krasner, ed., *International Regimes,* p. 63.

13. Janice Gross Stein, "A Common Aversion to War: Regime Creation by Egypt and Israel as a Strategy of Conflict Management," in Ben-Dor and Dewitt eds., *Conflict Management in the Middle East,* p. 73.

14. From the standpoint of international law, the sole binding agreement remains the Israel-Jordan Armistice Agreement signed on April 3, 1949, "in order to facilitate the transition from the present truce to permanent peace in Palestine." Until such time, the signatories pledged "No aggressive action by the armed forces—land, sea, or air—

of either Party shall be undertaken, planned, or threatened against the people or the armed forces of the other."

15. Karl Deutsch et al., *Political Community and the North Atlantic Area* (Princeton, N.J.: Princeton University Press, 1957), p. 5.

16. Jervis, "Security Regimes," pp. 173–194.

17. Barry Buzan, *People, States and Fear* (Brighton: Wheatsheaf, 1983), p. 106.

18. Charles Lipson, "Why Are Some International Agreements Informal?" *International Organization* 45, no. 4 (Autumn 1991): 527.

19. Young, "International Regimes," pp. 331–356.

20. Thomas C. Schelling, *The Strategy of Conflict* (London: Oxford University Press, 1960), p. 89.

21. Robert O. Keohane and Joseph S. Nye, Jr., *Power and Independence. World Politics in Transaction* (Boston: Little, Brownand Co., 1977), especially pp. 24–29.

22. These features and the historical record of the relationship are traced in the following: Yaron Ran, *Shorashei Ha-Optzia Ha-Yardenit* [The Roots of the Jordanian Option] (Tel-Aviv: Citrin, 1991); Avi Shlaim, *Collusion Across the Jordan* (New York: Columbia University Press, 1988); Ian Lustick, *Israel and Jordan: The Implications of an Adversarial Relationship*. Policy Papers in International Affairs, No. 6 (Berkeley: University of California Institute of International Affairs, 1978); Aaron S. Klieman, *Israel, Jordan, Palestine: The Search for a Durable Peace*. The Washington Papers, No. 83 (Beverly Hills, Calif. and London: Sage Publications, 1981); and Adam Garfinkel, *Israel and Jordan in the Shadow of War* (New York: Macmillan and St. Martin's Press, 1992).

23. The term *limited security regime* is employed by Richard Ned Lebow and Janice Gross Stein in "Beyond Deterrence," *Journal of Social Issues* 43, no. 4 (Winter 1987): 5–70.

24. Robert O. Keohane, *After Hegemony* (Princeton, N.J.: Princeton University Press, 1984), p. 244.

25. The most authoritative source on the Amman-Jerusalem dialogue is the Israeli journalist Moshe Zak, whose articles over the years in the Hebrew daily *Maariv* document the series of direct and indirect contacts. Accounts in English can be found in Moshe Zak, "Israeli-Jordanian Negotiations," *The Washington Quarterly* 8, no. 1 (Winter 1985): 167–176; and Moshe Zak, "The Ambivalent Diplomacy of King Hussein," *Global Affairs* 4, no. 2 (Spring 1989): 111–128.

26. See Aharon Klieman, *Statecraft in the Dark: Israel's Practice of Quiet Diplomacy* (Boulder, Colo.: Westview Press, 1988); also, Aaron S. Klieman, *Israel and the World After 40 Years* (Washington, D.C.: Pergamon-Brassey's, 1990), especially pp. 221–232.

27. Young, "International Regimes," pp. 348–355.

28. It needs to be recalled that the partition plan adopted by the General Assembly of the United Nations on November 29, 1947, actually provided for dividing Palestine west of the Jordan into two Jewish and Palestinian Arab states that would assume their place alongside the East Bank Hashemite kingdom.

29. David B. Dewitt, "Confidence- and Security- Building Measures in the Third World: Is There a Role?," *International Journal* 42, no. 3 (Summer 1987): 523. Profound insight into reciprocal Israeli and Jordanian vulnerabilities is to be found the classic treatment of the recurrent "security dilemma" by Robert Jervis, "Cooperation Under the Security Dilemma," *World Politics* 30, no. 2 (January 1978): 167–214, which builds in turn upon Glenn H. Snyder, "The Security Dilemma in Alliance Politics," *World Politics* 36, no. 4 (July 1984): 461–495.

30. Schelling, *The Strategy of Conflict,* p. 4.

31. Kenneth N. Waltz, *Theory of International Politics* (New York: Random House, 1979), pp. 91, 105–107.

32. On how Israel played the key role in defusing the 1970 crisis and reinforcing Hashemite control over the East Bank buffer zone is analyzed in Adam M. Garfinkle, "U.S. Decision Making in the Jordan Crisis: Correcting the Record," *Political Science Quarterly* 100, no. 1 (Spring 1985): 117–138. The only Israeli insider account is that of Israel's ambassador to Washington at the time, Yitzhak Rabin, *The Rabin Memoirs* (Boston: Little, Brown, 1979).

34. Robert Axelrod, *The Evolution of Cooperation* (New York: Basic Books, 1984).

35. On the GRIT strategy of "Gradual and Reciprocated Initiatives in tension reduction," see Charles Osgood, *An Alternative to War or Surrender* (Urbana: University of Illinois Press, 1962).

36. Jervis, "Cooperation Under the Security Dilemma," p. 180.

37. Before the crisis started, Israeli intelligence reported Jordan and Iraq had begun to operate a joint air force squadron based in Iraq that flew maneuvers along the Israeli border and later that the Jordanians were showing the Iraqis how to operate four batteries of U.S.-made hawk missiles captured in Kuwait. Joel Brinkley, "Israelis Say Jordanian Planes Fly Reconnaissance for Iraq," *The New York Times (*September 1, 1990). On August 7, 1990, Israeli Defense Minister Moshe Arens warned that the entry of Iraqi forces into Jordan would constitute a *casus belli* for Israel—thereby cautioning the king against going too far, while at the same time easing the pressures on him by also deterring Saddam Hussein. For Israeli sensitivities regarding the kingdom during the Gulf crisis, see Joseph Alpher, "Between Israel and Iraq: The Role of Jordan," *IDF Journal* (Winter 1991): 21–24.

38. On the limited, essentially symbolic engagement of Jordanian armor in the course of the 1973 War, see Chaim Herzog, *The War of*

Atonement (Jerusalem: Steimatsky's, 1975), pp. 30, 139–142; and Richard A. Gabriel and Alan Scott MacDougall, "Jordan," in Richard A. Gabriel and Alan Scott MacDougall, eds., *Fighting Armies* (Westport, Conn.: Greenwood Press, 1983).

39. The Samu'a reprisal raid in which 18 people were killed and 134 wounded, as well as the immediate aftermath, are described in Clinton Bailey, *Jordan's Palestinian Challenge, 1948–1983* (Boulder, Colo., and London: Westview Press, 1984), pp. 25–26; Samir A. Mutawi, *Jordan in the 1967 War* (Cambridge: Cambridge University Press, 1987), pp. 76–82; and James Lunt, *Hussein of Jordan* (New York: William Morrow, 1989), pp. 80–81.

40. According to the language of the 1978 Camp David framework accords, and in spite of its demonstrative refusal to endorse either the Sadat initiative or the Camp David formula, Jordan is mentioned in the document no less than fourteen times. A prominent place was reserved for it at each stage of the intended peace process: from instituting administrative self-rule in the territories to regulating and even policing the transitional arrangement until concluding negotiations over the final status of Gaza and the West Bank.

41. The question is posed in Ernst B. Haas, "Why Collaborate? Issue-Linkage and International Regimes," *World Politics* 32, no. 3 (April 1980): 361.

42. Insight into the staying power of conventional wisdom, and of the "Jordanian option" in particular, can be found in Efraim Inbar, *War and Peace in Israeli Politics. Labor Party Positions on National Security* (Boulder, Colo., and London: Lynne Rienner, 1991), especially pp. 60–66.

43. On July 31, 1988, King Hussein publicly and unequivocally announced Jordan's disengagement from the disputed West Bank. Second, he has repeatedly told Israeli interlocutors of his inability to accept less than total Israeli withdrawal. Moshe Zak, "Israeli-Jordanian Negotiations," *The Washington Quarterly* 8, no. 1 (Winter 1985): 172. Thirdly, the demographic breakdown of East Bank–West Bank population figures underscores the Hashemite predicament. Whether in a federation or a confederation framework, the Palestinians constitute a clear majority, with some 1.2 million and another 700,000 joining nearly 2 million Palestinians, their ranks swollen by over 300,000 refugees from the Persian Gulf, resident in Jordan proper.

44. The theoretical underpinning for such defections is derived from the logic of "bandwagoning" developed in contrast to "balancing" by Stephen M. Walt, *The Origins of Alliances* (Ithaca, N.Y.: Cornell University Press, 1987).

45. Stephen D. Krasner raises the question of whether regimes really make a difference in his own contribution to the *International Organization* special issue of Spring 1982, p. 189.

CHAPTER 7

Syria and Israel: Toward a Change?

Eyal Zisser

INTRODUCTION

All analysis directed to evaluating the chances for building a "Syrian-Israeli security regime" must first address the basic question as to how much Syria's long-term policy toward Israel has changed. The point of departure of this chapter, is Syria's acceptance of the American-Soviet invitation to the Madrid Middle East peace conference. Syria's acceptance of this invitation was a significant event, marking the first time in the history of Hafiz al-Assad's regime that Syria expressed its readiness to participate in a regional peace process that would include direct negotiations with Israel. Indeed, Syria entered the process even though the conditions it had once claimed were necessary for such participation remained unfulfilled. Syria's agreement to enter into these negotiations was all the more significant given the fact (which Syria could not ignore) that one of the American aims of these negotiations, as declared by President Bush in his address to the Madrid conference, was Syrian recognition of the state of Israel and the signing of a Syrian-Israeli peace treaty. Such a treaty would ensure Israel's security—and might even involve Syrian recognition of at least some of Israel's claims to the Golan Heights.[1]

Syria's very readiness to participate in a peace process of which it was not in control and to which it was forced to commit itself because of domestic and foreign constraints may be considered a significant change, in the Assad regime's two-decade-long policy toward Israel. It may also be an indication that Syria has altered its "national security concept," which had guided its policy toward Israel in recent decades. This concept is tied in with the dominant, realistic view pointed to by Lipson, according to which states must preserve their security by "arming themselves to deter wars if possible and fight them if necessary."[2] Indeed, Syria's notion of security was based predominantly on military strength, whether pan-Arab or—from the beginning of the 1980s—exclusively Syrian. This concept included the notion of achieving "strategic parity" with Israel and reliance on the Soviet Union for military and political backing.[3] However, Syria's ultimate inability to achieve such parity, mainly as a result of the collapse of the Soviet Union, made changes in its national security concept inevitable.

These policy changes are part of the Syrian reorientation in the past several years aimed at adjusting to an international reality in which the United States is the hegemonic power. The need to formulate a new national security concept could catalyze Syria's integration into the American-sponsored new order shaping up in the Middle East and perhaps also into an emergent security regime, based on peace and security agreements between the countries of the region, which are backed and supervised by the United States. Such regime could be considered by the Syrians as a "deliberate effort to manage regional affairs to capture joint gains or prevent common losses" (as Lipson puts it).[4]

The results of the Israeli national elections on June 23, 1992, were an additional factor strengthening this change in Syria. Although, the Syrians were concerned with the Rabin government's emphasis on seeking a solution to the Palestinian problem, the government's declared readiness to advance the peace process and make substantial territorial concessions—including on the Golan Heights[5]—encouraged Syria's readiness to participate in the peace process. On the other hand, one should bear in mind that this participation is not irreversible. If it is marginalized in the process by Israeli preference for achieving a separate solution to the Palestinian problem,[6] Syria may revert to its initial attitude toward Israel. Moreover, Syria did not lose its power to veto the process and has been capable of sabotaging it or stopping it by threatening the Jordanians and Palestinians.[7]

This chapter will analyze the reasons for the change in Syria's policy toward Israel, the changes in its national security concept, and the implications for the relations between the two countries in the near future.

SYRIA AND ISRAEL SINCE ASSAD'S RISE TO POWER: THE HISTORICAL PERSPECTIVE

Assad's rise to power in November 1970 was a landmark in the history of Syria. Before he assumed control of the regime, Syria had suffered from chronic domestic instability and outside Arab intervention. Thanks to his political talent and the existence of propitious conditions, Assad has succeeded in building a relatively stable and effective regime in the domestic and foreign policy spheres and in becoming an important actor in the Arab arena. On the home front, Assad firmly established himself as sole ruler in a fragmented country that formerly had had little effective centralized government.[8]

Assad's policy toward Israel, as shaped over the years, has comprised two basic components, reflecting two main objectives of the regime—that, on the face of it, appeared to be contradictory. On the one hand, there was an extremist and dogmatic attitude, manifest in the refusal to recognize Israel's right to exist and in the desire to vanquish it militarily. On the other hand, there was a realistic and pragmatic approach, made manifest in a series of understandings with Israel that eventually even included readiness to enter into negotiations for a settlement with it, in the hope of restoring the Golan Heights to Syrian hands.

The hostile and intransigent component in Assad's attitude toward Israel was and still is rooted in a number of interrelated ideological, psychological or emotional, and practical motives connected to protecting his regime. Ideologically,[9] Asad rejected the existence of the state of Israel, which he believed to be an entity alien to the region, illegitimately established by Western imperialism at the expense of the Arab Palestinian people.[10]

Assad's hostility toward Israel is also the result of an obsessive and increasing fear of the perceived Israeli threat to the existence of his regime, to Syria in particular, and to the entire Arab nation in general. In Assad's mind, Israel was a regional superpower with nuclear capability, holding military superiority. Moreover, Asad considered Israel aggressive by nature, with expansionist ambitions of gaining control over Arab lands to realize the vision of "Greater Israel."[11] This image of Israel made it hard for Assad to envision peace with it.[12] Instead, he strove to eliminate Israel, in a struggle that would not end in his lifetime but would go on for generations.[13]

Finally, Assad's hostility toward Israel also had its roots in constraints resulting from the nature of the Syrian regime, which was based on the Alawi minority's control of the foci of power in the country. The minority sense of insecurity underlies the Ba'thi regime's tendency (particularly manifest in 1966–1970) to divert the people's attention from internal to external affairs and especially toward the conflict with Israel. Furthermore, the struggle against Israel served to legitimize the Ba'th regime.[14]

Yet, despite Assad's ideology, obssessive fear of Israel, and internal constraints, he is actually first and foremost a pragmatist, who is well aware of the difference between vision and reality. His pragmatism is expressed in the domestic policies he has implemented, in the moderation that has occurred in Syria's attitudes in both the inter-Arab and international arenas, and in his policy toward Israel. Assad has recognized Syria's limitations in confrontation with Israel and that any additional defeat in a military encounter with Israel could have disastrous results for his regime. This pragmatic approach has been reflected, even before the present peace process got under way, in Syria's strict observance of the separation of forces agreement with Israel of May 31, 1974, and in the tacit understanding with Israel regarding Lebanon (for example, in 1976–1977).[15] It should be noted, however, that although between Syria and Israel there was a "well-articulated regime that combined both formal and informal institutions to produce shared normative understandings, shared rules of behavior, and common expectations about key issues,"[16] this has not constituted a security regime.

The pragmatic attitude toward Israel also stems from Assad's belief that the Syrian regime has a direct and immediate interest in retrieving the Golan Heights lost in 1967 (when Assad served as minister of defense and commander of the air force). The importance of the Golan for the Syrian regime cannot be overstated. After having failed to take the Golan by force in the 1973 War, Assad often expressed the hope of retrieving it through negotiations, even at the price of a settlement with Israel; a settlement whose nature he never defined. Assad probably envisaged a non-belligerency agreement rather than a full peace treaty with Israel.[17] However due to ideological, psychological, and political constraints, he refused to recognize Israel's right to exist and could not contemplate signing a peace treaty with it.

Recognizing Israel's right to exist runs beyond the utmost limit of Assad's pragmatism in Syrian policy over the past two decades. On the one hand, during the 1970–1973 period Syria tacitly agreed to Sadat's policy that did not foreclose negotiations as a means for resolving the Arab-Israeli conflict. Syria was even prepared, albeit with certain reservations, to accept U.N. Security Council Resolution 242. In 1974–1975, Syria did not dismiss out of hand the Egyptian-guided pan-Arab policy calling for a political solution to the conflict with Israel. At first, it did not oppose the idea of an interim settlement with Israel and even, as noted, signed a separation of forces agreement with it on May 31, 1974. Moreover, it expressed cautious and reserved willingness to be a part of Henry Kissinger's step-by-step process and thus bring about an improvement in its relations with the United States. Finally, in early 1977, Asad showed some interest in the comprehensive approach of the newly elected President Carter with whom he even met in Geneva on May 9, 1977. On the other hand, in each of these cases Assad hesitated to follow through. After the 1973 War, he refused to participate in the Geneva convention. Later, he refused to continue the interim agreements policy, harshly codemning the "Sinai II" agreement that Egypt had signed with Israel on September 1, 1975.[18] From Sadat's visit to Jerusalem in November 19, 1977, until the late 1980s, Syria again pursued a radical policy, which became more intransigent after the signing of the Israeli-Egyptian peace accords (March 26, 1979), Israel's annexation of the Golan Heights (December 14, 1981), and the Lebanon War (in June 1982).

Yet, a closer examination of the course of events, just referred to, shows that Assad's refusal to make peace with Israel also stemmed from other reasons, mainly the absence, in his view, of the necessity in terms of his own interest. First, Assad assessed that there was no chance for Israeli full or partial withdrawal from the Golan. He also felt that the Americans were neither willing nor able, under the conditions prevailing in the region during those decades, to force Israel to make such concessions.[19] Second, although the conditions surrounding the negotiations conducted in the region immediately after the 1973 War were considered by most Arabs as an achievement, Syria felt (mainly because of Sadat's adoption of independent moves) that cracks had been created in the wall of Arab unity, which Syria treasured so highly. Therefore Syria, insisted on conducting negotiations with Israel in a united Arab delegation, but in effect, continued, to confront Israel separately, thereby reducing its chances of retrieving the Golan. Third, the situation inside Syria and in the regional and international arenas did not, in Assad's view, oblige him to recognize Israel and to make peace with it, and certainly not at the price of relinquishing ideological principles. At home, certainly in the early 1970s, Assad's regime enjoyed relative stability with the strong backing of the Soviet Union, which bolstered his confidence that he could withstand the Israeli threat. Finally, Assad assessed that the Arab world, including Syria, was not yet ripe for a political move that would include recognition of Israel and therefore would not support him should he undertake such a move.

All these factors produced a situation in which Assad could not overcome the limitations he had imposed on his attitude toward Israel and enter into direct negotiations with it. Therefore, in Assad's view, joining a peace process that had a dynamic of its own, over which he had no control, would do him more harm than good.[20]

From Sadat's visit to Jerusalem in 1977 until 1991, a peace process involving Syria was never on the agenda, and the 1981 Israeli annexation of the Golan further reduced the possibility of such a move. Moreover, the Lebanese War in 1982 underlined the Syrian fears of the danger posed by Israel. So Assad dug his heels deeper and deeper into the radical, almost fatalistic approach, according to which Syria was destined to wage a protracted war against Israel, alone if necessary on the battlefield and even from a position of inferiority. The aspiration for strategic parity with Israel may have had its roots in this perception and was an expression of both despair regarding the political process and a deepseated fear of Israel.

THE ISRAELI FACTOR IN THE SYRIAN NATIONAL SECURITY CONCEPT

Syria's national security concept, developed over the past two decades, was based on two main components: deployment of independent military strength and the backing of the Soviet Union. As soon as Assad rose to power, he began building up the Syrian army. However, until the Egyptian-Israeli peace process began, Syria's plans to fight Israel were based on the assumed participation of other Arab countries' armies. They would force Israel to divert forces from the Syrian front or strengthen the Syrian forces, as the Egyptian army and the Iraqi expeditionery force did in 1973. However, after the Egyptian-Israeli peace accords, and especially in the wake of Syria's isolated confrontation with Israel, in the war in Lebanon, its regime adopted the policy of seeking strategic parity; and aimed at building up Syria's military strength both quantitatively and qualitatively, to the point of matching Israel's. Therefore, over three years following 1982, the Syrian army substantially increased in size[21] and efforts were made to improve its quality, mainly by procurement of advanced military equipment for its ground forces, air force, and air defense, from the Soviet Union.[22]

The second component of the national security concept was the backing of the Soviet Union, regarded as essential not only as a source of military and economic support, vis-à-vis Israel, but also to deter the United States from attacking it (a scenario that the Syrians believed relevant during the American involvement in Lebanon in 1983–1984 and after the American attack on Libya in April 1986). The Soviet backing lent Damascus considerable self-confidence, although the Syrians were well aware of the Soviet Union's limitations as well as of the dangers inherent in overdependence on it.

It is important to point out that although the Syrian national security concept developed in light of the threat posed by Israel, it also functioned to abate the general sense of insecurity that had been plaguing the Ba'thi regime ever since it came to power in 1963. For in this conection there was the threat posed by a broad strata of the Syrian population, mainly the urban Sunni community, which made no secret of its opposition to the path adopted by the Alawi regime, especially its socio-economic policies and its secular nature. Then there were the threats from Syria's rivals in the Arab world and even from Western countries such as the United States, which until recently were perceived by Damascus as major enemies.

But it was primarily Syria's threat perception concerning Israel that led to a belligerent orientation. Such an orientation, Syria hoped, would deter Israel from carrying out its "plots" against the regime, and perhaps even lay the groundwork for a military option that would, in the short run, force Israel into accepting a political settlement advantageous to Syria (i.e., one that involved the return of the Golan) and in the long run perhaps lead to the liquidatation of the Jewish state. As noted, the anti-Israeli stance and the building of a strong army also seemed to serve the Syrian regime as an effective means of grappling with domestic, regional, and international challenges. Therefore, the Syrian regime made use of its military power at home in putting down the Muslim Brothers uprising of 1979–1982, which peaked in the al-Hamma riots of 1982, and also abroad; for example, in Lebanon, where the Syrian army has been used to promote Syria's long-term political objectives since 1976.

THE CHANGE IN SYRIA'S POSITION

During the past five years, however, Syria's views regarding both the conflict with Israel and its own national security have apparently undergone a dramatic change, whose apex thus far has been the possible Syrian readiness to reach a peace agreement with Israel. This change is anchored in the modifications that have occurred in Syria's policies and worldview over the past several years as a result of domestic, regional and international developments. Since the mid-1980s, these developments have placed the Syrian regime in a serious bind both at home and abroad.

Domestically, since the mid-1980s Syria has suffered from an economic crisis caused primarily by the increases in defense expenditures—the result of its attempts at attaining strategic parity with Israel. This, coupled with the exacerbation of the basic structural ills of the Syrian economy, brought Syria close to bankruptcy during the 1985–1987 period. In those years, the country suffered from galloping inflation, a decrease in investments, dwindling foreign currency reserves, an increase in the deficit, and most serious, serious shortages in staples and supply problems.[23] The economic crisis led to deep dissatisfaction among the population and the emergence of groups opposed to the regime.[24]

Assad assessed correctly that economic and social stability and development would fortify the stability of the regime and its security no less than military might. Therefore he began in 1987 to slow, although not to cease, the military build-up, and to channel more resources to domestic needs.[25]

Syria's problems in the international and Arab arenas were no less serious; indeed, it found itself in total isolation. Following the signing of the Camp David accords and the Egyptian-Israeli peace agreement, Syria became completely alienated from Egypt.

Because it backed Iran in its war against Iraq, its relations with the Gulf states during the 1980–1988 period were chilly, and those states stopped granting economic and financial aid. During the years of 1985–1990, Syria ran into a dead end in its attempt in Lebanon to unite all local factions behind a "Syrian solution" to the country's ruinous civil war. Finally, since the end of the Iran-Iraq War in late 1988, Iraq has emerged as a significant threat to Syria, ready to retaliate against Syria, for its stand in that war. This threat partially materialized in 1990, when Iraq granted assistance to Syria's major opponent in Lebanon at that time, General Michel Aoun.

Syria's regional distress was exacerbated in the 1986–1987 period with the U.S. peace initiative advanced by U.S. Secretary of State George Shultz, and again in the course of 1989–1990, when, under the guidance of Secretary of State James Baker, harbingers began to appear of a regional peace process involving the United States, Israel, Jordan, and the Palestinians. At that point, Syria realized that it was in danger of becoming even more isolated and further away from realizing its goal of retrieving the Golan Heights. Syria's relations with most EEC countries were also poor, especially those with Britain, which severed diplomatic ties with it in 1987, after the Hindawi affair.[26] This incident also resulted in further damage to Syria's relations with the United States, when the American ambassador to Damascus was recalled.

But of all the difficulties on the international scene, however, the most dramatic was the collapse of the Soviet Union and the communist regimes in Eastern Europe. In the Syrians' view, this process, which reached its peak in 1991, posed a potential threat to the survival of the regime. For with the disintegration of the Soviet Union, Syria's main source of political, economic, and military assistance suddenly disappeared. Furthermore, East European communism had also been a source of ideological inspiration and even a role model for the Syrian regime and to its people.[27]

The Syrians, especially President Assad, appear to have discerned the impending disintegration of communism and correctly analyzed this process since Gorbachev's rise to power in 1985. Assad was well aware of the implications for Syria, which also were pointed out to him by the Soviet leaders themselves. In April 1987, during Assad's official visit to the Soviet Union, President Gorbachev told him that he must abandon his effort to achieve strategic parity with Israel. In November 1989, the Soviet ambassador in

Damascus, Alexander Zotov, declared that the Soviet Union would start taking into account Syria's ability to pay for future weapons deals and that it would supply Syria with only only defensive weapons.[28] Such statements made it clear to the Syrians that they would not be able to rely for long on Soviet backing and that the status of the Soviet Union as a world power was on the decline. Assad carefully witnessed these developments and in his inaugural address for his fourth term of office, in 1992, defined the changes affecting the Soviet Union as an "upheaval of international proportions" that was far more significant for the Arab cause and Syria than any other change that had occurred since the end of World War II.[29] The fall of the Soviet Union left the United States as the world's only superpower. And in Assad's eyes, the United States was an even more serious enemy than Israel, a feeling that intensifed during the hostility between Assad's Syria and the Reagan administration during the course of the 1980s.[30]

The stark realities of the situation in the domestic, Arab, and international arenas in the mid-1980s, led Assad to the preception that the very survival of his regime was in jeopardy. Therefore, since 1989 Assad has pursued a gradual but consistent process of change at both levels, Arab and international, adopting more moderate policies than before. In December 1989 he renewed relations with Egypt and in July 1990 he even visited Cairo, despite the previous unequivocal Syrian stand that, so long as Israel's flag flew in Cairo and so long as the Camp David accords were in effect, he would never set a foot on Egyptian soil.[31] By changing the policy toward Egypt, Assad hoped to bolster his status in the Arab world and also improve relations with the West.

Assad also improved his relations with the United States, because he realized that the quality of his relations with that country could decide the fate of his regime. In June 1990, after a six-year hiatus, ambassadors were exchanged between the two countries, and Assad began receiving a long line of American senators, business people, and government officials to whom he expressed Syria's willingness to have better relations with the United States. Realizing that one of the conditions the United States would impose for this would be a change in Syria's attitude toward Israel, Assad also began signaling vague but consistent messages that he was ready for negotiations with Israel.[32]

Interesting to note, however, is that, despite the changes in foreign policy, Assad has strictly prevented any change in the social, economic, and political spheres in Syria, because in his view the root of the trouble in Eastern Europe lay in the domestic openness instituted by Gorbachev. This policy highlights the regime's weakness domestically and the continuing fears it feels for its very survival.

IMPACT OF THE GULF CRISIS

The Gulf crisis that erupted in August 1990 did not precipitate a change in Syrian policy but merely accelerated a process of change that began earlier. Moreover, the Gulf crisis created a situation, in which the United States and Syria found that they required the support of the other. This facilitated the improvement in relations between the two countries. During the Gulf War, Assad aligned himself with the United States (which he earlier considered a deadly enemy) and even sent in military forces to the Gulf against an Arab sister-state, Iraq. It is true that Syria's relations with Iraq were strained since the beginning of the Iran-Iraq War, but Syria's notorious hostility toward the Iraqi Ba'thi was still a long way from siding with the West against Iraq, in such blatant contradiction to the idea of Arab unity and the pioneering, revolutionary image that the Syrian Ba'th regime had been at pains to cultivate.

Syria's role during the Gulf crisis greatly improved its strategic situation. Its relations with the United States improved, although by the end of 1993 these relations were still far from being truly cordial. Disagreements between Syria and the American administration continued, focusing on the issues of Syria's sheltering terrorist organizations, its sanctioning of drug cultivation and trafficking in the Lebanese Bekaa, its violation of human rights, and its attitude toward ethnic minorities.[33] Syria's relations with West European countries also improved greatly. Relations with Britain were restored, and Syria ceased to be a pariah in the international community. Syria's status in the Arab world improved as well, and its relations with the Gulf states flourished. In Lebanon, Syria received tacit American backing for the elimination of its main rival, General Aoun, and the installation of its ally, Elias al-Hirawi, in Beirut.[34] Finally, in return for its cooperation during the Gulf crisis, Syria received generous economic assistance from Saudi Arabia and Kuwait as well as grants from Western Europe, which enhanced its economic situation.[35]

Nevertheless, the Gulf crisis also demonstrated to the Syrians their basic weaknesses. The crisis underlined the superiority of Western technology and weaponry, such as that Israel had at its disposal, over the Soviet weaponry Syria possessed. The international community's sympathetic reaction to the Iraqi missile attacks on Israel once more demonstrated to Syria the support that Israel receives from the West. Moreover, the Gulf crisis provided ample proof to Syria that the United States was now the only superpower in the world. The crisis also created a very dangerous precedent from Syria's point of view: the international community, led by the United States, intervened with force in the affairs of an Arab state. Also detrimental from Syria's point of view was the destruction of the power of Iraq, which, despite longstanding Syrian-Iraqi hostility, Syria had viewed (and in 1973, indeed used) as a strategic hinterland in the event of a confrontation with Israel. Finally, the Gulf crisis exposed the schisms and factionalism in the Arab world, highlighting for Syria a lesson it had already learned: that Arab countries could not be relied on for support in the future.

Therefore, the Syrians concluded that the crisis had not brought any real change in Syria's status and its basic problem, the threat to the existence of the regime, had not disappeared. They believed that Damascus must accelerate the process, which had begun before the crisis, and adopt a more moderate policy and improve relations with the United States.

When the Gulf War ended, the United States launched a peace process designed to resolve the Arab-Israeli conflict. This process gained momentum as the Madrid conference was convened in October 1991 and the bilateral and multilateral talks between the countries of the region began. After difficult deliberations, and under heavy pressure from the United States, including eight rounds of visits to Damascus by Secretary of State Baker between March and July 1991 during which he held exhaustive talks with the Syrian leadership and mainly with President Assad, the Syrians announced on July 14, 1991, that they were ready to participate in the American-sponsored process. Syria showed up in Madrid and participated in a number of rounds of direct talks with Israeli representatives.

This marks the first time in Syria's history it explicitly participated in a Middle East political process that included direct talks with Israel. The underlying conditions of this process were especially difficult for Syria to accept in that they did not involve an international conference but direct, bilateral talks. Moreover, the Arab world did not show a unified front in the opening talks, and neither Europe nor the United Nations played a significant role in them (as Syria hoped they would). Even more worrisome for Syria was the fact that it had received no clear and solid guarantees from the United States for the return of the Golan Heights to Syrian hands.[36] Moreover, Syria entered Madrid as a full participant in a process whose goal, as defined by President Bush in his keynote speech, was to be Arab recognition of Israel's security needs and the signing of contractual peace accords with Israel involving certain border amendments. For Syria, this might mean having to relinquish part of the Golan Heights.

The new pragmatic components in Syria's approach undoubtedly constitute a turning point in its traditional policy toward Israel, reflecting a pragmatism that had always been part of that policy under Assad, but never given such clear expression before.

SYRIAN ATTITUDE TOWARD PEACE PROCESS

The political process was viewed as a necessary evil that would ensure the security and stability of the Syrian regime. It was seen as the price that Syria must pay to find its way to the heart and pocket of the United States; indeed, as the Syrian regime saw it, its fate hung on whether this path was to be successfully traveled. Second, the Syrians viewed the Bush administration as being easy to work with, the friendliest American administration and the one most open to Arab positions and most ready to exert pressure on Israel. In Syrian eyes the chances of getting the Golan back had never been better and might never present themselves again. This "now or never" perception of the Syrians became especially strong as the November 1992 presidential elections approached. Third, there has also been a change in the Arab world at large regarding the Arab-Israeli conflict, with the Arab world more prepared than ever to accept Israel. This general change was manifest also in Syria, as no demonstrations against the peace process took place. This absence of protest was not only the result of suppression by the regime; for during the Gulf War, for example, there were hostile public reactions to the regime's official anti-Iraq policy.

Nevertheless, it is still necessary to regard the recent change in Syria's position with great caution; in many spheres no real change occurred from 1991 to 1993. Syria still refuses, at least publicly, to recognize Israel's existence or to take any steps that might imply that it exists. Moreover, Syria's conditions for a peace settlement are tough: complete Israeli withdrawal from lands captured·in 1967 and the restoration of "Palestinian rights," implicitly including the right of return (which many Israelis fear would result in the destruction of Israel).[37] Nor, apart from a certain moderation in tone, has any substantial change occurred in Syria's public rhetoric regarding Israel. In the Syrian media and in statements by Syrian leaders, Israel continues to be described as an aggressive, expansionist state.[38] The Syrians also still prefer to remain vague on the subject of how they view peace with Israel. They claim that the goal of the political process is to bring about the restoration of Arab lands and the reinstatement of Arab rights, and they refuse to include a peace treaty between Syria and Israel as one of its final objectives. Even within the process itself, Syria has so far refused to participate in the multilateral talks. Moreover, Syria continues to grant its protection to terrorist organizations—Palestinian and Lebanese—and implicitly encourages, or at least supports, their operations against Israel, especially from inside Lebanon.[39] Syria also implicitly opposes the Israeli-PLO agreement of September 13, 1993. Finally, Syria continues to equip itself with new weaponry. The latest in this process was the acquisition from North Korea of scud-C surface to surface missiles, with a range of about 600 kilomeres.[40] In addition, Syria is attempting to establish an Iranian-Syrian defense axis in which Iran would provide Syria with a strategic hinterland, a role once played by Iraq.[41] To use Lipson's terms, this may be the Syrian way of "creating institutions to capture the potential gains from cooperation [the peace process and rapprochement to the West], while minimizing the real dangers of deception and nonperformance,"[42] which it sees in this process.

As we have indicated, Syria participated in the peace process without committing itself, at least publicly, to the objective of achieving a peace treaty that would express its recognition of Israel. This stance is perhaps what underlies Syria's tactics in the rounds of negotiations that took place up to the end of 1993, in which it refrained from making concessions and gestures (such as positive and moderate declarations and agreeing to meetings with Israeli leaders) from which it would receive no practical quid pro quo. However, these tactics may also have reflected Syria's need to preserve its prestige at home and in the Arab world to avoid unnecessary threats in the domestic sphere or dangers to the stability of the regime. Nevertheless, the equivocal stance toward the peace process that Syria displayed up to the end of 1993 seems to suggest that deep in the hearts of Assad and his colleagues in the Syrian leadership, there is still a sense of commitment to their radical and hostile conception of Israel and the policy that calls for its destruction. As noted, this conception has its roots in psychological, emotional, and ideological motivations; and these will not quickly disappear. Given these deepseated motivations, Assad and his colleagues in the leadership were clearly faced with a dilemma over what path to take in their policy toward Israel.

SYRIA IN THE WAKE OF THE 1992 ISRAELI ELECTIONS: PRESUPPOSITIONS FOR PEACE

The results of the elections to the Israeli Knessset that took place on June 23, 1992, and the establishment of a new Israeli Labor government headed by Yitzhak Rabin, exacerbated Syria's dilemma and brought the Syrian leadership closer to a moment of truth. These events obliged the Syrians to consider a series of questions that might be involved in the negotiations or in a peace treaty itself. For, as the peace process advanced, Syria found itself increasingly participating in it and hence increasingly committed to it.

Despite the expectations that Rabin's government would give priority to the Jordanian-Palestinian axis of the peace process over the Syrian one, Rabin later clarified that he would not neglect negotiations with Syria. Moreover, he declared that he was prepared to reach an interim settlement with the Syrians in the immediate future, as a step on the road toward peace.[43] These declarations, alongside Israel's readiness, as expressed in the round of negotiations that began in Washington on August 24, 1992, to implement Security Council Resolution 242 in the Golan Heights (although Israel refused to commit itself to full withdrawal)[44] not only improved the atmosphere in the discussions between the Israeli and Syrian delegations but also challenged the Syrians to formulate a response, perhaps on the assumption that Syria would soon be required to make a decision regarding the future of the process as a whole.

SECURITY ARRANGEMENTS AND SYRIA'S NEW NATIONAL SECURITY CONCEPT

It is important to examine the Syrian attitude toward three key issues: the nature of future security arrangements (in light of the changes in its national security concept), the possibility of reaching an interim agreement, and the possibility of reaching a separate agreement with Israel.

As we have seen, the Syrian national security concept has been badly disrupted over the past several years. First, the Soviet Union, which had been Syria's major prop, no longer exists. Second, although Syria continues, as if there had been no peace process or rapprochment with the United States, to build up its army and equip itself with deadly weapons, it seems that the Syrians now realize that their military option is a shaky one.

The warning signal that may have brought the Syrians to this realization was the American attempt to contain the worldwide spread of weapons supply. Bush's May 1991 initiative for arms control in the Middle East and the consequent American efforts to stop North Korean weapon convoys to Iran and Syria were interpreted by Syria as meaning that the United States was allowing Israel to retain its clear qualitative superiority over the Arabs and continue holding atomic weapons.[45] Alongside its refusal to accept the American arms control initiative, Syria began raising the issue of Israel's own military build-up, with special reference to its nuclear capability. This led the the Syrians to seek the formulation of a new security concept that would assure adequate defense. Integration into peace and security arrangements, or even a security regime, orchestrated by the United States was one of the ways not only of improving Syria's relations with America, but also of serving its own defense and security interests.

Therefore, a security regime in the Middle East is important to Syria no less than to Israel. Such regime could appear quite tempting to the Syrians, who, moreover, cannot afford to pass up the opportunity to reach an agreement over the Golan. An essential component in such arrangements, from Syria's point of view, would be "clipping Israel's atomic claws"—an issue that the Syrian press discussed at length in the course of 1992[46]—in addition, it seeks to contain the military edge that Israel has over Syria, especially in terms of advanced weaponry.

Indications of Syria's eagerness that controls be exerted over Israel's weapons of mass destruction were particularly evident in an interview Assad granted the BBC on June 2, 1992, in which he stated: at a distance of less than 100 kilometers from the heart of the city of Damascus, there are Israeli nuclear weapons and missiles that can carry various kinds of nuclear warheads, manufactured by Israel or with the assistance it receives from Western countries. We see that the international community must quickly prevent the manufacture of nuclear weapons in Israel and destroy the atomic weapons and thus prove its determination to preserve peace and prevent global human disasters that might occur; otherwise what meaning is there to the cry for a farewell to arms?[47]

During the first stages of negotiation, the Syrians refrained from referring to any other issues related to security arrangements. However, an analysis of Syria's past behavior, alongside recent press reports, may give some indication of Syria's future direction. For example, after the Israeli election there were hints of readiness for a demilitarized zone between Israel and Syria, in which U.N. or even American forces would be deployed, although Syria failed to deny or confirm such a possibility.[48] Moreover, Syria may be prepared to accept a supervisory mechanism (such as that which existed in the framework of the interim settlements signed between Israel and Egypt in 1975). The fact that for years Syria has permitted, or at least ignored, the flights of Israeli planes over Lebanese territory might be translated into its readiness to accept supervisory mechanisms that could include early warning stations on both sides, use of American intelligence data, reconnaissance flights, and the like. The Syrians clearly view these components of prospective security arrangements as a crucial, albeit not exclusive component, of a new security concept that takes into consideration the integration of Syria into a security regime, based on closer cooperation, or even friendship, between Syria and the United States.[49]

INTERIM SETTLEMENT VS. COMPREHENSIVE AGREEMENT

An interim settlement could have clear advantages for both parties. It would enable gradual progress and help both the Israeli and Syrian governments contend with public opinion at home that would be hard put to accept an overall settlement. For the Syrians, the clearest advantage of an interim settlement might be that it would not oblige them to recognize Israel and sign a peace treaty with it. Israel, for its part, would not be required, in such a settlement, to relinquish all of the Golan Heights. Moreover, an interim settlement would allow both sides time in which to contemplate the intentions of the other side and prepare the ground for future progress.

Such considerations apparently underlie Prime Minister Rabin's declaration in early September 1992 of his readiness to negotiate interim settlements with the Syrians[50]—in contrast to Israel's earlier policy that advocated seeking a comprehensive peace treaty. The Syrians, however, have refrained from responding to Rabin's declaration and have continued to insist on a comprehensive settlement. Indeed, one must bear in mind that Syria regards the May 1974 separation of forces agreements, achieved with the mediation of Henry Kissinger, as hindering the goal of retrieving the Golan.[51] Syria has traditionally been suspicious of interim agreements, fearing that they would perpetuate Israeli control of the Golan indefinitely. Moreover, the Golan is too small for any interim settlement that would allow the Syrian regime to boast territorial achievements. Therefore, the Syrians will probably continue to aim for a comprehensive settlement that would include the transfer of a significant chunk (or, if possible, all) of the Golan to their sovereignty, rather than for interim settlements that would not significantly enhance their claim to the Golan.

Syria's objective, then, is comprehensive peace. Therefore, Israel's primary attempt to reach an understanding with the Jordanians and Palestinians without similar progress with them is viewed by Syria with great concern. The resolution of the Israeli-Palestinian conflict, the Syrians believe, may leave them facing Israel alone, in a much inferior bargaining position and with even less chance of retreiving the Golan Heights. Such fears underlie Syria's outright rejection of any partial solution to the Arab-Israeli conflict and its reservations about the Israel-PLO September 1993 accord.

CONCLUSION

The current constraints to which Syria is subject, including the collapse of its traditional national security concept, the possible return of the Golan Heights, and finally, Assad's feeling that as far as the Arab-Israeli conflict is concerned he is treading on solid ground both at home and in the entire Arab world serve as the basis for his decision to cross the limits he had once drawn for himself and participate in direct negotiations for peace with Israel. This, of course, means that he has entered—and from a position of weakness—into a process over which he has little control, one that might result in Syria's recognition of Israel and the signing of a peace treaty incorporating security arrangements.

The Syrian change in approach to Israel has so far been expressed in a series of steps, some of them of a tactical nature, which, although constituting a substantial change in Syria's position, will still allow Assad to retreat from the peace process. So far, there has been no a strategic volte face such as Sadat's revolutionary visit to Jerusalem. Assad has yet to declare (in word or deed) his total, unequivocal acceptance of the existence of Israel in the Middle East. The absence of such acceptance in the first stages of the negotiations derives from a number of reasons, related to both his negotiating tactics and his fundamental ideological and psychological difficulty in changing basic conceptions about Israel.

A step such as Sadat's visit to Jerusalem would seem to be out of character for Assad, a cautious leader who does not like intiatives and changes. His greatness as a leader indeed lies in his calculated and gradual steps. Therefore, we see slow progress reflecting caution and inner struggles on his part. These inner struggles are genuine, because he does not want to abandon ideological principles and finds it difficult to cross psychological barriers. He also fears that Israel will not, in the end, return the Golan and that a favorable change in his attitude toward Israel may be detrimental to Syria's status in the Arab world and to the fate of his regime. Nevertheless, Assad is prepared to consider the possibility of basing his country's security on a security regime that would replace its traditional national security concept, and thus integrate Syria into the new world order.

The path to a peace agreement between Israel and Syria is still long and strewn with obstacles, but in his decision of July 14, 1991, to give a positive answer to the American initiative Assad stepped onto this path, and he is progressing slowly and cautiously. If there are no substantial changes in the present conditions, he will find it difficult in the future to step off it on his own initiative.

NOTES

1. The Syrians reacted with clear disappointment to Bush's speech, especially because it did not explicitly mention the formula of "land for peace," which Syria viewed as a central component of any future settlement with Israel. See, for example, the response of Syrian Foreign Minister Faruq al-Shar' to Bush's speech in R. Damascus, October 30—Daily Report: Middle East and Africa, US Foreign Broadcasting Information Service (DR), October 31, 1991.

2. See Charles Lipson "Are Security Regimes Possible? Historical Cases and Modern Issues," Chapter 1.

3. See also 'Amos Gilboa, "Syria's National Security Concepts" in Avner Yaniv and Moshe Ma'oz, eds., *Syria and Israel's National Security* [Hebrew] (Tel-Aviv: Maarachot, 1991), pp. 143–153.

4. Lipson, chapter 1.

5. This readiness was manifest in the declaration of the head of the Israeli team for negotiations with Syria, Professor Itamar Rabinovich, that Israel accepts tha applicability of Resolution 242 to the Syrian front as well, *Ha'aretz* (August 25, 1992).

6. This possibility was suggested in the declarations of Israeli Prime Minister Rabin, both before and immediately after he was elected. See, for example, Israel TV, June 16—DR, June 17, 1992.

7. On similar Syrian moves employed against Jordan and the Palestinians in the mid-1980s, see Patrick Seale, *Asad: The Struggle for the Middle East* (London: I. B. Tauris, 1988), pp. 464–473.

8. On Assad's personality and method of government, see Moshe Ma'oz, *Asad: The Sphinx of Damascus* (London: Weidenfeld and Nicholson, 1987); and Seale, ibid., pp. 339–350.

9. It is commonly believed that Assad's hostile attitude toward Israel is anchored in his vision of Arab unity and, as a stage along the path to that unity, the aspiration to establish what is generally known as Greater Syria. These two may indeed be Assad's long-term objectives. However, his policies over the last two decades have clearly been characterized by the desire—and effort—to achieve far more modest goals, mainly the improvement of Syria's status and maneuverability in the inter-Arab and international arenas. An understanding of Assad's direction, therefore, requires an examination not of his grand ideologies but of the lower, simpler, and more basic strata of his world-view; that is, his perception of himself as a loyal son of the Syrian people, which is an essential part of the Arab nation. For an analysis of the Greater Syria

conception, its roots, development, and influence on Assad's path, see Ma'oz, *Asad*, pp. 109–122; Itamar Rabinovich, "Stages in Syria's Policy on the Conflict With Israel" in Alouph Hareven and Yehiam Padan, eds, *Between War and Settlement? The Arab-Israeli Conflict Since October 1973* [Hebrew] (Tel-Aviv: Zmora, Bitan, Modan, 1977); Seale, *Asad*, pp. 24–40, 349–350. For a different approach, which regards the goal of Greater Syria to be a central component of Assad's worldview, see Daniel Pipes, *Greater Syria: The History of an Ambition* (Oxford: Oxford University Press, 1990), pp. 175–188.

10. Therefore, for example, Assad habitually compared the Jewish presence in Palestine to the Crusaders' presence in the region between 1099 and 1299. He also claimed, especially with the inception of the large wave of immigration of Soviet Jews to Israel in early 1990, that the real origins of the Israeli citizens of European descent were in the Khazar (Jewish converts) tribes of central Asia. See, for example, Asad's speeches of March 8, 1988, March 8, 1990 (*Tishrin* [March 9, 1988; March 9, 1990]. On Assad's comparison of Israel to the Crusaders, see Ma'oz, *Asad*, p. 104.

11. This claim reappeared in President Asad's speech of March 12, 1992, after the Middle East peace process was under way (R. Damascus, 12 March 1992.

12. See Ma'oz, *Asad*, pp. 188–189; Seale, *Asad*, p. 348.

13. See Seale, ibid., p. 495.

14. See, Yaacov Bar-Siman Tov, *Linkage Politics in the Middle East—Syria Between Domestic and External Conflict*, 1961–1970 (Boulder, Colo.: Westview Press, 1983).

15. See Ma'oz, *Asad*, pp. 123–134; see also Yair Evron, *War and Intervention in Lebanon: The Israeli-Syrian Deterrence Dialogue* (Baltimore: Johns Hopkins University Press, 1987), and Seale, *Asad*, pp. 278–280.

16. See Lipson, chapter 1.

17. In the past twenty years, Assad has only once, in an interview to *Newsweek* (February 25, 1975), declared that he was ready to sign a formal peace treaty with Israel in return for Israeli withdrawal to the 1967 borders. This interview is considered an aberration, as it contravenes the whole range of Assad's other statements on this issue, in which he refrained from expressing readiness for a peace treaty with Israel.

18. On Syria's policy during this period, see Ma'oz, *Asad*, pp. 97–107; Rabinovich, "Stages;" Seale, *Asad*, pp. 226–250.

19. On Assad's attempt to obtain an American commitment to support Syria's demand that all of the Golan Heights be returned to it, see Ma'oz, ibid., pp. 97–108; Seale, ibid., pp. 226–249.

20. In his book on Assad, Seale argues that in those years Assad was ready to participate in a real peace proccess in the region, but the stub-

bornness of Israel, backed by the United States, prevented the achievement of peace. Although Seale's claims, which are based on Assad's, are not totally without substance, they ignore the ideological component that is central to Assad's thinking, as well as the constraints facing his regime. See Seale, ibid., pp. 202–315.

21. From 313,000 regular soldiers in 1983, there was an increase to some 500,000 in 1985; also in 1985, the Syrian army had a force of some 4,000 tanks of various types and some 650 aircraft. See Gilbo'a, "Syria's National Security Concept," in Yaniv and Ma'oz, *Syria*, p. 147; Mark A. H. Heller (ed.), *The Middle East Military Balance* (Tel-Aviv: Tel-Aviv University; Jaffee Center for Strategic Studies, 1983, 1984, 1985).

22. For further information, see Zeev Eytan, "The Syrian Army" in Yaniv and Ma'oz, *Syria;* Seale, *Asad*, pp. 398–399.

23. For more information on the Syrian economic distress in the mid-1980s, see Eliyahu Kanovsky, *What's Behind Syria's Recent Economic Problems?* (Dayan Center, Occasional Papers (Tel-Aviv: Tel-Aviv University, 1985); Moshe Dayan Center, Tel Aviv University, *Middle East Contemporary Survey* (MECS), vol. 10 (1986), pp. 610–611.

24. MECS, vol. 10 (1986), pp. 608–610.

25. MECS, vol. 11 (1987), p. 640.

26. On April 17, 1986, a woman, boarding an El Al airplane was arrested at Heathrow Airport while carrying an explosive charge. Her boyfriend Nizar al-Hindawi, an agent of Syria's secret services was also arrrested. After trying Hindawi, the British government pointed an accusing finger at the government of Syria as responsible for the attempt to blow up an El Al plane and severed diplomatic ties with it. See "Syria," in MECS, vol. 10 (1986), for the Syrian version of this affair, see Seale, *Asad*, pp. 475–483.

27. This was well manifest in the preoccupation of the Syrian press during the late 1980s in their interpretation of events in Eastern Europe, which sought to prove to the Syrian public that the Syrian system was superior to its Soviet model. For example, from *Tishrin* (October 2, 1991): "The collapse of the regimes that used to call themselves socialist in Eastern Europe does not mean the end of socialism and the collapse of socialist thinking. Rather, it signals the collapse of a pattern of socialist practice that will be rightly judged and assessed by history." (R. Damascus, October 2—DR, October 4, 1991.)

28. See Helena Cobban, "The Nature of the Soviet-Syrian Link Under Asad and Gorbachev", in Richard Antoun and Donald Quatert (eds.), *Syria: Society, Culture and Polity*, (Albany: State University of New York Press, 1991).

29. *Tishrin* (March 13, 1992).

30. See Seale, *Asad*, pp. 394–420, 461–491; and Asad's speech on March 8, 1988, (R. Damascus, March 8, 1988).

31. Mena, August 16—DR, August 17, 1990.

32. For example, former American President Carter's declared following his visit to Damascus in March 1990 that Assad had authorized him to propose the convening of an international conference for resolving the Arab-Israeli conflict, after which he would be prepared to conduct bilateral talks to settle the dispute between Syria and Israel, on the condition that these talks include the issue of the Golan Heights (*Ha'aretz* [March 19, 1992]).

33. See "Syria," in MECS, vol. 13 (1990).

34. The American ambassador to Damascus declared shortly after the Syrian attack that the United States supported the implementation of the Ta'if agreement and that the Syrian moves in Lebanon had been made in an effort to help the legitimate Lebanese administration expand its sovereignty over all of Lebanon (Sana, October 24—DR, October 25, 1991).

35. The Gulf states granted Syria $2.5–3 billion in return for the military aid it gave them during the Gulf War and as compensation for the damages that the war caused Syria (*al-Hayat,* London [July 6, 1991]).

36. It is worth mentioning that the content of the American letter of guarantee to Syria was not made known and that, later, Secretary of State James Baker was forced to deny Syrian claims that it included an American commitment to Syria for full Israeli withdrawal from the Golan Heights (*Jerusalem Post* [July 26, 1991]).

37. Those conditions were set forth in the speech of the Syrian foreign minister, al-Shar'a, at the Madrid peace conference. (R.Damascus, October 30—DR, October 31, 1991).

38. See the editorials in *Tishrin* [May 26 and July 1, 1992].

39. In the State Department annual report for 1990 on "Patterns of Global Terrorism," published in April 1991, Syria is still considered to be a country that grants patronage to terrorism. (*Jerusalem Post* [May 1, 1991]).

40. *Ha'aretz* (July 5, 1991).

41. After a visit to Iran by the Syrian chief of staff, Hikmat Shihabi, on September 25, 1991, there were rumors, later denied by both sides, about the possibility of military cooperation between them, including a joint project for the development of surface to surface missles. (Tehran Television, September 25—DR, September 26, 1992; R. Damascus September 19—DR, September 19, 1991.)

42. See Lipson, chapter 1.

43. See Rabin's speech on September 7, before the general assembly of the World Organization of B'nai Brith (*Ha'aretz* [September 8, 1992]; see also *Ha'aretz* [June 24 and 25, 1992]).

44. *Ha'aretz* (August 25, 1992).

45. See, for example, Assad's speech to the Syrian parliament on March 12, 1992, in which he attacked the United States for its efforts to prevent Syria from purchasing advanced weaponry, while at the same time providing such weaponry to Israel or helping Israel to produce it (R. Damascus, March 12—DR, March 12, 1992).

46. See, for example, an article in *al-Ba'th* under the title "Full Peace Demands the Removal of Israel's Atomic Fingernails" (*al-Ba'th* [June 9, 1992]).

47. *Al-Ba'th* (June 3, 1992).

48. *Haaretz* (October 31, 1991).

49. Against this background one can understand a certain Syrian disappointment at the result of the elections in Israel, which pointed to an improvement in Israel's relations with Washington, thus deflating Syrian hopes to benefit from the rift between Israel and the United States (see inter alia, *Tishrin* [July 1 and 11, 1992]).

50. *Ha'aretz* (September 8, 1992).

51. For Assad's views on this issue, See Seale, *Asad*, pp. 227–266.

CHAPTER 8

Arms Control in the Middle East: Global Regimes vs. Regional Dynamics

Gerald M. Steinberg

INTRODUCTION

The efforts to limit and control the transfer of advanced weapons provide a very visible and complex example of an international regime. Indeed, arms control and nonproliferation provide the most visible and complex example of an existing international security regime. More clearly than any other set of issues, arms control combines the idealist concepts of collective security and the transcendence of the Hobbesian "state of nature," with the requirements of realism and the preservation of national security interests. As Lipson has noted in this book, the ultimately unstable combination of realism and deterrence has stimulated the exploration of "more cooperative efforts to provide national security." This is the essence of arms control.

The initial elements of this regime can be traced to the 1925 Geneva Convention, which prohibited the use of chemical weapons. The major components, consisting of the Nuclear Nonproliferation Treaty (NPT) and the system of controls operated by the International Atomic Energy Agency (IAEA), were developed in the late 1960s and early 1970s and have been in operation for over two decades. Other elements were added in the 1980s, such as the London Nuclear Suppliers' Group (LNSG) and the Missile Technology Control Regime (MTCR), and in 1993, the Chemical Weapons Convention (CWC) was opened for signature. Together, these measures and institutions meet Krasner's definition of a *regime*: "sets of implicit or explicit principles, norms, rules, and decision-making procedures around actors' expectations converge in a given area of international relations."[1]

However, although the major analytic and legal frameworks for the existing arms control regime are global, the dynamics of proliferation and arms races are based on distinct regional factors. This is particularly true for the Middle East, a region characterized by numerous and overlapping ethno-national conflicts, which lead to geometrically accelerating arms races. In addition, factors such as a high degree of asymmetry between small states and large ones, rich oil producers and poor overpopulated states, and sharply contrasting political systems must be incorporated in any regional arms control regime. These regional factors determine the requirements for negotiation, verification, sanctions, crisis management, and other key aspects.

In contrast, the basic elements of the existing arms control regime are global and not designed specifically for application in the Middle East. The NPT, the activities of the Safeguards Division of the IAEA, the MTCR, and the CWC are all designed to apply on an identical basis to all regions and states. As will be demonstrated in this chapter, this global framework has failed to encompass the factors responsible for the proliferation of both conventional and unconventional weapons in the Middle East. Moreover, in some cases, the effort to apply the global regime to the area is counterproductive; with respect to Israel, for example, this effort has threatened to weaken national security.

In the place of the existing global framework, a regional arms control regime, designed to include the particular factors characteristic of the Middle East, has been suggested. These include non-conventional-weapons-free zones, based on the concept of nuclear weapons free zones but including chemical and biological weapons, missiles, and limits on conventional weapons. To develop these approaches further, however, the current emphasis on the existing global structures, including the NPT, IAEA, and MTCR will have to be shifted to the regional model.

Recent changes in the Middle East, including the beginning of political negotiations beginning in Madrid in October 1991 and the focus on arms control in the multilateral talks, have created the opportunity for change in the relationship between conflict and cooperation. For the first time, the development of arms control in the Middle East has become conceivable, if still very distant. The evolution of this potential will depend on the degree to which regional frameworks and regime structures are emphasized.

ARMS CONTROL IN THE MIDDLE EAST: REQUIREMENTS AND VARIABLES

The development of an arms control regime is extremely complex in any context, and the difficulties in the Middle East are significantly more formidable than those that plagued the negotiations between Moscow and Washington for decades. The U.S.-Soviet arms race was essentially confined to the two superpowers, whereas the Middle East is a multipolar system, where military conflicts involve shifting coalitions among many states. A United Nations General Assembly report on the requirements for "effective and verifiable" arms control in the region concluded that over twenty states, including all the members of the Arab League, Iran, Israel, and perhaps Pakistan are part of the regional arms dynamics.[2] The core of the U.S.-Soviet confrontation was largely ideological, but the wars in the Middle East are based on the explosive combination of ethnic, nationalist, religious, and cultural conflict.

Some of the greatest difficulties in reaching the level of cooperation necessary for arms control agreements, in any context, result from the inherent problems of the surrounding conflict situation. In his analysis of the inherent obstacles to the development of security regimes, Lipson notes that as a result of the anarchical nature of the international system, "information is poor, deception and cheating are possible, and, most important, basic rights of property and contract (and enforcement mechanisms for those rights) are simply absent at the international level." This is particularly true in the Arab-Israeli context.

Moscow and Washington maintained diplomatic links throughout the Cold War, and despite the distrust and threat of conflict, multiple channels of communication existed. In the Middle East, however, many states do not even recognize the legitimacy of others. Lebanon, Jordan, Kuwait, Saudi Arabia, and even Iraq are considered by some to be artificial creations of the colonial period. Iran, which is rapidly becoming a major proliferator in all areas, is boycotting the Arab-Israeli peace talks and calls for the destruction of Israel. In such an atmosphere, it has been difficult both politically and logistically to even discuss issues pertinent to arms control.

The process of arms control is further complicated by the overlapping nature of the conflicts in the region. In the wake of its war with Iran, Iraq was able to purchase billions of dollars in weapons and military technology; this arsenal was later used in the invasion of Kuwait and to threaten Israel. Iranian and Iraqi capabilities led Saudi Arabia to spend billions of dollars on new weapons and technology, including American F-15 combat aircraft and Chinese CSS-2 intercontinental ballistic missiles. Based on previous Saudi contributions to the Arab wars in 1967 and 1973, these weapons represent a potential threat to Israel. As such, Israel has voiced concern regarding this military build-up. It can thus be seen that no single aspect of the Middle East can be isolated, and regional arms control must be wide-ranging.

The region is also characterized by extreme asymmetry in the geopolitical situation and military forces. Israel's small population (under 5 million) and geographic area (20,000 square kilometers prior to 1967), led to a major emphasis on advanced technology and an offensive strategy. The major Arab states such as Iraq and Egypt have much larger populations and base their military power on very large groundBen-Gu forces, which could potentially overwhelm Israel. The massive oil revenues some states in the region receive enable them to spend large sums on weapons and military deployments, whereas other states, and Israel in particular, lack these resources.

In response, Israeli leaders, beginning with Ben-Gurion, saw the development of a nuclear deterrent as the only means of securing national survival in the face of the Arab quest for overwhelming conventional superiority.[3] This led to the Israeli nuclear weapons program, based on the reactor located at Dimona, and according to various unconfirmed reports and the testimony of Mordechai Vanunu, separation and other facilities, and the development of the Jericho missile.[4] Although possession of nuclear weapons has never been officially acknowledged, Israel is assumed to possess a nuclear deterrent. Faced with the threat to national survival posed by Arab conventional forces, Israel will not agree to limits on its nuclear deterrent unless limits on conventional forces are included as well.[5]

Thus, in the Middle East, no single issue or area can be separated from the full range of weapons, and all states must be included. To be successful, arms control processes must encompass both conventional and unconventional weapons from the beginning and must include limitations on all the Arab and Islamic states in addition to Israel. This issue area cannot be separated from the overall process of political negotiation and conflict amelioration.

VERIFICATION REQUIREMENTS IN THE REGION

Regimes based on restraints and limitations in the area of national security are inherently extremely difficult to achieve. The absence of a reliable external enforcement mechanism makes any such limitations very risky and always leaves open the option of defection.[6] In addition, although, as Lipson notes, "regimes can provide or facilitate sanctions for rule violations," in the international arena, the credibility of externally imposed sanctions is generally open to question and must be demonstrated.

In the area of arms control, this "Prisoners' Dilemma" is focused on the issue of verification. In any arms control regime, verification is the key element, and effective limitations in the Middle East will require major efforts in this area. In general, the efficacy of verification systems is based on timely warning of diversion of nuclear materials and credible penalties sufficient to deter such diversion. In contrast to other regions, the threat of international economic or political sanctions have not been adequate to deter violations in the Middle East.[7] Many countries have consistently failed to comply with international agreements. Although Iraq and Libya signed the NPT and are ostensibly bound by the IAEA safeguard system, the leaders of these states have not been prevented from actively seeking nuclear weapons. (Iraq is even a member of the IAEA Board of Governors.) Similarly, Iraq signed (but did not ratify) the 1972 Biological and Toxin Weapons Convention, which prohibits the development and possession of biological weapons, but Saddam Hussein invested heavily in the development of deadly toxins.[8]

In general, the inherent anarchy of the international system is particularly pronounced in the Middle East. In many cases, agreements in this region have been treated as temporary tactical measures that are readily ignored or renounced when circumstances change. In addition to Iraq, there are numerous other examples in the Middle East, such as Nasser's expulsion of the U.N. forces in 1967.[9] Under these circumstances, effective safeguards, verification, and assurances against sudden "breakout" will have to be monitored directly by the nations involved. A proposed international satellite reconnaissance agency that "filtered" the unprocessed data in any way would be considered unreliable for similar reasons.[10]

Limitations and agreements concerning nuclear, chemical, and biological weapons as well as surface-to-surface ballistic missiles must also solve the problems posed by the ambiguities of dual-use systems. These are technologies, materials, and facilities that can be used for both civil and military purposes. Many states have attempted to disguise missile development as a form of research for space launchers, chemical weapons in the form of pesticides, and nuclear weapons facilities as a nuclear energy research program (even though Iraq is one of the world's largest petroleum producers). Effective safeguards will require that dual-use facilities and materials are operated transparently and open to full inspection and verification. Secret programs and dual-use technologies are a source of distrust and would endanger a system of arms control and restraints.

Functionally, verification requires much closer cooperation between states than currently exists. No progress can be made as long as Syria refuses to participate in the multilateral talks in the context of the U.S.-sponsored Middle East peace negotiations, including the sessions on arms control. Major political changes will be necessary before a reliable system of verification can be developed.

THE EXISTING GLOBAL REGIME

In contrast to the particular factors that characterize proliferation and warfare in the Middle East, the existing arms control regime and its major components are global. A single standard of behavior and system of verification exists for each type of weapon and technology, including nuclear, chemical, biological, and missile systems. In this system, countries with unique concerns and genuine threats to national survival, such as Israel, are treated in the same way as international pariahs, such as North Korea and Iraq. A general pattern of political, military, and economic symmetry is assumed, whereas in the Middle East, asymmetry is the norm. As a result, the global system of agreements has failed in the Middle East and is viewed with suspicion and distrust.

In many ways, the NPT, which was signed in 1968 and entered into force in 1970, is the core of the global arms control regime. The NPT recognizes two groups of states: the five nuclear weapons states—United States, Soviet Union, United Kingdom, France, and China—and the nonnuclear weapons states (NNWS)—to which all other nations belong. The nuclear weapons states pledged to make efforts to reduce their stockpiles though arms control agreements (Article VI—France and China did not sign the NPT and have only recently announced the intention to accept this agreement). These countries also agreed not to provide other states with any form of assistance, technology, or materials that might be used to develop nuclear weapons (Article I). The nonnuclear signatories promise not to develop nuclear weapons (Article II), but are allowed to acquire materials, technology, and facilities for civil nuclear applications.

The global nature of the treaty creates two forms of problems and limitations. In the first place, all NNWS signatories are treated according to a single set of regulations. Every state that signs the NPT is allowed access to nuclear research facilities and is entitled to assistance from the other states, including the five nuclear powers. States eager to pursue a nuclear weapons program signed the treaty to acquire an infrastructure that could later be applied to the development of a military capability. Second, the treaty provids no answer for states that determine nuclear weapons to be necessary to deter threats to national survival. By considering all NNWS on an identical basis, the NPT, like most other international agreements and regimes, is unable to incorporate important political differences among states or between status-quo and revolutionary systems. Those states with a commitment to the status quo and stability in the international system, such as the United States, Canada, and Western Europe, view international agreements such as the NPT as binding obligations and the basis for stability and survival in the nuclear age.

In contrast, for nondemocratic leaders with territorial ambitions and no interest in the status quo, international agreements are meaningless or minor obstacles to be overcome. The leaders of the radical regimes in Iraq, Libya, Iran, and North Korea do not share an interest in international stability or the prevention of war. They have proven to be willing to sacrifice millions of lives and take enormous risks to advance their own interests and agendas. The NPT treaty begins by noting "the devastation that would be visited upon all mankind by a nuclear war." Leaders such as Saddam Hussein, who used chemical weapons to destroy entire villages in his own country and who had no hesitation in sending hundreds of thousands of soldiers to their deaths in the wars against Iran and the U.S.-led coalition, are not likely to be effected by concerns for "all mankind."

Indeed, by signing the NPT, such states are guaranteed access to the very technology and materials necessary to acquire nuclear weapons. Article IV notes that "Nothing in this treaty shall be interpreted as affecting the inalienable right of all the Parties to the Treaty to develop research, production and use of nuclear energy for peaceful purposes without discrimination and in conformity with articles I and II of this treaty." The NPT goes on to assure access to this technology "on a non-discriminatory basis." As noted in the first section of this chapter, the effort to place Iraq and Libya in the same category as Canada, Sweden, or Japan has failed.

In general, the NPT framework was based on the assumption that most, if not all, "Third World" nuclear arms efforts were the result of the activities of "a small coterie of scientists and bureaucrats working with political leaders."[11] Until recently, there was little, if any discussion of efforts to develop a nuclear capability for military or political purposes.

In addition, the NPT system does not recognize any legitimate need for nuclear deterrence. During World War II, the United States began developing atomic weapons to match similar programs in Germany. In 1945, after the Nazis had been defeated, President Truman employed these weapons against Japan to avoid a ground invasion and the casualties that this would have caused. Truman and subsequent American leaders have defended the decision to use nuclear weapons as entirely legitimate under the circumstances.[12] The subsequent decisions to develop nuclear weapons by the Soviet Union, France and the United Kingdom were defended in terms of deterrence and the requirements of national security.

Geoffrey Kemp notes that "On some occasions, weapons proliferation has led to greater caution between adversaries, and may have strengthened deterrence." He cites the specific example of

Saddam Hussein's failure to use chemical weapons against Israel, attributing this caution to the fear of massive retaliation promised by Israel.[13] Israel faces threats to national security even greater than those faced by the United States or any of the other nuclear powers. Arab states have acquired massive conventional forces and continue to reject the legitimacy of a sovereign Jewish state. As noted previously, Israeli nuclear deterrence is seen as entirely legitimate in this situation. The NPT and other elements of the global approach to nonproliferation provide no answer to these vital and legitimate concerns.

IAEA

The International Atomic Energy Agency was created in 1957 as an independent international agency, although it is linked to the United Nations, and the IAEA Board of Governors reports to the U.N. Security Council. In 1970, when the NPT entered into force, the IAEA became responsible for the negotiation and administration of safeguards on nuclear materials and facilities transferred under the terms of the treaty.

The IAEA, like the NPT, is also based on the principle (or the fiction) of equality among states. The IAEA has 110 members, which elect the Board of Governors (consisting of 34 nations). The board, in turn, appoints the director general of the agency, and the director general controls the Department of Safeguards and Inspection. Under the terms of the regime, each state within the system negotiates a specific safeguards agreement. Because some states asserted that intrusive safeguards would impinge on national sovereignty, and nosy inspectors could compromise proprietary information or reveal industrial secrets (this had more effect in the 1950s and 1960s when the nuclear industry was growing), the safeguards and inspection procedures were designed to be largely nonintrusive. Safeguard agreements and reports were also secret, ostensibly for the same reasons. Evidence of a diversion or violation, if detected, is reported to the director general, who then is authorized to bring it to the attention of the Board of Governors. The board, consisting of representatives of states, is of course highly political and can be expected to act on some violations or suspected violations, while ignoring others for political reasons. For example, the Arab members of the IAEA did not press for action to slow the Iraqi nuclear weapons program. At most, the board can report its findings to the U.N. Security Council for action.

All these factors raised serious questions regarding the effectiveness of safeguards with respect to would-be nuclear weapons states. Even if IAEA system provides timely warning of a diversion, the effectiveness of this measure in terms of deterrence depends on the credibility of sanctions. Closed nondemocratic states would be able to hide evidence of a nuclear weapons program much more successfully than open democratic states, putting the latter at a distinct disadvantage. In addition, nondemocratic regimes are able to resist the impact of sanctions and survive in power for a significant period. Thus, leaders who conclude that a nuclear program could escape detection until the last stages, that likely sanctions are acceptable, or that the threat to apply sanctions was not credible are not deterred by the IAEA safeguards system.

Iraq provides the most blatant, but not the only, example of such a response to the existing regime and the universal approach of the IAEA system. Iraq is an NPT signatory and signed an IAEA safeguards agreement. In the late 1970s Iraq acquired a French reactor, under safeguards, but IAEA inspectors later testified that the inspection system was inadequate. Iraq was able to choose the nature and timing of the inspections and limit the nationalities of acceptable inspectors to those who would not necessarily have detected evidence of diversion.[14] As a result, the Israeli government acted to destroy the reactor. The Iraqi nuclear program, however, continued, with the assistance of technology and materials acquired from Germany, the United States, and other states (in violation of the terms of the NPT). Iraq built two independent facilities for the enrichment of natural uranium (centrifugal and isotopic separation), which were never reported to the IAEA and never under safeguards. Had it not been for the Iraqi invasion of Kuwait, the American-led attack in January 1991, and the dispatch of the U.N. Special Commission under the terms of the cease-fire, the Iraqis would have succeeded in manufacturing nuclear weapons in a short period of time.

The case of Iraq, although most blatant, is not unique. Spector reports that in September 1981, the IAEA inspectors feared that material had been diverted from reactors in India and Pakistan. Although the deficiency at the Indian plant was apparently cleared up, the Pakistani case is less clear, and Spector concludes that spent fuel containing plutonium might have been diverted from the Pakistani reactor.[15] No action, however, was ever taken. In the Middle East and South Asia, it is clear that the IAEA's global system of safeguards and inspections has failed to stop nuclear proliferation.

CONTROL OF CHEMICAL AND BIOLOGICAL WEAPONS

Although the Arab and Islamic states, including Iraq, are signatories of the 1925 Geneva Convention banning the use of chemical weapons, this has not prevented many of them from manufacturing, storing, and in some cases, using these weapons. In the early 1960s, Egypt used chemical agents in Yemen. Since then, chemical weapons have proliferated widely, and large stockpiles exist in Iraq, Syria, and Libya.

As in the case of nuclear weapons, the efforts to limit chemical weapons proliferation are based on international forums and negotiations. To supplement the 1925 convention, the Committee on Chemical Weapons of the Conference on Disarmament negotiated the CWC. The goal of the CWC is a "complete and total ban on chemical weapons" in all states. This activity, however, has failed to slow or impede the development of chemical warfare capabilities in Iraq, Iran, Syria, or Libya.

In the area of chemical and biological weapons, as in the case of nuclear weapons, verification and safeguards are very important issues. Indeed, given the broad applications of legitimate civil chemical and biological processes that can provide a ready base for conversion to military use, such as pesticide production and pharmaceuticals, verification requirements in these area are more complex than in the case of nuclear technology. These considerations have led to development of a highly intrusive approach to CBW verification, including resident inspectors and challenge inspections. Such intrusive measures, however, have been opposed by the United States and other states, who are concerned about the abuse of the verification system for industrial or military espionage. Inspectors from other states could, for example, demand entry to a U.S. nuclear weapons lab or drug development facility, to gain information that would be applied to the development of weapons.

The complexity of these verification issues again illustrates the difficulty of developing a single global system for limiting chemical and biological weapons. The technical and political requirements in North America or Europe are significantly different from the requirements in the Middle East. The global approach in this area suffers from many of the defects apparent in the NPT and IAEA systems.

SUPPLIER-BASED ARMS CONTROL

In addition to limiting the activities of "recipient states," the NPT and IAEA systems also include restrictions on "supplier states." Article I states that the signatories agree not to provide any form of assistance, technology, or materials that might be used to develop nuclear weapons. Other agreements, developed by the London Nuclear Suppliers' Group, provided guidelines and a "trigger" list of technologies and materials that were to be limited.[16]

In the case of Iraq, however, the guidelines were totally ineffective and did not prevent Saddam Hussein from acquiring the technology necessary to develop nuclear weapons. Billions of dollars of nuclear weapons technology were sold, particularly by German and American firms, without safeguards of any kind.

Supplier agreements have also been developed to limit the proliferation of missile technology and chemical weapons. The MTCR, formed in 1987, was designed to prevent the flow of ballistic-missile-related technology throughout the world. This global agreement had some immediate impact in the Middle East; the agreement effectively ended the Condor missile project, which was based on European-supplied technology and included Argentina, Iraq, and Egypt. The MTCR, however, was not effective in preventing Iraq from obtaining the ability to modify and manufacture Scud-B missiles, capable of carrying Iraqi chemical warheads, which were used against Israel and Saudi Arabia during the Gulf War. MTCR signatories such as Germany, Britain, and the United States were instrumental in the development of the Iraqi missile program, and the United States even provided loan guarantees that were applied to these purchases.[17]

The application of the MTCR in the Middle East has been particularly problematic. In 1991, the United States succeeded in pressuring Israel to join the MTCR system and restrict its exports of missile-related technology, despite the high economic cost.[18] The Israelis expected, however, that the U.S. government and other signatories would act effectively to prevent other regional powers, including Iraq, Iran, Syria, and Libya, from obtaining ballistic missiles. The United States apparently gained reluctant Chinese cooperation, and Beijing has reportedly cancelled the agreement to sell M-9 missiles to Syria. However, North Korean deliveries of Scud-C missiles to Iran and Syria were not halted. If the MTCR is to be successful in the Middle East, it must lead to an end to all missile deliveries in the region, including Iran and Syria.

In a broader sense, the effort to use the global approach to the problem of ballistic missile proliferation in the Middle East is flawed in the same way as the NPT. As many analysts note, there is a vast difference between Israeli requirements for an assured second-strike deterrent, as provided by ballistic missiles, and the impact of such a capability on Iraqi or Syrian capabilities. The report of the Aspen Strategy Group recognizes that the differences between Israel and Iraq "mandate different goals" in responding to their respective missile programs.[19]

Supplier-based limitations have also been developed in the area of chemical weapons. During the Government-Industry Conference Against Chemical Weapons (GICCW) in Canberra, Australia, in 1989, a list of chemical agents was developed, and members of the "Australia Group" have agreed to control exports of these agents.[20] However, the efforts to develop international agreements among supplier states have failed to prevent the sales of chemical warfare materials and facilities. Much of the verification system depends on the voluntary cooperation of chemical firms, who are supposed to alert national governments of sales to foreign interests.

The large plants at Samarra in Iraq and Rabta in Libya were based on technology, equipment, and raw materials imported from Germany, Belgium, and other European suppliers. Although German law technically forbids the sale of military equipment to states involved in armed conflicts, the export of precursors used to make deadly chemical weapons was allowed as "civilian material"—largely in the form of pesticide plants and materials.[21] The exemptions for dual-use technology and civilian material that can be used to make chemical weapons constitutes a major flaw in global supplier-based measures.

The Middle East has also had experience with attempts to limit the supply of conventional weapons. In 1949, the United States, France, and Britain announced a coordinated effort to "regulate the flow of arms." The Tripartite Declaration was formalized in May 1950, which led to the establishment of the Near East Arms Coordinating Committee. However, this agreement failed to slow the flow of arms to the region and illustrates the limitations of supplier-based agreements. Britain, France, and the United States continued to provide arms due to both political and economic factors.[22]

Additional efforts to limit conventional arms sales after the 1967 and 1973 wars, which focused on the role of the superpowers, failed for similar reasons.[23] In 1977, President Carter announced that arms transfers would be regarded as "an exceptional foreign policy implement." The dollar volume of government-to-government arms sales was to be reduced, and Carter pledged that the United States would not be the first supplier to introduce newly developed advanced weapons systems into a region. However, within four months of announcing the policy, the Carter administration had agreed to substantial arms sales to the Egypt, Saudi Arabia, and Iran. These sales included a number of highly advanced weapons, including AWACS (airborne warning and control system) aircraft and sixty F-15 combat aircraft for Saudi Arabia. Jordan received military grant aid, and Israel (along with NATO members, Japan, Australia, and New Zealand) was exempted from the overall ceiling. In this atmosphere, efforts to gain restraints from other suppliers had little impact. Iraq purchased thirty-six F-1 Mirage aircraft from France, leading to responses in kind from Iran, Israel, and Saudi Arabia.

As the number of suppliers of advanced technology and materials increases in the Middle East, and the availability of billions of dollars in oil revenues to pay for such purchases continues to grow, the global supplier-based agreements will become even more difficult to enforce. The disintegration of the Soviet Union and the creation of many new and unstable states in this region, some of which may develop close links with Iran, have increased the number of potential suppliers and made it more difficult to monitor compliance.

THE MISSING LINK: CONVENTIONAL AND NONCONVENTIONAL WEAPONS IN THE MIDDLE EAST

The major components of the existing global arms control regime focus on specific types of weapons in isolation. The NPT and IAEA system are concerned exclusively with nuclear weapons, and the chemical warfare convention and negotiations deal only with the proliferation of chemical agents. Similarly, the mechanism to limit biological weapons is based on the 1972 international agreement, and the MTCR concerns ballistic missiles independent of warheads or other weapons. Finally, conventional weapons are generally outside the existing global arms control regimes, although, as already noted, some unsuccessful efforts have been made to regulate the flow of conventional arms to the region.

Although each of type of weapon is subject to an independent set of limitations and verification system, from the perspective of national security, they are closely interrelated and interdependent, particularly in the Middle East. As noted earlier, the Israeli nuclear deterrent capability was originally developed to counter massive Arab conventional stockpiles, including tanks and combat aircraft, which threaten Israeli national survival. As a result, in the Middle East, the negotiation of limits on nuclear weapons cannot be considered in isolation from conventional weapons.

Similarly, the regimes in Iraq, Libya, and Syria link their acquisition of chemical weapons to the Israeli nuclear option. In international discussions of chemical warfare limitations, the representatives of these states have referred to this capability as the "poor nations' nuclear weapons." In the Middle East, nuclear, chemical, biological, and conventional weapons are inextricably linked, and the existing international arms control regime treats each area in isolation.

THE ALTERNATIVE: A DEDICATED MIDDLE EAST ARMS CONTROL REGIME

Given the defuse nature of regional proliferation patterns and causes, it would be surprising if any global approach and regime were successful in dealing with all regions and factors. Instead, a regionally based nonproliferation regime, linking nuclear, chemical, biological, and conventional weapons, would provide a better approach, particularly for the Middle East. The 1990 Aspen Strategy Study Group notes that the "global approach has reached a point of diminishing marginal returns."[24] The existing regime, although necessary, is "not sufficient. . . . What is needed are regional and country specific policies to complement those pursued at the global level."[25]

Regional arms control frameworks have been proposed by a number of states, such as a Middle East Nuclear Weapons Free Zone (MENWFZ), which includes mutual inspection and real-time safeguards, is based on direct, face-to-face negotiations, and provides a basis for responding to the particular conditions and problems of the Middle East. The creation of a Middle East section of the IAEA, in which Israel, Syria, Egypt, Libya, Iraq, Iran, Saudi Arabia, Algeria, and other states would operate a system of safeguards and inspection, has also been proposed. Such a regional forum would force the states to address each other's security problems and concerns, rather than attempt to use the international organizations, such as the IAEA, to impose limitations on the others. The tendency to use the meetings of the IAEA and other international arms control negotiation forums for political attacks would also be removed. Given Israel's concerns regarding the threat to national survival posed by conventional, chemical, and biological weapons deployed by Arab states, such a regional framework will also be able to include limitations on these weapons.

The concept of a Middle East Nuclear Weapons Free Zone has been under discussion since 1974, when Egypt and Iran raised the issue in the United Nations.[26] Although the initial conception was simply a call for all states in the region (and Israel in particular) to adhere to the NPT, the framework has since been broadened. The outlines for a regional NWFZ are based on the Latin American model as negotiated in the Treaty of Tlatelolco. This model also served as the basis for the South Pacific Nuclear Free Zone established in 1985.

In 1975, Israeli Foreign Minister Yigal Allon declared support for the concept of a regional NWFZ based on direct negotiations and mutual inspection.[27] In large part, this initiative was a result of the difficulties inherent in the structure of the IAEA and the operation of the safeguards system in the Middle East. Many of the states in the region have declared themselves in favor of an NWFZ, although the terms of reference vary. Under the Israeli proposal, inspection would be performed by teams consisting of the countries in the region, with Israeli personnel monitoring activities in the Arab states and the reverse. With the spread of chemical and biological weapons, both Israel and Egypt have proposed to include these agents in any regional agreement.[28]

In 1988, the United Nations General Assembly created a committee to examine the issue. The report, published in October 1990, explicitly examines the terms required for "effective and verifiable measures" which would facilitate the establishment of a MENWFZ.[29] The committee discussed the problems of defining the states to be included, suggesting that all the members of the Arab League, as well as Iran, Israel, and perhaps Pakistan be included. The report also discusses the need for a system of "verification and control," noting the weaknesses of the IAEA safeguards in guaranteeing compliance with the terms of the NWFZ.

A regional verification system, however, requires much closer cooperation than currently exists. The negotiation and operation of an NWFZ would require direct discussions between the states, and a moderate level of cooperation. With the exception of Egypt, the Arab states have been unwilling to recognize the legitimacy of Israel or to hold formal direct negotiations. As the U.N. committee concludes, the negotiation of a NWFZ must be related "to other measures to reduce the danger of hostilities and to strengthen Israeli confidence that a true and lasting peace was being built." In general, arms control proposals are predicated on a significant political change and an amelioration of the basic conflicts.

THE BUSH PROPOSAL AND ARMS CONTROL IN THE PEACE PROCESS

In May 1991, the Bush administration published an initiative specifically designed to further arms control in the Middle East. The proposal included limitations on the transfer of conventional weapons, as well as missiles, chemical and biological weapons, and nuclear technology, materials, and components. By placing these elements in a single framework, the proposal marked a major change in U.S. policy. In addition, the American effort included a broad range of countries including Iraq, Iran, Libya, Syria, Egypt, Lebanon, Israel, Jordan, Saudi Arabia, Maghreb, and the Gulf states.

The conventional weapons limitations focused on restraints among the major weapons suppliers, including the five permanent members of the United Nations Security Council, and incorporating the other members of the "G-7" (the group of seven advanced industrial nations, which also includes Germany, Italy, and Japan). Together, these countries account for the bulk of military sales to the Middle East. The U.S. initiative called on these states to avoid destabilizing transfers and to establish effective export controls.

With regard to missiles, the proposal called for a freeze on the acquisition, production, and testing of surface-to-surface missiles and their ultimate elimination. The states in the region were also called upon to join international bans of chemical and biological weapons and to undertake confidence-building measures in these areas. The initiative also called for a verifiable ban on the production and acquisition of enriched uranium and separated plutonium, adherence to the NPT, and acceptance of IAEA safeguards. Although these measures were described as steps to the longer term goal of creating a nuclear weapons free zone, the focus on the NPT/IAEA system left this critical issue in the context of global regimes, with their inherent limitations, as noted previously.

These proposals represented a major new effort to establish restraints in the Middle East and were welcomed by some of the states, including Israel, as a useful basis for further discussions. The Israeli minister of defense, Moshe Arens, even suggested that Israel would accept a comprehensive freeze on conventional weapons if it was properly verified. However, a high degree of ambiguity still surrounded these measures.

The U.S. government was criticized for announcing arms sales totalling over $24 billion to Saudi Arabia, Egypt, and Israel at the same time, thereby undermining its own proposal. In addition, the Syrian government, which received $2 billion from Saudi Arabia, used these funds to purchase Scud-C missiles from North Korea and again sought M-9 missiles from China. The Iraqi obstruction of efforts by the United Nations to enforce the terms of the ceasefire resolution, which stipulated the supervised destruction of Iraqi missiles and chemical, biological, and nuclear materials and facilities also did not increase the prospects for voluntary restraint on the part of the other states in the Middle East.

Regional arms control was included in the agenda of the multilateral meetings of the Arab-Israeli peace process that began in

Madrid in October 1991. The initial discussions were held in the context of the first round of the multilateral talks in Moscow, and in May 1992, the first working group meeting on arms control was held in Washington. All the multilateral talks, including arms control, were boycotted by Syria (and Lebanon), which immediately limited the possible effectiveness. Had the Syrians attended, the obstacle posed by the lack of direct negotiations would have diminished. The session began with a series of "seminars" on the history of U.S.-Soviet arms control and crisis management.

The Egyptian delegation sought to introduce an agenda item focusing on the elimination of weapons of mass destruction, including nuclear weapons, but with no mention of conventional weapons. This position has been part of a sustained Egyptian effort (known as the Mubarak plan) aimed at freezing the production of nuclear material in Israel. Israel sees this as an effort to obscure the linkage between nuclear weapons and the conventional threat. If this pattern continues, the talks could quickly become divisive, and like discussions in the IAEA annual meetings, become more of a propaganda forum rather than an opportunity for discussion and basis for negotiations.

To begin the process of arms control in the Middle East, a number of confidence-building measures (CBM) have been suggested. Potential CBMs include prenotification of military exercises and missile launches, the development of crisis management centers, and tacit restraints on weapons deployment. Many of these examples are based on the experience developed in the context of the CSCE process in Europe. However, the fundamental political and military contrasts between the situation in Europe in the 1980s and the Middle East raise questions regarding the applicability of this model.

PROSPECTS FOR A REGIONAL ARMS CONTROL REGIME

Security regimes in general can provide a means to manage the inherent anarchy and uncertainty in the international system and the nature of the "security dilemma." As Lipson notes, "By creating an inclusive framework with well-defined norms, regimes lower the transaction costs of negotiating and implementing specific agreements. By encouraging repeated transactions, they lengthen the shadow of the future."[30]

In the Middle East, the "shadow of the future" is often threatening, and arms control is still seen as a distant and strictly idealist enterprise. Arms control, whether in the Middle East or anywhere else, cannot be developed outside the context of fundamental political change, cooperation, and the sense of common interests. Efforts to impose arms control without this basic element are doomed to failure and are likely to contribute to increased conflict.

In addition, as has been demonstrated in this chapter, arms control in the Middle East is closely linked to the particular nature of conflict and political relations in the region. The multitude of major actors, the asymmetries, and the deep ethnic and national conflicts all add to the complexities of arms control in the Middle East.

The global regime, based on the NPT and IAEA systems, was established during a period characterized by bipolar stability, in which Washington and Moscow were able to exercise a high degree of hegemonic control. With the collapse of the Soviet Union and the creation of large number of unstable successor states, the NPT structure has been weakened; the new Islamic republics that have been formed are a source of particular concern regarding the transfer of materials and technology to the Middle East, underlying the need for a regional mechanism.

In addition, the global approach to arms control, and the existing global regime, including the NPT, IAEA, MTCR, and CBW conventions, have failed when applied to the Middle East. Some efforts have been made to strengthen the NPT and IAEA systems in the wake of the Iraqi (and, more recently, North Korean) case, but with limited results.[31] Indeed, much of the analysis of the Iraqi case emphasizes the inherently limited nature of the global approach, and the limitations on efforts to apply the type of safeguards regime necessary for the Middle East on a global and nondiscriminatory basis.[32]

Only a regional approach, based on a dedicated regime, negotiated and operated by the various states in the region, can provide a useful framework. Arms control limitations must encompass both conventional and nonconventional weapons, and mutual verification inspections systems must be negotiated and managed within the region itself.

This will require not only a major change in the approach by the states involved, but also a radical shift in U.S. policy toward arms control. The existing global regime largely reflects the U.S. perspective and approach, and the American government has generally failed to support regional alternatives to the existing global structure. Until the United States, as the main supporter of arms control, shifts to a regional approach, in which all forms of weapons and technology, including conventional weapons, are linked and limitations are interdependent, the prospects for arms limitation in the Middle East will remain low.

NOTES

1. Stephen D. Krasner, ed., *International Regimes* (Ithaca, N.Y.: Cornell University Press, 1983), p.2.
2. *Establishment of a Nuclear-Weapon-Free Zone in the Region of the Middle East.* Study on effective and verifiable measures which would facilitate the establishment of a nuclear-weapon-free zone in the Middle East. Report of the Secretary General, United Nations General Assembly, A/45/435, 10 October 1990.
3. For a history of the motivations behind the development of Israeli nuclear deterrence, see Yair Evron, *Israeli's Nuclear Dilemma,* [Hebrew] (Tel Aviv: Hakibutz Hameuchad, 1987); and Gerald Steinberg, "Israeli Nuclear Ambiguity: Evolution and Evaluation," in *Security or Armageddon: Israel's Nuclear Strategy*, ed. Louis Rene Beres Lexington, Mass.: Lexington Books, 1985), pp. 29–44.
4. See Leonard Spector, *Nuclear Ambitions* (Boulder, Colo.: Westview Press, 1990).
5. The link between these issues is included in the speech by Yitzhak Shamir before the U.N. General Assembly, June 7, 1988, reprinted in *Arms Control in the Middle East*, ed. Dore Gold (Boulder, Colo.: Westview Press, and Tel Aviv University, JCSS Study No. 15, 1990), p. 141 See also Gerald M. Steinberg, "Arms Control in the Middle East," *Encyclopedia of Arms Control and Disarmament*, ed. Richard Dean Burns (New York: Charles Scribner's Sons, 1993).
6. Lipson, Chapter 1 in this book. The problems of regime enforcement and sanctions, in general, were first discussed by Thomas Schelling, *The Strategy of Conflict* (New York: Oxford University Press, 1960).
7. See, for example, the discussion of this issue in *New Threats: Responding to the Proliferation of Nuclear, Chemical, and Delivery Capabilities in the Third World*, An Aspen Study Group Report (Lanham, Md.: University Press of America, 1990), p. 18.
8. Seth Carus, *The Genie Unleashed: Iraq's Chemical and Biological Weapons Production* (Washington, D.C.: Institute for Near East Policy, 1989).
9. See Raymond Cohen, *International Politics* (London: Longman, 1981), pp. 127–140.

10. John Tirman, "International Monitoring for Peace," *Issues in Science and Technology* 4, no. 4 (Summer 1988): 53–58.

11. *New Threats;* p. 21.

12. Martin Sherwin, *A World Destroyed* (New York: Alfred Knopf, 1975).

13. Geoffrey Kemp, *The Control of the Middle East Arms Race* (Washington, D.C.: Carnegie Endowment, 1992).

14. Nuclear Nonproliferation Policy, Hearing before the Subcommittee on Energy, Nuclear Proliferation, and Government Processes,Committee on Governmental Affairs, United States Senate, June 24, 1981.

15. Leonard Spector, *Nuclear Ambitions: The Spread of Nuclear Weapons, 1989–1990* (Boulder, Colo.: Westview Press, 1990), p. 422.

16. Ibid. pp. 433–434.

17. Gary Milholin, *Licensing Mass Destruction: U.S. Exports to Iraq* (Washington, D.C.: Wisconsin Project on Nuclear Arms Control, 1991).

18. Israel signed a bilateral agreement with the United States agreeing to adopt the MTCR guidelines, with the expectation that full membership in the MTCR would be granted at the next meeting of the current members. Israel has applied for MTCR membership to expand its commercial space launcher program and bid on international contracts in this area, as specified under the MTCR.

19. Aspen Strategy Group, p. 22.

20. S. J. Lundin, "Multilateral and Bilateral Talks on Chemical and Biological Weapons," *SIPRI Yearbook 1990: World Armaments and Disarmament* (Oxford: Oxford University Press, 1990).

21. Jean Pascal Zanders, "Chemical Weapons Proliferation: Mechanisms Behind the Imhausen/Rabta Affair," Centre for Polemology, Free University of Brussels, March 1990.

22. J. C. Hurewitz, *Middle East Politics: The Military Dimension* (New York: Praeger Publishing, 1969).

23. H. Y. Schandler, R. G. Bell, R. F. Grimmett, and R. D. Shuey, "Implications of President Carter's Conventional Arms Transfer Policy," Foreign Affairs and National Defense Division, Library of Congress, Congressional Research Service, Washington, D.C., September 1977; see also Andrew Pierre, *The Global Politics of Arms Sales* (Princeton, N.J.: Princeton University Press, 1982).

24. Aspen Strategy Group Report, p. 20.

25. Ibid., p. x.

26. Avi Becker, "A Regional Non-Proliferation Treaty for the Middle East," in *Security or Armageddon;* p. 125.

27. See Efraim Inbar, "Israel and Nuclear Weapons Since October 1973," in ibid., p. 69.

28. See Becker,"A Regional Non-Proliferation Treaty for the Middle East," Security or Armageddon: Israel's Nuclear Strategy, Louis Rene Beres, ed., Lexington Books, 1985, pp. 119–132.

29. *Establishment of a Nuclear-Weapon-Free Zone in the Region of the Middle East.* Study on effective and verifiable measures which would facilitate the establishment of a nuclear-weapon-free zone in the Middle East. Report of the Secretary General, United Nations General Assembly, A/45/435, 10 October 1990.

30. Lipson, this volume.

31. See Hans Blix, "Verification of Nuclear Nonproliferation: The Lesson of Iraq" *The Washington Quarterly*, Autumn 1992; Rolf Ekeus, "The Iraqi Experience and Multilateral Approaches to Controlling Nuclear Proliferation," Center for Security and Technology Studies, Lawrence Livermore National Laboratory, March 16, 1993; and Lawrence Scheinman, "Nuclear Safeguards and Non-Proliferation in a Changing World Order," *Security Dialogue*, Vol. 23, No. 4, December 1992, p.40.

32. Eric Chauvistre, *The Implications of IAEA Inspections Under Security Resolution 687*, UNIDIR, Geneva, 1992.

PART 4

Nonmilitary Aspects

CHAPTER 9

An Observation on Arab Culture and Deterrence: Metaphors and Misgivings

Adam Garfinkle

The Middle East is fast approaching the revolution in military technology and doctrine that confronted U.S. and Soviet planners in the late 1940s and 1950s. This is to say that, for the first time ever, aircraft and ballistic missiles tipped with weapons of mass destruction offer to an increasing number of countries the ability to inflict enormous damage on enemy civilian populations without first having to meet and defeat their armies in battle.

These looming military-technical changes raise important questions about the future of the Middle East and, indeed, most of the world. The most important questions are these: How will Middle Eastern elites conceive the military and political uses of new military technologies? Will deterrence along the lines of that which has applied between the United States and the Soviet Union in the last forty years apply also to Middle Eastern antagonists within the region and between the region and states outside it? If not, will other forms of deterrence apply?

Another way of putting this last question is: Might a security regime develop among major protagonists in the Middle East, attuned to local circumstances, that will parallel but not replicate the security regime that arguably obtained in U.S.-Soviet strategic relations from the mid-1960s on? A security regime describes an informal and generally tacit but nevertheless effective set of conventions governing the behavior of decision units. As developed in chapter 1, a security regime is less than a treaty or a contract, but more than mere coincidence of interests.[1] What are the prospects that such a regime could come into being in the Middle East? Even short of effective formal arms control, might the major states of the region find ways to deal with one another short of horrific warfare using weapons of mass destruction?

The answer, of course, must be "maybe." There is no way to know for certain. In general, prospects for the evolution of a stable security regime between dissimilar ethno-linguistic units seem poor. For tacit cooperation to be sustained over time, there must be a certain degree of reciprocity with respect to intent, the integrity of the communications channel, and with respect to certain pertinent values. Between Israel and most of the Arab states or Iran, such reciprocity is not generally in evidence. Nor does it seem to be in evidence between Turkey or Iran and the Arab states. Nor is it in evidence when it comes to Kurds, Copts, and other minorities within the Arab world. As Lipson put it, security regimes "must be premised on some compatible configurations of preferences, reasonable information about others' choices and behavior, and some limits on the risk of cooperating." But, he adds,

> If states view politics as a zero-sum struggle, if they actually desire wars of expansion, if they cannot seek joint gains for domestic political reasons, if they fail to recognize that their policy choices are interdependent, if they cannot distinguish between offensive and defensive weapons and military deployment, if they are unwilling to reassure other states by permitting adequate verification, then the prospects for security regimes will be poor indeed.[2]

It would seem at first blush that each of these obstacles obtain in full in relations between Israel and the Arab states, and perhaps less fully in relations between the Arab world and both Iran and Turkey. Yet, there are important exceptions. Israel's relationship with Jordan qualifies as a tacit security regime,[3] and Israel's relationship with Syria, buttressed by the 1976 red lines agreement, may qualify, as well, in a more limited way. Israel's relationship with Egypt is not tacit—there is a peace treaty—but beyond that, given the importance to each state of its relationship with the United States, one might say that the triangular relationship, which contains within it certain understandings about security relations in the region as a whole, also resembles a security regime.

Generally, where security regimes may be said to work between the Arab states and Israel, they do so bilaterally. Often, too, as in the Israeli-Egyptian example, they are aided by an outside power—in this case the United States. Possibly, however, a different, multilateral security regime may be working among the Arab states themselves. There is at least a chance that the special political character of the Arab world augers for the development of a different kind of security regime within the inter-Arab system.

Inter-Arab relations are far from placid. There have been many minor skirmishes, a certain amount of semi-clandestine low-level violence (as between the Syrian and Iraqi Ba'th, for example), competitive assassinations, and much internal repression and violence, especially in Arab countries with heterogenous populations along ethnic or sectarian lines. But certain Western images notwithstanding, the record of cross-border aggression in the Arab world is not a particularly bad one. With three relatively minor exceptions and one major one, Arab states have not gone to war with each other in the postindependence period.

The first exception was Egyptian and Saudi intervention in the Yemeni civil war in the 1960s, the second the very brief Syrian invasion of Jordan in September 1970, and the third Syrian intervention in the Lebanese civil war in the mid-1970s and beyond. Of these, the first did not involve classical cross-border aggression, but was more of a proxy war fought by expeditionary forces. The second was part of a slow-motion coup d'etat and did not have the full backing of the Syrian political echelon at the time. The third, too, started out less as aggression directed by one state against another and more as a semi-legitimized intervention within an ongoing civil war.

The one major exception, of course, was the Iraqi invasion of Kuwait. About this there are no conditional statements to be made, except to note that the aggression, in the end, failed.

In short, it would not be terribly surprising if, looking back with many years' hindsight, analysts of the future have little difficulty explaining why Arab countries with unconventional weapons refrained from using them against each other. They could simply conclude that it was not the political habit to war within the Arab domain.

THE QUESTION OF CULTURE

What explains the relative calm in the inter-Arab politico-military realm compared to less well-restrained Israeli-Arab and Iranian-Arab relations? I suggest that there is a regulatory model of inter-Arab relations derived ultimately from the cultural metaphor of the feud, and that it operates cognitively just beneath the line of sight of day-to-day consciousness. The greatest force of such metaphors lies in their capacity to organize everyday life by becoming so much a part of it that they acquire a "taken for grantedness" so natural that the generative assumptions they bear disappear in the flow of events.[4] This is how the dynamic equilibrium social metaphors of American liberalism work, and this is how I think the basic assumptions of thousands of years of Arab social life based around the centrality of primordial ties work, too.

Before explaining what is and is not meant by this assertion, we need to step back and say a few words about the role of culture in political analysis.

The sources of national policies in the politico-military sphere are an amalgam. One may start with national interests and end with idiosyncratic factors, but in between are the filters of both bureaucratic subcultures and culture more generally. In other words, culture does not explain everything; but as part of the sphere of causality, it cannot be ignored and sometimes it is particularly important. It is also a subtle and abusable field of inquiry. As for the abusable, we can point to the racist national-character stereotyping of the past, to World War II–era theories holding, for example, that Japanese were prone to violence because they were short—a sort of collective Napoleonic complex. As to the subtle, when social anthropologists talk of culture differences, they are speaking about relative emphases, not polarities. Arabs are said to be especially sensitive to matters of honor and shame, but that does not mean that Swedes or Zulus have no concept of honor and shame. The *suk* model of negotiations in Arab life is sometimes analyzed with relevance to its political significance, but that does not mean that buying a used car in Topeka is like purchasing a diamond broach at Tiffany's just because both happen in America.

Therefore, because all human beings share their basic humanity, and because culture furnishes only part of the explanation for politico-military behavior, Middle Easterners are by no means wholly inscrutable to Westerners. They often act in ways that

Westerners can easily understand. But sometimes they do not. Just as it is an exaggeration to claim that culture explains everything, so it makes no sense to argue that it explains nothing. It defies reason to argue, as some have, that despite having a different language, a different religious experience, and different historical memories, Arab leaders will not act differently in roughly analogous situations from Americans. Let one example illustrate.

Few Western analysts, for example, thought that Saddam Hussein would fail to take advantage of a last-minute escape hatch on or about January 15, 1991 to avoid war with the United States and its allies. It would be, they suggested, irrational for him not to do so. But because rationality is context—and culture—dependent, what is and is not rational is not always obvious from the outside. Saddam acted rationally in the situation in which he found himself because there are times in Middle Eastern political cultures when it is better (e.g., literally safer) to be defeated (so long as one is not totally destroyed) than to be dishonored. Saddam probably believed before mid-December 1990 that the United States would not attack and that, even if it did, which he seemed to accept in the three weeks before the war, Iraqi armed forces would do well enough to prevent a rout. He probably believed these things partly because of how cultural predispositions led him to interpret American behavior. He was wrong, yes; irrational, no.

There are times, therefore, when cultural factors rise to prominence in explaining decision behavior or at least seem to *post hoc.* In my view, one reason that a multilateral security regime is unlikely to arise in the Middle East in cases of states with dissimilar ethno-linguistic backgrounds, but is possible among the Arab states, is the same: culture. An understanding of culture is necessary (but not sufficient) to understanding the politico-military realm in any part of the world. With Kant and every philosophical idealist since, I take it as obvious that Middle Eastern leaders' definitions, attitudes, and perceptions of deterrence are influenced by basic core beliefs no less than everyone else's. Although elements of strategic interaction no doubt have elements that can be universalized at a high level of abstraction, they must find a real human context. That means cultures, following von Herder and Isaiah Berlin, must be recognized as irreducible wholes, their languages archives of distinctive syntaxes for apprehending the world, and their internalized histories distinctive mythologies for ordering action within that world.

Happily, now that the dark ages of behaviorism and positivism are lifting, most scholars acknowledge the concept of strategic culture, a term coined by Jack Snyder in the mid-1970s. Speaking about the Soviet case, Snyder wrote:

> It is useful to look at the Soviet approach to strategic thinking as a unique "strategic culture." Individuals are socialized into a distinctively Soviet mode of strategic thinking. As a result of this socialization process, a set of general beliefs, attitudes, and behavioral patterns with regard to nuclear strategy has achieved a state of semipermanence that places them on the level of "culture" rather than mere "policy." Of course, attitudes may change as a result of changes in technology and the international environment. However, new problems are not addressed objectively. Rather, they are seen through the perceptual lens provided by the strategic culture.[5]

The concept of a strategic culture is related closely to observations of national style. The function of military organizations, too, is not merely a matter of insular bureaucratic politics divorced from the broader cultural milieu, but is instead a particular expression of that milieu. Culture predisposes military institutions in a way that affects their decisions and operations.[6]

This is not really a new idea. Clausewitz argued, for example, that war and defense test a society in such a way that its essential values and means of social organization emerge. When normal life is disrupted by war, and when sacrifices are asked of people by their rulers to either prosecute or deter war, the very bonds of social order are stretched tight. It is illogical to suppose that culture plays no role in defining social relations under such circumstances and, as Sir Michael Howard has usefully reminded us in his writing on "The Forgotten Dimension of Strategy," social relations generally go far toward determining whether any politico-military strategy will work.

Aside from Clausewitz and common sense, there is much contemporary evidence for the relationship between culture, history, and national styles in politico-military decision making. In Europe, where deterrence has a self-conscious literature, differences between British, German, and French approaches are understood and accepted universally. Therefore, as David Yost points out, "terms such as creneau, donion and sanctuaire, which spring naturally to French lips, seem curiously antiquarian to an American; but they evidently reflect France's historical experience with castles and fortresses from the Middle Ages through Vauban in the seventeenth century."[7]

Even local experience can be compelling. Chadian soldiers of Tuareg extraction employed Toyota flatbed mini-trucks mounted with machine guns to defeat a far superior (on paper) Libyan invasion force in 1986–1987 by adapting old techniques of brigandage to new instruments.[8] On paper—Western paper—the Chadians should have been deterred or defeated, but within their cultural experience lay a novel formula for success.

Culture can matter at different levels in the politico-military sphere. It may matter directly when local religious and cultural patterns are consciously raised to the level of a template for planning—as has been the case in Islamic Iran, among the Hizbollah in Lebanon and other fundamentalist groups, and in a more attenuated way in Saudi Arabia. But culture may work in less direct ways, too, as virtually all those with diplomatic experience in the Middle East will attest.

Understanding culture promises great treasure. But like all treasure, it is very hard to acquire. However difficult, some combination of inductive and deductive methods can be used to gain cultural understandings. It is possible to generalize about populations, at least to some extent, and the effort is worth making if the intrinsic importance of the subject is great enough. Such understanding will never allow perfect analysis of the past or present, and certainly cannot be used reliably for purposes of predicting exactly how Middle Easterners will act in the future in a new technological environment. After all, analysts cannot even predict most of the time what their own political system will do, let alone those of others.

Happily, however, whether in astrophysics or political analysis, it is not necessary to know everything to understand something. Even a level of knowledge that enables one to "know it when one sees it" is better than nothing; at the very least it can enable experts to alert those responsible for public policy as to what to look for in others' behavior.

Not everyone shares even this modest level of optimism about culture-based analysis. Some believe that individual characteristics do not matter when it comes to politico-military matters because broad patterns of national interest have pride of place. Statesmen's biases and theories do not matter because the relative power of countries as they interlock geographically instead determines their essential strategic choices. Others hold that similarities in thinking about deterrence among cultures is ordained by the logical universality of the primary elements of strategic interaction. Still others argue that, even if cultures are different, it does not mean that political decision-making units are. Politics is a special realm, they say, and one cannot extrapolate from general culture to the behavior of political elites.

Still others argue more specifically that, although culture may matter marginally in the politico-military sphere, the subjects in question here—Middle Eastern leaders—are likely to bring to problems of military deterrence and strategy the same cognitive predispositions as those of Westerners. Western models clearly predominate among Israelis and, as for the Arabs, local traditions of military science have been heavily influenced by Europe from the diffusion of European military science to the Middle East in Ottoman times to the fact that military academies established by France and Britain during the interwar period were responsible for educating military and political leaders still on the scene today. The military brass of many Middle Eastern countries has been and still is trained professionally outside of the region, and the relationship between Middle Eastern armaments industries and the technical bases from which they have been derived outside the region are as closely linked today as they were half a century ago. Extensive military supply relationships between Middle Eastern countries and those outside the region, too, have brought with them advisors, weapons manuals, and in many other ways communicated not just implements but ways of thinking about using them. There is also perhaps some truth to the contention that the weapons themselves predispose their own uses, as when, for example, agricultural technology embodying certain capital/labor ratio in the land of its creation tends to reproduce itself when exported to other lands.

Also, in this regard, some argue additionally that Middle Easterners have long carried on a love-hate relationship with the West in which they have frequently been imitative. William R. Brown has argued that contemporary Arab statesmen (and intellectuals) incline to be eclectic in their politics and techniques,[9] and Ami Ayalon has shown how political terminology among the

Arabs evolved against European patterns over the last two centuries.[10] So perhaps they will be imitative here, too, particularly those Arab political and military elites conversant with Western ways.

More specifically with respect to method, even those who grant in theory that culture matters often despair of studying it in practice. Not only may it be impossible to extrapolate from general social relations to the political sphere, but how can one know in top-heavy political cultures whether the idiosyncrasies of the leader mirror the culture in any significant way? There is also a serious problem distinguishing causality: Are Iraqi politics under the Ba'th the way they are because of culture or because it is a fascist dictatorship? When two different templates *fit* the evidence, how does one know which one *accounts* for the evidence?

Moreover, social anthropologists do not agree on Arab social traits to begin with and neither do Arabs. It is also hard to talk about Arabs in general: there are urban and there are rural, rich and poor, educated and illiterate; and this is not to speak of regional and "national" differences. Some hold that the difference between an Iraqi and a Tunisian is just as great as that between a Greek and a German. This is an exaggeration, because all Arabs have Arabic in common, and most have Islam in common, too. Nevertheless, despite a substrata of commonality that comes from language, religion, and roughly similar historical experiences over the past century, there are important differences among the Arab countries such that one must take special care before generalizing about "the Arabs" when one speaks of political culture. There may be an Egyptian strategic culture, and an Iraqi strategic culture, and a Saudi strategic culture, in Snyder's sense of the term defined previously. There is an Arab strategic culture only to the extent that Egyptians, Iraqis, Saudis, and other Arab-state elites share certain characteristics. How extensive that sharing is remains a subject for study.

Last, there is the specter of orientalism, not as dangerous as communism, perhaps, but just as irritating. The entire following discussion admittedly treads on slippery emotional soil. Those who wish to do so can read all that follows as inappropriate, inadmissible, or even racist, willfully ignoring all of the expressions of limits I have just described. I cannot help what others may do, but I regard as absurd the contention that cultural groups "own" their own histories to the point that outsiders are prohibited from commenting upon them.[11] Moreover, to communicate anything about Arab culture to an English-reading, mainly Western, audience, it is necessary to use Western ways for contrast. I am trying to communicate *differences* in so doing, however, not judgments about differences, even though, admittedly, only an automaton can perfectly uphold the distinction. Those who insist on reading what follows as willfully judgmental do so on their own dime.

STUDYING ARAB STRATEGIC CULTURE

It would be nice if we could just eavesdrop on Arabs' conversations about the problems outlined previously and find out what we wish to know. But we cannot do this because there is little self-reflective literature on Arab (or Iranian) views of deterrence.[12] An indirect way, keying in on understanding language, culture, and experience, can be used to acquire, in effect, an Arab "operational code"; that is, a particular group's orientation to gaming in a situation of strategic interaction.[13] One wants answers to questions like these as they apply to everyday face-to-face behavior:

- How does a given culture define a bluff?
- How does a given culture view dissimulation?
- How does a given culture define the requirements of honor (i.e., how far from now is "the future")?
- By what criteria does a given culture define a prominent "other"?
- Under what circumstances does a given society condone violence in face-to-face relations?
- How does a given culture value the individual as opposed to relevant collectivity (like the extended family) of which he is a part?

With answers to questions about core social definitions of resolve, credibility, fabrication, and related concepts, one can try to extrapolate to the politico-military realm, trying to take into account the important systematic differences between face-to-face behavior and collective decision-making units operating in a political environment. Having done that, one can then search the actual record of recent politico-military experience, listening for echos between what has been inductively adduced and what can be deductively observed. The hope is that by going back and forth in this fashion, one can make a better educated guess about what Middle Eastern countries, thought of as cultural units, will do with IRBMs and aircraft fitted out with dangerous substances.

Data for the inductive side of the analysis can come from three domains: language-based anthropological literature on the structure of daily life; evidence gathered from high culture, predominantly the historical experience of Islam; and general studies of Arab political culture. From such data one could build a maximal speculative case with which to sort through the politico-military experience at hand.

To give just one example of how this might work, many observers have noted that when it comes to truth telling and game playing, Arabs and Westerners have different styles. Westerners tend to conceive of political bargaining processes as a way to satisfy fairly the basic aspirations of all parties, but a "fair" settlement is less the aim of political bargaining for Middle Easterners than maximizing one's own values. Observers also note that in the *suk* model of negotiation, threats to break off talks, use of outrageous claims and demands, and endless haggling are common. Protracted and even dissimulative tactics are within bounds, and it may even be that a negotiation that has these features at some point in its progress gives a sense of satisfaction and honor upon completion that a quick and pat negotiation does not.[14]

This difference in perception is said to be based on the presumption that people, not issues, are at the center of the Arab concept of negotiations. To simplify: in the West, a relationship is struck to close a deal, but in the Arab world, a deal is struck to create a relationship. The personal relationship is seen to be more concrete and what counts, not a deal that, when one thinks about it, is in truth a more abstract matter.

This also seems to resonate with other aspects of Arab politics and history. Political loyalty was and remains to a considerable extent a function of personal oaths and family ties. There were cases where pacts made between Mohammed and other chieftains had to be renegotiated when Mohammed died or enforced with violence.

There are, possibly, modern implications, too. Raymond Cohen has shown that, in Egyptian-Israeli relations, the main problems never were "irreconcilable interests, megalomaniac ambitions, still less soaring ideals, but a cultural chasm." Cohen illustrated how Israelis use language directly, Egyptians indirectly. Israelis tend to understatement, Egyptians to hyperbole. Israelis are preoccupied with security, Egyptians with face or honor. The differences in protocol and bargaining, therefore, make negotiations difficult and the need for mediation extreme.[15]

Moreover, for the Arab leaders to engage in direct negotiations with Israel after 1967 presupposed the personalization of the conflict—haggling not to make a deal but to establish a relationship. If Arab bargaining styles are such that deals are made to encourage relationships, then the predominant Israeli view that meeting face to face was just step one and the real problems would come in discussing details may be exaggerated. This suggests that the peace process between Madrid in October 1991 and the Rabin-Arafat handshake on the White House lawn in September 1993 made much more progress than was generally estimated and, indeed, the former event may have made the latter event almost inevitable.

And finally by way of preliminary example, a note on the future. If negotiations have at their core assessments of people and expectations of ongoing relationships, Arab leaders may be more inclined to take the measure of the person than the measure of his arsenal. Stable strategic deterrence, on the other hand, requires some capacity to coldly calculate the balance of force and acknowledge at least privately that one is the weaker party. Saddam Hussein seemed to try to take the measure of George Bush between August 2, 1990, and January 15, 1991, not that of the American arsenal. He did not do a very good job of it, and Iraq suffered grievously. If a similar mistake should occur in an environment suffused with nuclear weapons, the disaster will doubtlessly be far more ecumenical.

The Feud Model

In the short space of this chapter, it is not possible to review even cursorily all of the hypotheses that can be derived from the method just described. The remainder of this chapter explores only one idea: the possibility that a macrocultural metaphor animates contemporary Arab thinking about political life both within and without the idealized Arab nation. Here we return to the metaphor of the feud raised at the outset.

If one aggregates observations about daily life and Islamic experience, one has the raw theoretical material for an analysis of contemporary Arab political culture. One would expect therefore to find a resonance between the former literature and that which directly deals with contemporary Arab political culture. And one does.

Two central observations emerge from this latter sort of literature. The first is that there is a crisis of legitimacy in the Arab states, and second is that the Arabs as a whole are afflicted by an inferiority complex when it comes to dealing with the West.[16] From the first observation comes subsidiary points about the role of pan-Arabism, the function of violence in and between societies, the character of modern political leadership, and the nature of the Arab political community, all of which echo observations about the nature of face-to-face relations and the legacy of Islamic history. From the second comes points about how Arabs see the West and how they think the West sees them; here too we hear echoes of observations about honor and shame and the Islamic conception of historical teleology.

Both the legitimacy crisis and the inferiority, or victimization, complex with the West may well rest upon a substrata of metaphor modeled on the feud. There may well be an implicit model of inter-Arab relations and Arab international relations based on the fundamental concept of feud, and it approaches, in some respects at least, a rudimentary security regime.

When I use the word *feud,* I use it as would an anthropologist, not a newspaper columnist. Once again, by raising this suggestion, I am not implying that Arabs are primitive or brutal or aboriginal or anything of the sort. As everyone knows, it is Europeans who have excelled in recent centuries at genocide, militarism, racism, and other forms of cultural insanity. Rather, I mean to point out only that social structures from the past in any civilization are carried forward metaphorically even as new contents are being poured into them, and this is liable to be as true of Arabs as it is of, say, the English people who settled the East Coast of America and whose assumptions and manners have without question infused American political culture to this day. As previously alluded to in passing, Anglo-Saxons are captivated by the metaphor of the dynamic equilibrium, as such phrases (and institutions) as *checks and balances*, *E Pluribus Unum, the invisible hand, federalism, political pluralism*, and so many others suggest.

Russians seem to be capitivated more by organismic metaphors, epitomized by Andrei Amalrik's statement that anything that does not grow and expand must die. For the Arabs, let it be suggested, the reigning social metaphor has been that of feud. So let me draw out the feud metaphor, for it may have important implications for future deterrence relationships.

Arab feuding is a complex phenomenon that has taken place historically among relative or potential equals, whose paradoxical aim it is to establish temporary dominance to prevent permanent dominance by one group over another.[17] The establishment of dominance has both an outside purpose, to deter attacks of aggression or retribution from other parties, and an inside purpose, to solidify hierarchical authority within the *hamula*. The result of feuding is to create conditions for equilibrium, parity, self-esteem, and personal and familial vindication and concord. Feud, writes Jacob Black-Michaud, is a "form of publicly recognized and accepted physically violent reaction in retaliation for a wrong inflicted in the absence of more sophisticated penal institutions and a means to enforce them."[18]

Because feud is a means of law and order in the absence of any more formal institutional framework to produce it, what is classified in the West even today as penal law is traditionally regarded by Islam as a matter of private vengeance.[19] The guiding metaphor for such exchanges seems to be status quo or balance; the Islamic concept of justice (*'adl*) is rooted in the notion that a disturbance of balance requires rectification either by blood or by a suitable equivalent.

One can go further. "The very violent and socially debilitating effects of feuds," writes Black-Michaud, "themselves thus provide powerful incentives for its rapid 'conclusion' if parties involved cannot in some way contrive to avoid each other."[20] Thus, "fear of feud is the only possible deterrent to feud, since a necessary prerequisite for its existence is the absence of more elaborate types of social control and of all those formal institutions which, under other social conditions, serve to inhibit the unrestricted use of violence by individuals to their own ends."[21] Put another way, feuding is a controlled exhibition of violence to deter still worse violence. Feuds may therefore be defended *post hoc* "on the irreproachably logical grounds that, in the absence of government, there existed no logical alternative to feud but anarchy."[22]

Anthropologists have related feuding to the question of personal and tribal honor in the Arab world. It is widely said that "the only legitimate motive for murder is slighted honour."[23] In feuding societies, writes Black-Michaud,

> honour and power are synonymous. The one implies the other. A group's defence of its honour is thus in a very real sense the defence of its right to live in a given area and to exploit its birthright of natural resources. Through the exercise of physical violence, which causes fear and leads to a network of alliances, each group ensures respect of its rights to an equal place for itself in the social system which is feud. For the individual, on the other hand, defence of his own honour and that of his group provides an opportunity for self-aggrandizement and the acquisition of prestige. . . . Feud is then, simultaneously, a violent affirmation of the rights of all to treatment on a footing of equality and a means of selecting those most qualified to orient the co-operative efforts of the majority.[24]

This analysis projects what to a Westerner might seem to be a somber view of traditional Arab culture, and anthropologists note that feuding and exacting personal vengeance constitutes a morally ambiguous act and is so seen by its executors. On the one hand, taking vengeance is customarily right and the only possible course of action given certain circumstances. But that does not efface the individual pain involved or make the act itself any less difficult even in the eyes of the avenger. Taken together, a picture emerges of the individual captured by a set of social norms and forced to do things that are inwardly distasteful.

Of course, because Arab political elites today are not members of isolated bedouin tribes, it is fair to ask: Of what relevance is this to the study of contemporary affairs? The answer is, as already suggested, that social forms tend to be more stable than individual personalities such that, even if many members of a society become Westernized, they do not thereby destroy their society's form of doing business so much as adjust it to new contents. Hence it is not necessary that Arab leaders be traditional bedouins or villagers for anthropological observations to be relevant, because Arab society still bears signs of traditional ways, just as every society reflects its past. Anthropological analysis still applies, albeit less surely in proportion to the distance traveled away from traditional forms.

Thus, for example, the Palestinian scholar Hisham Sharabi has argued that "the neopatriarchal state, regardless of its legal and political forms and structures, is in many ways no more than a modern version of the traditional patriarchal sultanate."[25] This is not a direct assertion of the feud model of inter-Arab relations, but of a key precondition for it: that Arab politics are still largely organized essentially according to *hamula*, or extended family. I think Sharabi is right.

Owing to the paradoxical circumstance in which separate Arab states exist within an idealized pan-Arab national domain, it is not farfetched to suggest that the logic of feuding that used to apply between extended families has been abstracted to apply now among Arab countries. Consider Black-Michaud's comment, just quoted, in this light. Does not each Arab state consider honor and power together, consider itself in theory as one among equals, ally with others in the face of challenges from outside the nation? Does not the picture of leadership given fit Gamal Abdel Nasser to a tee? If so, this would help explain why the Arab countries express their sense of oneness and mutual brotherhood, yet often behave toward each other with cynical aggressiveness. At some level there seems to dwell the notion that minimal social equipoise and survival require demonstrations of resolve, just as in feuds of old, and that occasional aggressive behavior (short of unritualized warfare) is a normal and even healthy aspect of inter-Arab relations.

In other words, it may be that the structure of feud has been transposed as metaphor from operating between families or tribes to operating among Arab countries. There is at least anecdotal evidence for this. First, Arab diplomats often speak explicitly in such terms. The separate Arab states are almost universally referred to in pan-Arabist rhetoric as families of the Arab nation. A senior Egyptian official described Yasser Arafat's siding with Saddam Hussein as making "a crucial error by tying the Palestinians' lot to the losing side of a deep Arab blood feud in which most key Arab nations, including Egypt, Saudi Arabia and Syria, all stand against Iraq."[26] Around the same time, an associate of Yasir Arafat's stated that as long as Arafat headed the PLO, "none of the gulf Arabs will speak to us again. They are of Bedouin stock and they will not forget he stabbed them in the back."[27] In other words, Arafat committed the opening act of a feud.

Still others interpreted Saddam Hussein's postwar pursuit of nuclear weapons as motivated by revenge, just as one would expect in the blood feud model. As Elie Kedourie put it: "With Saddam, you either make a deal with him or you kill him. There is no third way."[28] In other words, one ends a feud through honorable reconciliation between symbolic equals or one raises the feud to winner-take-all warfare. Do not think, Kedourie warned, that after you have slighted Saddam, your ignoring him will cause Saddam to ignore you. If, indeed, the Iraqis tried to assassinate former president Bush during his trip to Kuwait in April 1993, this would seem to bear out the point.

If the model of blood feuding does apply to relations among the Arab states, what general implications for the politico-military sphere might flow from it? One is that the isolation of any Arab country from the consensus of the moment is an especially painful trial for an Arab leader. It would be akin to being ostracized from one's extended family, and in traditional Arab society, those so shunned have no honor, which is, as noted, bound to family. Indeed, it often strikes Western analysts as odd the extent to which Arabs drop in on one another unannounced, comment on each others' conditions, and insinuate themselves into each others' affairs. It really does resemble the life of an extended family in many ways. To be kicked out of the tent, as it were, as Egypt was after Camp David, is a serious matter, even though Egypt was willing to bear it, far more serious than for a given Latin American country to be outside of the Latin family.

Another implication is that monetary compensation might play a more significant role in local politics than it does in the West. Recalling the discussion about negotiations, the significance of blood money (*diya*) is not to be underestimated in the popular culture of the region. When accidents cannot be repaid eye for eye, financial compensation is an honorable way to restore a balance between rough or potential equals. It may work on the larger political level, too. In October 1989, Syrian MiGs shot down a civilian Turkish plane inside Turkish airspace, and Syria claimed innocent error. Turkey demanded $14.6 million in compensation, and the Syrian government at first refused. Every country pays compensation if it mistakenly downs an aircraft; there is nothing "Arab" about the act itself. But how it may fall into a cultural pattern is another matter. If blood feuds and blood money are as important as anthropological evidence suggests, this was not a trivial or a culturally naked event, nor was the eventual Syrian decision to pay up.

Also, if feud metaphors apply, Arab leaders might more easily see themselves as inexorably pushed toward tragedy than other statesmen. There are some suggestive examples. Jordan's King Hussein wrote in 1962 that in the Middle East: "Life is all too often held cheaply and death passes unheeded."[29] Then, in May 1967, captured by his own pessimism, he joined the Arab war coalition that resulted in Jordan's losing the West Bank and East Jerusalem. In later memoirs he speaks retrospectively of his family's honor being at stake, and the fatalism that he expresses is close to the feeling of the individual who must do the unpleasant no matter what the consequence. Who can assure us that Arab leaders with ballistic missiles and nuclear warheads at their fingertips will see themselves as optimistic free agents in control of their destinies? Given the cultural context, they may instead see themselves as agents of an inexorable destiny that, like society, is larger than themselves and implacable.

Moreover, given the positive traditional role of violence in maintaining the equipoise of an anarchic society, the inhibition against unleashing military force might be less in a confrontation among rough equals. In other words, if it is second nature to be suspicious of others and see violence as a legitimate means of personal and familial defense, is it not possible that such frames of reference will be projected onto the world at large?

To mention rough equals is to bring up another point and to see an echo with the brief discussion, brought out earlier, of how Arab negotiating assumptions differ from Western ones. The requirements of feuding stem from conditions of scarcity in circumstances where the competitors are assumed to be essentially equal. Both bedouin society and Islam inculcate a strong sense of individualism and egalitarianism among traditional (and not-so-traditional) Arabs. These may seem like opposites, but they are not. Striving for honor can be described, in other terms, as striving to maintain potential or extant equality with others. This is why, perhaps, Arab leaders often go to great lengths to create conditions, sometimes real and sometimes symbolic, for balanced transactions. They do not easily cooperate with one another so long as one side needs to restore honor. Therefore, it is frequently the case that diplomatic fixes to common problems are accompanied by symbolic acts that create balanced transactions, without which agreements could not go forward. These symbols can be so important that they are considered more important than the exchange of concrete values they allow. Consider Brown's description of Egyptian-Saudi diplomacy in the 1960s in this light:

> Following the 1967 war the antagonisms between Faisal and Nasser were overcome . . . at the Khartoum Conference. Just months before, as the two struggled over the outcome of the civil war in Yemen, Faisal had been castigated by Nasser as an enemy of the Arab people. In their reconciliation, Faisal offered monumental foreign exchange support for the defeated Jordanians and Egyptians. In Arab eyes, it appeared that Nasser was forgiving Faisal.[30]

This may be why Arab governments generally find it difficult to deal with outside parties that cannot be construed as near or potential equals. To be plundered, say by the West or Israel, and not be able to pay back the deed as would be the case in feuding societies is to be dishonored.

If one substitutes state in international politics for family in feuding society, a number of interesting observations emerge. Suggestive hypotheses from the Arab-Israeli conflict abound. Israel's humiliation of Arab armies in 1967 was so total that Arab honor was demeaned. Most Israelis expected to be able to trade territories for a political settlement after the war, but because the Arabs could not find a means to create the possibility of a balanced transaction, the Arab states could not engage in negotiations. Later they could, because of "the crossing" of 1973. Henry Kissinger's view that the restoration of Egypt's honor would have been undone by Israel's annihilation of the trapped Third Army seems a justifiable conclusion.[31] There are those who have argued, too, that Palestinians could not have considered a compromise peace with Israel before the *intifada*, which allowed Palestinians to hold their heads up and look Israeli military personnel squarely in the eye. This may well be true.

The most dramatic examples of the thesis that contemporary Arab countries often see themselves as "families" and that questions of honor and shame play prominently in relations among their political leaderships come to us from the Kuwait crisis. Virtually all Arabs view the intercession or intervention of outside powers into the affairs of the Arab world as a humiliation, as an occasion for shame. Fear of being seen as too close an ally of the United States, for example, drove President Mubarak to seek an Arab League mandate before Egypt would commit troops to the defense of Saudi Arabia. In a live news conference on August 8, 1990, Mubarak accused Saddam of shaming the Arab world by forcing foreign intervention into the Middle East by refusing to facilitate an Arab solution to the problem. He said directly to Saddam:

> The world is moving freely in the region. . . . You are not accepting the Arab umbrella. Well, you are getting the foreign umbrella. American and French and British forces are being forced on you. . . . You cannot put me in a bind like this. You cannot commit such a crime and then ask me for the impossible. Don't embarrass me. Just like you have interests, I have interests. I am trying as much as possible to protect Arab honor.[32]

If these words were not known to be about the Kuwait crisis of 1990 spoken between the leaders of sovereign Arab states in the twentieth century, with different proper nouns they could easily be fitted into the mouths of tribal chieftains of the Syrian desert in any one of a dozen prior centuries and be none the worse for the journey.

If the social dynamics of the feud are transposed from inner-Arab society to inter-Arab relations and relations between Arab states and the rest of the world, the implications for deterrence relationships are stunning. Possession of unconventional weapons would be seen in this context both as a means of establishing leadership of the Arab nation, and as an equalizing device with the stronger West. Many Arabs suspect, regrettably with some cause, that many Westerners think of them as wogs, and quite naturally, they are not about to act civilly toward those who reject their essential equality and dignity. Thus, paradoxically, possession of unconventional weaponry might enable Arab leaders to moderate their diplomatic behavior with respect to Western countries and interests. There is a danger, however, that this might not work out as planned, especially if some Arab leaders believe that possession is not enough, but use is required, too.

In either case, it stands to reason that if the Arabs believe that the West will deny them the accouterments of modern military power that advanced states possess because they believe the Arabs inherently inferior, the United States and kindred societies cannot expect friendship and understanding. It is galling to Arab elites that others doubt their credibility, and there have been practical implications: during Kissinger's 1973–1975 negotiations between

Egypt and Israel, Israeli intimations or outright accusations of Arab infidelity always produced counterproductive results in negotiations.[33]

If Arab political elites remain dishonored in their own eyes, what would they do if the feud metaphor is accurate? They would, as with vengeance killing, try to create some equality of pain. The Iran-Iraq War seems to have illustrated this well, and so in a way did the Gulf War of 1991. In the former case, the reaction of both sides to mutual military incompetence was to try to find a way to hurt the other side indirectly with economic pressure—like Iran getting Syria to shut off Iraqi oil pipelines—and their populations directly with artillery and missiles. The Iraqi reaction to prospective defeat at one point was to resort to chemical warfare, not just to prevent collapse, but to punish the other side. In the Gulf War, too, Iraqi tactics aimed at hurting Americans, Kuwaitis, and Saudis—even if Iraqi losses were disproportionately high. How else to explain the militarily irrelevant plunge into the Saudi border town of Khafji, the ecoterrorism of dumping oil into the Persian Gulf, and setting Kuwaiti oil wells ablaze?

The uses of terrorism and the oil embargo, too, as the Arabs seem to have understood them, appear to fit this metaphor as it pertains to the West. So has the *intifada* as pertains to Israel. To quote Brown again: "The real difficulty is not some special Arab potential for treachery. It is an image that the Arab sense of weakness has reflected into Western perceptions, an image of Arabs seeking equality through the only means that in the past has been available to them—through the equalization of hurt."[34] If certain Arab states and substate organizations can hurt with embargoes on the one hand and rocks on the other, it does not take much imagination to anticipate what they could do with IRBMs and biological warheads.

The general level of Arab frustration in recent decades at not having been able to repay a slight with a slight has been enormous. In the 1950s, Western countries decided how much arms Arab countries received, and so negotiations about such subjects, notably with the British government, were not really negotiations at all, so long as the West alone had what the Arabs wanted. Then entered the Soviet Union after 1955, first in Egypt, later in Syria, Algeria, Iraq, and elsewhere, but even the Russians demanded substantial control over weapons and policy. It has only been very recently, thanks to a proliferation of sources of advanced military technology, the end of the Cold War, and the development of some indigenous munitions manufacturing capabilities, that some Arab states have had a modicum of control over their own military potential. Iraq's invasion of Kuwait was, in this sense, too, the first shot of a new era.

The internal dynamics of feuding societies—the use of feud as a means to generate internal leadership—may also have implications for contemporary affairs. Most would appear to revolve around the much discussed contradictions of pan-Arabism, the fact that there is a structure of social and cultural identification that exceeds the administrative and political control of any one country's elite. The general implication for deterrence is clear: possession of nuclear weapons and ballistic missiles would more nearly approximate a force proportional to the size of the ambitions of the Arab nation.

Quite aside from deterrence issues, then, possession of nuclear and biological weapons by an Arab leadership would intimate Arab-wide political prestige and authority at home. In the feud model, powerful leaders are honored leaders, and honored leaders are leaders who retain a firm grip on power. Clearly, the aspiration of pan-Arabism has always been, and remains, mainly about power. This is why Mu'ammar Gadhafi's frequent remarks that an Arab bomb is a precondition and catalyst for Arab unity makes perfect sense in the cultural context of Arab politics. It may never happen, but many Arab leaders believe that whoever attains maximal power will become a political magnet, drawing power over the Arab states and the Arab state system. This is perfectly logical in the context of modern Arab nationalism and perfectly compatible with the feud metaphor. Such internal and regional considerations may be the most important reason that some Arab leaders want to acquire unconventional weapons.

More broadly, too, the feud metaphor is permeated with images of force within and between Arab communities; force is seen as a natural tool of political power in general. Edward Mortimer has suggested that Samir Khalil was correct to link Saddam Hussein with Hajjaj ibn Yusuf, a figure of Iraqi folklore. Ibn Yusuf, explains Mortimer, an Umayyad governor of Iraq at the end of the seventh century, used extremely brutal measures to tame the province and "is held thereby to have laid the foundation for 'the whole splendiferous drama of Iraq's rise to preeminence under the Abbasids'."[35] According to Khalil, "Every Iraqi schoolchild can quote the famous speech which Hajjaj made to the populace upon assuming the governorship: 'I see heads before me that are ripe for plucking, and I am the one to pluck them, and I see blood glistening between the turbans and the beards.'"[36] Mortimer goes on to suggest that the intensely violent creed of the Iraqi Ba'thi is a function of both history and a deep historical memory. He added that whereas in the West, the use of violence by a regime against its people tends to deligitimize it, in Iraq "the ability of the regime to use [coercion] may actually be evidence of its legitimacy, rather than the reverse, in the eyes of much of the population."[37]

The question nevertheless remains: If Arabs view force in this way when it comes to relations among themselves, how do they look at the use of force either toward outsiders, or outsiders' use of force against them? The most compelling way to put the answer is this: the same way. The evidence suggests that Arabs expect the stronger West to use force against weaker Arabs just as Arabs would use force against the West if the power relationships were reversed. This reflects, again, a "symmetrical" assumption of equality within the feud metaphor.

This notion of "do unto others before they can do unto thee" is consistent with the element of feud that stresses the importance of restoring honor by doing unpleasant but obligated things. The willingness to do unpleasant and violent things is in itself often a mark of courage in the Middle East. Why else would Syrian schoolgirls bite into live snakes in the presence of Hafiz al-Assad? The Iranian army did not crack in 1981–1982 although it found itself in very unpleasant situations. Suffering, especially for Shi'ites and especially around *ashura*, may have actually boosted morale. Similarly, the privations of an economic embargo of Iraq should never have been expected to break the will of the Iraqi government or erode genuine, albeit misguided, popular support for the regime. Why do so many Arabs still admire Saddam Hussein? Not because he won, but because he was brave enough to lose.

Loss of honor is coupled in the feud metaphor with loss of nerve, or sentimentality. Joseph Pierce once described local informants speaking of a tribe "without honor" because its leader so loved his daughter that he refused to kill her when she was found engaging in premarital sex. Applying this concept to broader political relations, he argued (in 1971) that:

> The highest point of United States prestige was when American troops landed in Lebanon in 1958. Westerners have a tendency to think that the people of the area might feel that we were interfering with the internal policies of an independent country and think less of us. . . . It must be remembered that the average Middle Easterner looks upon his government as an "enemy." . . . The United States was generally admired and respected almost everywhere by the man in the street because it had the force, and used it, to carry out its wishes.[38]

Conversely, some Arab governments were fearful of trusting American guarantees after what was, in their view, Washington's defeat in Vietnam, its failure to protect the Shah, its ignominious experience in Lebanon in 1983–1984, and its feckless conduct in the Iran-Contra debacle of 1986–1987. Even Saddam Hussein said so; he made special note of American's retreat from Vietnam and concluded from it that America could not stand the casualties from a large battle. Also, U.S. destruction of a few Iranian oil platforms in 1986—after alerting those on them to leave in advance—did not impress a government in Tehran already locked in a brutal war, nor did it impress anyone else in the region. To the contrary, it probably encouraged Iranian speedboat attacks against U.S. vessels at that time and Iraqi conclusions that Americans lacked serious tolerance for pain. Only when the United States did something very major, accidentally shooting down an Iranian airliner in 1988, did the Iranians take notice and, believing the attack to be deliberate, sued for an armistice in the war with Iraq under the erroneous belief that U.S.-Iraqi coordination was now too strong to defeat.

CONCLUSIONS AND IMPLICATIONS

Judging from both cultural analysis and a reading of the newspaper, the leaders of most major Arab states seek to acquire unconventional weapons. They have both good and diverse reasons. One reason has nothing to do with Arab culture but is universal: possession of such forces connotes first-class international status. In the Arab context, however, this motive graduates from merely compelling to obsessive because of the inferiority complex of Arab politics toward what it believes to be its tormentors—the West, the United States, and Israel.

In addition, however, there are important inter-Arab and intrastate motivations for most Arab leaders to wish to obtain such weapons for, through attainment of such weapons, they can cement their status domestically; acquire a coercive capability nearly proportional to pan-Arab ambitions as opposed to those of any given Arab state and thus raise their status regionally; gain the ability to bypass dependence on politically unreliable and often literally incompetent conventional armies; and gain the ability to establish an equality of pain with local and international adversaries directly, depending on a small loyal core of technicians instead of on a sprawling officer corps.

Cultural analysis also suggests that most Arab leaders retain a zero-sum notion of deterrence, which tells them that the better they can deter others, the safer they are. They appear to have little sense of the "security dilemma," the insight that deterrence beyond the minimal need looks to others like preparation for aggression and thus promotes mutual insecurity. Also, whereas at least some Western leaders think of deterrence as an attainable, desirable form of dynamic equilibrium, Arab leaders are more likely to see political equilibria as unnatural and even undesirable. The more they are influenced by a specifically Muslim worldview, too, they are liable to see deterrence as a condition to be overcome on behalf of one's own interests and values, not a mutual value to be attained by joint effort.

As far as many Arab leaders are concerned, therefore, no amount of conventional or unconventional armament is too much because stable peace is believed far more often to be the exception than the rule in human affairs. Governments like that of Iraq and Syria regularly allow normal public welfare and economic functions to lapse in order to purchase weapons, and there is no reason to believe this will stop anytime soon. Part of the reason is that one's value as an ally to others is a function of the power that can be brought to bear in the regional politico-military equation. For all these reasons, therefore, formal arms-control regimes for the region that require the explicit approval of the Arab countries are unlikely to succeed.

Last in this regard, Middle Eastern leaders tend to believe—for good reason, it might be added—that, because they live in a region of shifting and fluid alliances, they must try to achieve a level of military preparedness that enables them to deter all their neighbors simultaneously. In general, too, alliances with external powers are seen as supplements, not substitutes, for one's own power, the more so as great-power competition is sharply reduced in the region. This is so because of the perceived unreliability of external guarantees and aid, and because too visible a dependency on an external power is bad for political legitimacy at home in most cases. Unconventional weapons of mass destruction are especially attractive, therefore, for fear that others will get them first, and attractive because, all else being equal, they seem a relatively inexpensive way of deterring everyone at once.

So much for the desire to possess. What about the propensity to use? Arab political experience has generated a view of political accountability that is not democratic in the Western sense, and that leaves little room for pluralism; the constraints against militarism inherent in democratic pluralism are absent in the Arab world and are likely to remain absent. Arab history has fostered the idea that centralized and even brutal political authority is normal. When a state can brutalize its own people, those people are helpless to prevent the state from brutalizing its neighbors.

More important, the feud as a tacit model for the behavior of Arab states toward one another may incline Arab leaders to see themselves held within the grasp of fate and to see violence as having a more positive role in society—and by extension in international society—than Westerners. The willingness of someone to endure the unpleasantness on behalf of one's honor is traditionally esteemed. All else being equal, this may incline Arab politicians to "bite the bullet" of using weapons of mass destruction more easily than Westerners.

On the other hand, it is possible that mere attainment, short of use, of unconventional weaponry will sate Arab desires for enhanced status. It is also possible that the frequency of votive acts in face-to-face behavior, in which the saying of something is considered nearly equivalent to the doing of it, will carry over to threats made with unconventional weapons, and that any miscalculation will be on the side of caution. The Iranian regime, arguably the most dangerous in the region, may totter and fall. An Arab-Israeli peace, not so farfetched anymore, may reduce regional tension significantly, removing at least some of the precipitants to violence and war.

More to the point of security regime theory, both the Israeli-Jordanian and Israeli-Syrian relationships show that at least bilateral and limited arrangements can come to exist and be maintained over time. There is no reason to assume that new technological conditions will radically change this. Moreover, the generally good record of inter-Arab relations when it comes to overt aggression suggests that there is a framework of expectation and a sense of reciprocity, based on the feud model, that, although it will not lead to light, frolic, and laughter, can encourage an austere deterrence at least most of the time.

On balance, then, cultural factors appear to play a mixed role. In some respects, culture militates for the use of weapons both to threaten and to actually be employed, but culture has also erected limits to violence, at least among Arabs if not also between Arabs and others. There is the substitution of violent language for violent behavior in votive acts. There is the perception of general kinship, of being enmeshed in an essentially familial relationship. There is, too, the softening agent of orthodox religion that, like all such religions, views peace in a positive light. More important, there is the attenuated metaphor of the feud that, although it allows for violence, is essentially a violence-limiting, order-keeping institution.

It would seem, in conclusion, that although the deliberate and premeditated use of weapons of mass destruction by Arab leaders against each other, against elements of their own populations, or against regional "others" like Israel, Iran, and Turkey cannot be ruled out, the greater danger is war by miscalculation or accident. This was also the case during the Cold War between U.S. and Soviet power. Efforts to create full security regimes in the Middle East are not likely to succeed when deep animosity and fears persist; but with the concerted effort of external third parties, limited and semi-imposed security regimes might at least reduce the danger of war by miscalculation or accident—through establishing hot lines, increasing intelligence transparency in crises through selected sharing of satellite photography, and by promoting regionwide functional cooperation. That would be perhaps not so small a mercy.

NOTES

1. See chapter 1, and Charles Lipson, "Why Are Some International Agreements Informal?" *International Organization* 45, no. 4 (Autumn 1991).

2. See, chapter 1.

3. See Aaron Klieman's chapter in this book, and my *Israel and Jordan in the Shadow of War* (New York: St. Martin's Press, 1992).

4. I am referring generally here to the body of phenomenological sociology and philosophy represented by such writers as Charles Schutz, Ernst Cassirer, Peter Berger, Thomas Luckmann, and Erving Goffman.

5. Jack L. Snyder, *The Soviet Strategic Culture: Implications for Limited Nuclear Operations*, R-2154-AF (Santa Monica: Rand Corporation, 1977), p. v.

6. See Ken Booth's "The Concept of Strategic Culture Affirmed," in Carl Jacobsen, ed., *Strategic Power: USA\USSR* (New York: St. Martin's Press, 1990); Colin S. Gray, *Nuclear Strategy and National Style* (Lanham, Md.: Hamilton Press, 1983); Joseph Rothschild, "Culture and War," in Stephanie Neuman and Robert Harkavy, eds., *The Lessons of Recent Wars in the Third World,* vol. 2 (Lexington, Mass.: Lexington Books, 1987); and David S. Yost, "Nuclear Deterrence and Western Societies: Strategic Culture and Public Opinion in Britain, France, Germany and the United States," unpublished, February 26, 1991.

7. Yost, ibid., p. 39.

8. Captain Muak-Keofeed, "Routing the Libyans," *Marine Corps Gazette* (August 1987), pp. 26–27.

9. William R. Brown, *The Last Crusade* (Chicago: Nelson-Hall, 1980), pp. 71–72.

10. Ami Ayalon, *Language and Change in the Arab Middle East: The Evolution of Modern Political Discourse* (New York: Oxford University Press, 1987).

11. Here, see Bernard Lewis, "Other People's History," *American Scholar* 59, no. 3 (Summer 1990).

12. Some military professionals and academics do write in Arabic about current politico-military issues, especially in Egypt, but there is little theoretical or abstractive quality to this literature. As data on future attitudes on deterrence, it is nevertheless worth examining more closely than it has been so far.

13. The reference is to Nathan Leites, *The Operational Code of the Politburo* (New York: McGraw-Hill, 1963).

14. See William B. Quandt, "Egypt: Strong Sense of National Identity," in Hans Binnendijk, ed., *National Negotiating Styles* (Washington, D.C.: Foreign Service Institute, 1987), pp. 118–120.

15. Raymond Cohen, *Negotiating across Cultures* (Washington, D.C.: United States Institute of Peace, 1991); and *Culture and Conflict in Egyptian-Israeli Relations: A Dialogue of the Deaf* (Bloomington: University of Indiana Press, 1990).

16. Michael Hudson, *Arab Politics: The Search for Legitimacy* (New Haven, Conn.: Yale University Press, 1977); and Karen Dawisha,

"Arab Regimes: Legitimacy and Foreign Policy," in Dawisha, ed., *Beyond Coercion* (London: Croom-Helm, 1988).

17. Jacob Black-Michaud, *Cohesive Force: Feud in the Mediterranean and the Middle East* (New York: St. Martin's Press, 1975). This section borrows also from Raymond Verdier, *La Vengeance* (Paris: Editions Cujas, 1982).

18. Black-Michaud, ibid., p. 8.

19. Joseph Schacht, *An Introduction to Islamic Law* (Oxford: Oxford University Press, 1964), p. 175.

20. Black-Michaud, *Cohesive Force*, p. 89.

21. Ibid., p. 118.

22. Ibid., p. 134.

23. Ibid., p. 142.

24. Ibid., p. 178.

25. Hisham Sharabi, *Neopatriarchy: A Theory of Distorted Change in Arab Society* (New York: Oxford University Press, 1988), p. 7.

26. Quoted in Youssef M. Ibrahim, "Arafat, the Survivor, Now Finds Support Vanishing," *New York Times* (February 13, 1991), p. A16.

27. Ibid., p. A16.

28. Kedourie quoted in Thomas L. Friedman, "A Rising Sense That Iraq's Hussein Must Go," *New York Times* (July 7, 1991).

29. *Uneasy Lies the Head* (New York: Bernard Geis, 1962), p. 24.

30. Brown, *The Last Crusade*, p. 34.

31. Quandt, "Egypt: Strong Sense of National Identity," pp. 114–45.

32. Mubarak quoted in the *New York Times* (August 9, 1990), p. A18.

33. Brown, *The Last Crusade*, pp. 97–99.

34. Ibid., p. 96.

35. Edward Mortimer, "The Thief of Baghdad," *New York Review of Books* (September 27, 1990), p. 12.

36. Mortimer quoting Khalil quoting Ibn Yusuf, ibid., p. 12. Probably not just every Iraqi child, but every Arab child, knows this verse.

37. Ibid., p. 12.

38. Joe E. Pierce, *Understanding the Middle East* (Rutland, Vt.: Charles E. Tuttle Company, 1971).

CHAPTER 10

The Politics of Water in the Middle East: The Current Situation, Imaginary and Practical Solutions

Amikam Nachmani

The subject of water in the Middle East (ME) is extremely problematic, and raises unique emotions as well as extraordinary findings. Between the facts, myths, cliches, and doomsday predictions, this chapter will attempt to suggest a way, perhaps a modest one, out of the labyrinth.

But first, what is water? The definition below is an English one, yet the surprise, indifference, and ignorance imputed to the average Briton are found also among many Middle Easterners:

> [It] Pours from our tap at an average weekly cost of about 1.5 p. a head and few of us think of the massive operations that are necessary to get it there. It may be suddenly brought home to us when we read that our favourite valley in a national park is to be turned into a reservoir.[1]

However, when it comes to ME water a less benign language is used—indeed, a language that is probably unique to the ME. For example, when users were facing a decline in the water level of the Dead Sea, various remedies were proposed, the better known being the Mediterranean-Dead Sea (Med-Dead) project and the Red Sea-Dead Sea (Red-Dead) project. But since these two projects were very expensive, a cheaper and more economical solution was allegedly suggested: to bomb and strike militarily at the diversion plants on the Yarmuk river; huge amounts of water would thereby be released and find their way into the Dead Sea through the Jordan.[2]

In the case of Lebanon, water problems are directly linked to intercommunal feuds. Lebanon uses water to produce electricity and, of course, for irrigation. But the rise in the standard of living of the Christian community calls for the building of hydroelectric projects rather than irrigation plants. This means that the supply of air-conditioning to Beirut Christians impedes agricultural development for Shi'ites in the south.[3]

As for Turkey—a key element in any Middle East regional water plan—it gives us piquant advice concerning the Middle East water shortage. A Turkish businessman, involved in the prospective project of exporting his country's water by sea tankers, used a poetic flourish in attempting to sell his merchandise: "Countless millions of people have lived without love, but none without water."[4] However, perhaps the following quotation regarding Iraqi water interests in the Euphrates could be an alternative title for this chapter: "They [the Iraqis] have oil, we have water; let them drink their oil."

THE GLOBAL WATER SHORTAGE

The most disturbing aspect of water scarcity worldwide is the speed with which it has come about. Net renewable water resources per capita have declined dramatically over a single generation, and in little more than thirty years from now will have reached dangerously low levels. By the year 2025 the average annual net water resources in the Middle East are expected to be less than 700 cubic meters (m^3) per capita, half what they are today.[5]

The sharp growth in global population and development has badly depleted and polluted the world's water sources. This situation is keenly felt in India, China, and Mexico; even in the United States where there is a problem of deteriorating quality of water. More and more a dilemma arises between using water for industry and agriculture and using it for household purposes. Every day 40,000 babies die worldwide, many from side effects directly related to extreme shortages of clean drinking water. Of the 5.5 billion people in the world today, 3.5 billion are forced to live with less than 50 liters of water per person per day, one-seventh the quantity used by the average American.[6] Agriculture uses 73 percent of the world's fresh water, and the world needs more agriculture because of increasing food needs. In many poor countries, famine is prevented only by taking grains and cereals from the global grain stocks. Lately, however, these stocks have dropped sharply: in 1987 they were sufficient for 101 days, but as of 1989 for only 54.[7] Furthermore, experience shows that when available water resources drop to between 1,000 and 2,000 m^3 per capita per year, large investments are then generally required to meet ongoing water demand. However, when resources are below 1,000 m^3 per capita per year, difficult socio-economic adjustments are required to cope with such scarcity. Most countries of the region are now having to make these painful adjustments. Water withdrawals in several countries already exceed renewable supplies; others are at or close to the limits.[8]

Water conflicts exist in many places: between India and Bangladesh, Israel and its neighbors, Egypt and Ethiopia, Turkey and Syria, Turkey and Iraq. At the same time, distribution of water sources is highly uneven: many countries with small populations possess large amounts of water whereas many populous countries face acute shortages. Yet there is a limit to the human ability to bring water from one place to another by building dams, tunnels, and hydroelectric projects without causing irreversible ecological catastrophes. And in such circumstances where environmental damage is likely, financial assistance usually available from organizations such as the World Bank and International Monetary Fund will be denied for developing these projects.

The global shift from rain-fed to irrigated agriculture has increased the salinity of the earth in many areas; evaporation of fresh water has left chemicals (pesticides, fertilizers, etc.) and salinity in the ground. In addition, experience has shown that attempts to dam floodwaters have prevented the normal flow of destructive salts out of the soil to the sea, thereby rendering the soil unusable. Furthermore, it has already been proven that deforestation causes a reduction in the amount of rainfall. In Western Africa, deforestation is in part accountable for shorter rainy seasons. In Florida, a lack of vegetation has led to a 10 percent drop in rainfall over the past thirty years. Once exposed, land reflects more sunlight, producing atmospheric processes that reduce rainfall by drawing dryer air into a given area. Similarly, the worldwide tendency to utilize fresh river water just before it reaches the sea has proven disastrous because a river's most biologically productive part is the brackish zone where fresh water and saltwater meet.[9]

THE MIDDLE EAST WATER SHORTAGE AND "SECURITY REGIMES"

The problem of water shortage can be intriguingly compared with the existential danger posed by nuclear weapons. Indeed, in the Middle East the water scarcity has already caused armed clashes and presents a danger of major military confrontations.

Water is an existential element on a par with air; without it there can be no life. Therefore, lack of water, like nuclear weapons, could have fatal consequences. But unlike nuclear weapons, the problem of water shortage will never deter the use of weapons altogether; for whereas a nuclear war will presumably leave no survivors, in a water confrontation the stronger contender will gain the precious resource and survive, and only the weak will perish. Thus, the incentive for a "security regime" concerning Middle East water is weaker than the one that existed for a U.S.-Soviet security regime during the Cold War.[10] Furthermore, although widespread suffering from thirst might become an incentive for Middle East water cooperation, such combining of efforts would not yield more or new Middle East water sources; all are already in maximal or near-maximal use. Likewise, for reasons that will be explained later, combining national water systems is practically out of the question. Hence, from the outset, it should be clear that the best approach for Middle Eastern countries is to expedite the development of their own national water sources to the highest potential; and this basically means concentrating, as we shall see, on desalination.

The water supply in the Middle East is facing enormous pressures. Egypt's population is growing by 1 million every nine months and its water needs accordingly. Many Jordanian towns get water only once a week. Immigration into Israel is increasing the stress on that country's already taxed water sources. In the Gaza Strip, the salination of agricultural lands and fresh-water wells has reached catastrophic levels. The low level of the Euphrates River, together with pollution from pesticides, chemicals, and salt, has forced the Syrian government to cut back on the supply of drinking water and electricity to Damascus, Aleppo, and several other cities. Damascus is without water most nights and is estimated to lose as much as 30 percent of its water from old, leaking pipes. (In Jordanian cities the situation is even more severe: water losses from leaking pipes can reach 60 percent.[11]) Poor water quality and ecological catastrophes pose a threat of such immense and sinister proportions that the average Middle Easterner may be forgiven for feeling helpless in this regard.

DIMENSIONS OF THE MIDDLE EAST WATER PROBLEM

Over 50 percent of the population of the Middle East and North Africa (excluding the Maghreb) depend either on water from rivers that cross an international boundary before reaching them or on desalinized water and water drawn from deep wells. What is more startling, two-thirds of all Arabic-speaking people in the same region depend on river water that flows to them from non-Arabic-speaking countries, and another 24 percent live in areas with no perennial surface streams whatever. That is, the latter must rely either on well water from rapidly depleting sources or seawater, which is expensive both to purify in sufficient quantities and to pump to its places of use.[12]

The size of these water-dependent populations is rapidly increasing. World Bank data show, for 1983, a total population of 217.4 million in the area under discussion. It is conservatively estimated that by the year 2000 an additional 119.6 million will be added to this figure, a population increase of 55 percent. Water will be needed not only for these people as individuals, but also for industry and all other urban uses. Irrigation water will also be needed so as to prevent, as far as possible, dependence on potentially unreliable imports.[13]

DEPLETED SOURCES, GROWING CONFLICTS

There are four sources of water in the Middle East: precipitation; exotic rivers, or those that rise in amply watered areas but eventually grow smaller as they flow through deserts to the sea or inland sinks; aquifers, or underground water-filled strata; and desalinized seawater. In areas that exotic streams do not reach, particularly the Arabian Peninsula and the Libyan Sahara, millions more Arabs must rely on wells and desalinized seawater. In the peninsula south of the Jordanian and Iraqi borders, with an area of 1,160,481 square miles, not a single permanent surface stream exists. If we add riverless Libya to the list, the total for the Arab world becomes 1,839,839 square miles without one permanent surface stream.[14]

Water has indeed always been a source of conflict in the Middle East, but growing pressure on the already depleted sources aggravate this situation. In the period before the June 1967 Six-Day War, armed clashes broke out between Israel and Syria over the Jordan River sources. There is also growing tension in the Nile River basin, where the nine riparians (Egypt, Sudan, Ethiopia, Tanzania, Zaire, Uganda, Kenya, Rwanda, and Burundi) plan and execute water development projects that hardly take into account each other's needs. Any water taken by the upstream riparians for their own needs means that the downstream riparians get that much less. Similarly, growing immigration into Israel causes anxiety among the Arabs that Israel will supply water to these immigrants from the two remaining rivers whose waters have not yet been completely exhausted; namely, the Litani and the Yarmuk. Indeed, the average Israeli uses five to six times more water than the average person in Arab countries, and the new immigrants to Israel come mainly from countries where water is plentiful and lavishly used. Jordan, already one of the poorest countries in terms of water, needs more water for the 350,000 Palestinian refugees who were forced to leave Kuwait following the Gulf crisis. Overall, population growth in the Middle East now averages a staggering 3 percent annually, which can only increase both the pressure on the already exhausted water sources and the pollution of the water.

What solutions to this problem are there? Because agriculture consumes 80 percent of Middle East water, one remedy might be to switch to nonagricultural production. But can traditions of Middle East agriculture going back thousands of years be substantially changed? Would the Middle Easterners, who gained their independence from the colonial powers during the last fifty to sixty years, agree to depend on food produced outside the region? Would the Zionist dream of return to the land, to agriculture, be so easily relinquished? Would the Palestinians abandon their dream of returning to their villages, to their olive and grape tree orchards? For that matter, would Lebanese Christians give up their air-conditioning for the sake of Shi'ite farmers? One might expect that droughts and water shortages would encourage people in the Middle East to switch from agriculture to other kinds of production. But the reality has proved different: droughts have led only to a demand to move from rain-fed agriculture to irrigated agriculture. Thus, the pressure on the already dwindling sources increases. In addition, irrigation water has the disadvantage of causing higher salinity levels in soil than actual rainwater which is known for its purity. Furthermore, intensive farming, which utilizes large amounts of irrigated water and fertilizers, initially yields more food produce but ultimately increases salinity levels and renders the soil unusable.[15]

How could water development projects be financed by the International Monetary Fund if the latter conditioned the granting of money on unanimous agreement among all the riparians? Israel refuses to grant its consent to Jordan's Unity Dam over the Yarmuk River because it demands its share in the river's water as a riparian; Syria (also a Yarmuk riparian) refuses to sign a triple agreement because this would imply tacit recognition of Israel.[16] As a result, Jordan gets no money from the International Monetary Fund.

A remedy could exist in a shift from highly water-intensive crops (cotton in Egypt and Israel, citrus in Israel). But here, too, the opposition would be strong; people in the Middle East do not want to be dependent on others for food.

If sharing is a remedy, how would the Middle East riparians share their water? Do upstream riparians, or countries within which a river (e.g. the Nile) originates, have priority over downstream riparians (Egypt)? Perhaps history would decide; that is, the riparian that historically has consumed most of the river's water (Egypt) would have priority over the present or future needs of other riparians. But do population growth and other needs in one riparian give it priority over another? Should a riparian be demanded to consume water in more economical ways (e.g., Turkey's demands of Iraq and Syria to stop irrigation by flooding)? Should it be demanded of one riparian to use only certain sources of water and leave a specific source for supplying the needs of others?

Another remedy might be to take a regional approach to the problem. That is, water from certain countries could be diverted to others, according to need. But Middle East countries tend to be suspicious and unfriendly toward each other: for example, Egypt refuses to divert Nile water to Israel; likewise Lebanon with the Litani. There is also a danger, in this connection, of what Joyce Starr termed a "domino effect": for instance, Turkish-Syrian water relations and their possible detrimental impacts on the national Syrian water system might affect Israeli-Syrian water relations, and vice versa;[17] such problems would make a regional diversion scheme all the more difficult.

MAIN FEATURES OF THE MIDDLE EAST WATER CRISIS

An added complication in water project development is the fact that Middle East countries are reluctant to make honest disclosures concerning actual water usage and available resources: information is an asset which parties to negotiations do not easily surrender. This has led states outside the region, who in principle are prepared to help alleviate the problem, to express frustration at the tendency of Middle Eastern countries to use data relevant to their water problems as political bargaining chips, in the multilateral talks connected to the peace process. This has led these non-Middle East states to establish an independent water data bank as a basis of objective evaluation of Middle East water needs, and as a prerequisite for understanding the real dimensions of the water problem, which consists of the following elements:[18]

1. Water quality, hitherto a problem of the industrial world, has become as immediate a problem in the Middle East as water quantity.
2. Past water development projects, like the 1950s plan of Eric Johnston, the U.S. special ambassador, for the development of Jordan River water, have failed to anticipate the rapidly growing water needs of Middle Eastern countries. In addition, population growth, immigration, and so on have not been adequately coped with. Hence, the average Israeli, for instance, uses 400–500 m^3 of water per year, which is on a par with the rates in industrial or other countries that have plenty of water. However, in

Israel as in most of the countries of the Middle East, there is no possibility for expanding resources, as actual water usage has reached the level of potential water availability. (As a comparison, annual water potential per capita in the US is 10,000 m^3; Iraq, 5,500; Turkey, 4,000; Syria, 2,800; Egypt, 1,100; Israel, 460; Jordan, 260; West Bank and Gaza, 135.[19])

3. Water conflicts in the Middle East have been zero-sum: water for one user means lack of water for the other.[20]
4. Factors of ideology, nationalism, and recent decolonization, prevent Middle East states from relinquishing food production and making themselves dependent on food-producing countries with plenty of water (which are, in most cases, the ex-colonial powers). Deemphasis of agriculture has more potential for savings than conservation or reallocation of water, which would cover only a fraction of the projected shortfalls, but is ideologically painful.
5. The surplus of water in a few Middle East protagonists (Lebanon and Turkey) is both temporal and misleading. In particular, Turkey's population growth is enormous (1 million every nine months); furthermore, the uneven distribution of water within Turkey itself and the lack of local energy sources mean that Turkey has to supply more water to its own population and to produce more hydroelectricity.[21] Therefore, for instance, Turkey will be faced with the need to defuse Kurdish ethnic unrest by developing eastern Turkey where most of the Kurds reside, and this will require a greater allocation of water resources.
6. Although cooperation among the riparians is an essential prerequisite for all regional water development projects, such cooperation is very hard to achieve because it means tacit recognition of the legitimacy of various demands. A Syrian-Israeli water agreement would imply Syrian recognition of Israel; a Syrian-Turkish agreement concerning the Orontes River would imply Syrian recognition of Turkish sovereignty over the Hatay region, which the Orontes crosses on its way to the Mediterranean (Hatay, called Alexandretta by Syria, was taken in June 1939

from Syria and given to Turkey by France, then the colonial power that controlled Syria); a Turkish-Syrian-Iraqi agreement to share Euphrates water would mean, according to Ankara, the imposition of Iraqi and Syrian sovereignty on a Turkish asset. Turkey, instead, is prepared to discuss only the technical aspects of allocating water to the downstream riparians.

7. The intermittent civil wars and civil strife with which Middle East countries are plagued (Sudan, Ethiopia, Lebanon) frustrate the development of water sources. The civil war in the Sudan, for instance, prevents draining the Sudd marshes that otherwise would have added 35 billion m^3 of water annually to the Nile.
8. Middle Eastern water development projects have had deleterious effects on the environment. The Aswan Dam, the Ataturk Dam, and the draining of the Huleh marsh in Israel have all had very negative ecological impacts. Today there is a growing tendency to prefer the preservation of the environment over development projects.[22]
9. Combining national water systems is extremely complicated. An example is the Nile-Negev project: none of the upper riparians could be counted on to restrain their own development so as to allow water to flow down to Egypt for purposes of export to Israel—not to mention that most of the upper riparians are intermittent ideological enemies of Israel.[23]
10. In the absence of unanimous agreement, international monetary bodies cannot finance water development projects. Facing opposing Iraqi and Syrian demands, Turkey, for instance, is not able to acquire enough money for the GAP (the dams on the Euphrates River) and is very much behind schedule in terms of completing the project. Jordan, for similar reasons related to disagreements between Israel and Syria, is unable to begin work on the Yarmuk River Dam.
11. Water—clearly in the Middle East, perhaps also in other places—can serve a military function. When Turkey forced its neighbor Syria to withdraw its support for the Kurdish rebels, the quid pro quo was that there would be

no interruption in the flow of Euphrates River water to Syria. In 1970, Israel, to force Jordan to stop the infiltration of armed Palestinians into the territories occupied by Israel, bombed the East Ghor Canal, which carries water from the Yarmuk River southward to the Jordan Valley.

WATER IN THE WEST BANK AND GAZA STRIP

Israel is blamed for stealing Palestinian water by unilaterally pumping it from the aquifer under the western part of the West Bank; Israel is also said to be preventing the Palestinians from drilling new wells in the West Bank, thus keeping the water of that aquifer for itself. The Palestinians claim that Israel pumps up to 80 percent of West Bank water resources for its own use and thereby meets up to one half of its total water consumption in this way. The Palestinians further claim that they are left with only 137 million m^3 per year for their own needs—less than one-fifth of the West Bank water. They therefore refuse to consider suggestions that they acquire water from other outside sources, until they are allocated the entire supply that they claim is theirs.[24] Aquifers, however, know no human-made boundaries; the aquifer in question accumulates water from under the Israeli coastal plain as well as from the West Bank. The Palestinians argue that, because the aquifer is fed by rain falling on the West Bank, the water is theirs. Arab states, however, as downstream riparians (Egypt and the Nile River; Syria and Iraq and the Euphrates River; Jordan and the Jordan River), object to the notion that the upstream riparian has priority over the downstream user.

Another issue regarding Palestinian water is the mid-1950s Johnston plan for the allocation of Jordan River water. At the time the plan was suggested to the riparians, the West Bank was Jordanian territory, and its needs were to be supplied from the 770 million m^3 per year allocated to Jordan.[25] Israel argues that today the Palestinians must request their share from Jordan, or more specifically, from the Yarmuk River, not from Israel (which reportedly uses no more than the Johnston-quota allocation of 400 million m^3 annually).

Even without polemics and name calling (in recent water negotiations in Washington, D.C., Palestinian and Jordanian negotiators objected to the Israeli use of the term *Judea and*

Samaria for the West Bank and threatened to refer to Israel as the *area between the Sea and the River*. Israeli negotiators countered by threatening to call Jordan the *area which is north of the Hedjaz* or as the *Southern Sandjak of Damascus*[26]), the facts of the situation are bleak and the outlook gloomy, as Joyce Starr points out:

> Volumes of articles have been written on the subject of Israel's apparently robbing Palestinian waters and counter-claims to these allegations. The parties to the conflict are quibbling about numbers that may or may not be true. The reality is that Israel, the West Bank and Gaza, and Jordan, are facing a combined deficit of at least 300–400 million cubic meters per year (and some estimate the figure to be as high as 500–600 million cubic meters).[27]

Indeed, the area between the Jordan River and the Mediterranean Sea, which in a generation is expected to have a population of 14 million people total, is already currently suffering from "water stress," which means that only 500 m^3 per capita per year are available.[28]

SEAWATER POLITICS

The Mediterranean Sea, on which several Middle Eastern states border, is usually not dealt with in discussions of the Middle East water problem. Yet the sea is one vast concentration of water that knows no human-made boundaries; ecological phenomena in the Equator cannot be explained unless we understand climatic conditions in the North and South Poles and vice-versa.[29] The effects occurring in the littoral states show the need for a Mediterranean cooperation—alas an almost non-existent element.

The Mediterranean and its waters affect the littoral countries in ways that often are curiously intertwined. During the last four years the eastern Mediterranean coasts have been infested by jellyfish (or medusae) that are much more lethal than the species to which people had been exposed before. Tourism, cooling units of power stations and ships, fishing nets, and so on, were all seriously affected by the medusae. The source of this new species is probably the Indian Ocean and the Red Sea; in any case, it migrates to the Mediterranean via the Suez Canal in what is known as the Lessepsian Migration (after Ferdinand De Lesseps who planned the Suez Canal).[30]

On the other hand, a dramatic decrease has occurred in the amount of tar along the Israeli coast.[31] The rise to power of Khomeini and the civil war in Lebanon led to an almost total cessation of the functioning of the oil industry in Iran and in the Mediterranean oil terminals in Israel and Lebanon. Intermittent friction between Syria and Iraq have had similar effects on the oil terminals along the Syrian coast. On the other hand, in 1977 the oil carried by the pipeline from Iraq to Turkey reached the Mediterranean terminal at the Bay of Iskanderun (in 1987, 75 million tons of oil were unloaded there). As a result, Libyan and Turkish coastal tar pollution has increased considerably.[32]

TWO SUGGESTED SOLUTIONS

The two solutions that are most discussed are combining national water systems (e.g., the Turkish "peace pipeline," the Nile-Gaza-Negev-Jordan project, the Litani-Jordan River projects) and diverting seas (e.g., Med- or Red-Dead projects). The difficulties involved, however, are most formidable. For instance, the littoral countries as well as the riparians must agree to seawater diversion otherwise international loans will not be made available. In addition, it is absolutely clear that there could be no room for both a Red-Dead Seas Jordanian project, and an Israeli Med-Dead Seas one, because the Dead Sea would not be able to contain water from both the Red Sea and the Mediterranean. Furthermore, the diversion of seas in an earthquake prone area such as this, in the vicinity of the Syrian-African Rift, can lead to the contamination of pure aquifers that lie beneath the diversion routes.[33] Hence, the Middle East water crisis can be coped with only in a regional framework. Indeed, there is a growing tendency among global financial bodies to provide monies only for regional water projects. Joyce Starr suggests that, among other reasons, Egypt joined the war against Iraq out of fear of losing the international finances for the Nile-Sinai water project.[34]

Care must be taken, however, to avoid plans that are grandiose or impossible. As noted, nobody will be able to put an end to agriculture in the area and replace it with food imports from outside the Middle East; dependence is a dirty word in the Middle East even though many of the states are not able to survive without considerable import of food. Similar drawbacks bedevil the plan to produce electricity in Africa, from Nile River water, and export it to the EEC countries in return for EEC agricultural products.[35] The EEC countries would not be eager to subject their standard of living and supply of electricity to the whims of Nile riparian rulers.

The Turkish "peace pipeline" would carry the water of the Ceyhan and Seyhan Rivers (now emptying into the Mediterranean) to the entire Middle East and Persian Gulf. But with the pipeline's two arms exceeding a length of 6,500 kilometers, its projected cost of more than $20 billion, and its building expected to last more than fifteen years, this is hardly a practical plan. Not to mention the near-insurmountable psychological barriers: the Arabs will not want to depend on the Turks, Kuwait, on water coming from Iraq, and so on. Likewise, Jordan's plan to import Iraqi water from the Euphrates River is highly problematic. The envisaged 650 kilometer pipeline would be very vulnerable and would depend on the Euphrates River, which originates in Turkey.[36] However, Turkey's growing use of the Euphrates already leaves diminishing amounts for water to the downstream riparians.

In any case, all this puts Turkey at the center of Middle East water planning:

> Water is as important as oil. The days may not be far off when Turkey starts filling water into bottles and market them in the Middle East. . . . Water is not something that we should permit to flow away. We are the lucky ones in the Middle East. So we have to make the maximal use of this potential.[37]

In addition to the "peace pipeline," another of several proposed plans would involve the shipping of water by tankers or "medusa" plastic bags from the Manavgat River (which also empties into the Mediterranean) to potential buyers in the Middle East. Israel had originally thought that the Manavgat project could provide a source of water for the country's needs. However, current official thinking has virtually rejected this opinion given two recent winters that had substantial rainfalls; but, even more important, due to the apprehension shared by potential buyers of Turkish water, of placing Turkey into a position of power that comes with the ability to "turn off the tap."[38]

At present, the building of Turkish dams on the Euphrates River is causing growing conflict with Syria and Iraq. ("We *give* the [Syrians and the Iraqis] the water—they *can't share* it," declared the Turkish secretary of state responsible for the southeast Anatolia project [GAP]. "Ninety percent of the Arab population is dependent on water originating outside it and therefore it is normal that the tension in the region will escalate."[39]) Overall, the picture is again less than rosy: there is an internal Turkish objection to sharing and exporting a national raw material and asset such as water, and the Arabs, for their part, are reluctant to depend on Turkey.

Furthermore, the official Turkish stance poses almost impossible conditions. For instance, anyone who wants to import water by tanker from Turkey (from the Manavgat River) must undertake that the Turkish Republic of Northern Cyprus (whose water originates in the southern, Greek part of Cyprus, another place where a political conflict is exacerbated by the geography of water) will receive a certain percentage of this water at a relatively low price.[40] Ankara also stipulates that before it will supply its water to Middle Eastern countries a peace agreement must first be signed between Israel and its neighbors. Interestingly, observers note that Turkey (and Egypt which is a downstream riparian) has displayed a low profile at the multilateral water negotiations, for fear that precedent making decisions in the Arab-Israeli arena might also be applied to Turkey vis-à-vis its neighbors. It is no wonder therefore, that Turkey's delegation to the water talks held in Vienna (May 1992) downplayed pessimistic assessments of the water situation in the Middle East, presumably for concern that Turkey would be called upon to alleviate these problems from its sources.[41]

DESALINATION: THE ONLY REALISTIC HOPE

The fact remains, however, that lately Middle East water needs have considerably increased. The rebuilding of Kuwait, Lebanon and Iraq, the absorption of newcomers in Israel, and so on all point to the need for a "Marshall Plan" for Middle East water.[42] Is desalination a practical solution? The Israeli official view, for one, as presented in Moscow in January 1992 to the multilateral water summit of the Arab-Israeli peace conference, is that desalination is the only long-term remedy for water-poor areas such as the Middle East.

Indeed, the cost of a desalination project for 10,000 people equals the cost of one tank, and a project for 100,000 people costs about the same as a jet fighter aircraft. It is cheaper to invest in desalination of brackish water, seawater, or recycled sewage water than to try to settle disputes over available water sources, most of them already overused. Similarly, diversion of water from one place to another is much more expensive than the development of new technology for cheaper desalination.[43]

Globally, the major proportion of desalination capacity is already installed in the Middle East: Saudi Arabia has 26.8 percent of the world desalination capacity; Kuwait, 10.5 percent, the United Arab Emirates, 10 percent (in comparison, the United States has 12 percent). Arab countries also top the list in installation of major desalination plants rated at more than 4,000 cubic meters a day (m^3/d) per unit, and they continue to be the most important buyers. Close to 70 percent of the world's desalination plants are located in the Middle East, in the area from Algeria to Iran.[44] Israel desalinates 4 million cubic meters per year (m^3/yr) in thirty-three desalination units, scattered in twenty-three places all over the country, thus supplying 0.2 percent of its total water consumption.[45]

Concerning the costs of desalination, the cost of one major desalination plant which can produce 0.25 billion m^3/yr, is about $1 billion ($600–700 million for basic overhead, with about $250 million required over a period of fifteen years of operating expenses). This means that the needs of Jordan, Israel, and the West Bank could be met by two plants, which together could produce 0.5 billion m^3/yr of water, at a cost of $2 billion. Although this option is promising, one needs to keep in mind, however, that costs of desalination come to 25 cents per m^3, which is higher than the 15 cents Israeli farmers currently pay. These calculations are admittedly theoretical, and therefore in practice real costs might actually be significantly higher. We do know for certain, however, that commercial companies offer to desalinate seawater for 65 cents per m^3, and brackish water for 45 cents.[46]

At the beginning of 1990 there were 70,000 desalination plants worldwide, purifying 13 million m^3/d, or more than 4 billion m^3/yr. Desalination today is a viable option for regular domestic use, and not only for island-resort or oil-rich states. Especially advanced technologies are applied nowadays in desalination of both brackish water and seawater, making the process more and more economical and commercially feasible, while saving both energy and work and enabling longer membrane life.[47] Desalination of brackish water, rather than seawater, enables the use of solar energy ponds and parabolic mirrors (technology used in the production of solar energy) rather than burning oil for energy production.[48]

A word of caution is necessary, however. Despite the potential cost reduction involved in use of large plants, it is not reasonable to expect that desalination can solve the problem of water supply for agriculture in the near future. For the time being, desalination will serve mainly household and some industrial water supply requirements.[49] Most countries in the region also receive intensive solar radiation that can be used domestically, though until now it has been used mainly for rooftop heaters for homes. In addition, the use of solar ponds for the production of electric energy is already a proven technology. In both fields—desalination and use of solar energy for power production—sufficient knowhow exists in the area, whether among private companies or research institutes.

A few consecutive dry years have emphasized even more strongly the gravity of the Middle East problem. It is no wonder that desalination, notwithstanding its limitations, has assumed a central place in negotiations and all future development schemes. For we can even project a scenario whereby the country that builds a desalination plant, thereby enlarging the regional water supply, exhibits greater flexibility over natural resources, and could induce a positive chain reaction of tension reduction in the area.[50]

CONCLUSION

As we have seen, the combining of national water systems in the Middle East is virtually an impossible task. Likewise, the barriers to diversion of the Mediterranean or the Red Sea into the Dead Sea are insurmountable: international concord that would be required does not exist. Diversion of rivers, that is, national assets, as well as the relinquishment of agriculture and consequent dependence on foreign food producers are, again, unfeasible. As for recycling water: can yield only marginal quantities. Hence, in an area where all the available water sources are being used close to exhaustion, the only remaining option is independent desalination projects. Perhaps a generation from now we will possess economical technology for the mass desalination of water.

However, time is of the essence, decisions made now to implement water schemes will begin bearing fruit only in decades, and in some cases planning horizons can extend up to fifty years! Therefore, updated assessments of water experts that the two previous water-rich winters in the Middle East, plus conservation measures such as reduction of waste in irrigation, phasing-out of water-intensive crops, and price increases toward real value, have postponed the water crisis ought not to draw us into lethargy.[51] For it is still expected that critical shortages will emerge within ten to fifteen years. We have been granted a reprieve before the great crisis but not an annulment. We need to utilize this reprieve to our benefit by choosing our options and planning now.

Neither time, money, nor hope then should be wasted on regional water development projects. Even if cooperation were politically feasible, the region's water needs are growing to such an extent that in any case there will not be enough water to go around. The conclusion, therefore, is to help each of the Middle East states to act independently and desalinate as much water as possible.

NOTES

1. Peter Greswell, *Environment. An Alphabetical Handbook* (London: John Murray, 1971), p. 268.

2. Thomas Naff and Ruth C. Matson, eds., *Water in the Middle East: Conflict or Cooperation* (Boulder, Colo., and London: Westview Press, 1984), p. 26.

3. Ibid., pp. 71–72. In 1951, the highest consumption of electricity in Lebanon was in December. In 1964, because of a sharp rise in air-conditioning, the highest consumption shifted to the month of August. However, the lowest flow of water in Lebanon's rivers also occurs in August. As a result, more water than planned is diverted for the production of hydroelectricity and less water is left for agriculture.

4. Uzeyir Garih, aide-memoire (Istanbul, March 14, 1991). Garih is a Turkish businessman and owner of the Turkish company ALARKO.

5. Statement by the World Bank Delegation, Middle East Peace Process, Multilateral Talks, The Water Working Group, Washington, D.C., September 15–16, 1992, p. 1.

6. Eugene Linden, "The Last Precious Drops," *Time* (November 5, 1990).

7. Ibid.

8. Statement by the World Bank Delegation, p. 2.

9. Linden, "The Last Precious Drops."

10. On the two superpowers' security regimes, see Gordon A. Craig and Alexander L. George, *Force and Statecraft* (New York: Oxford University Press, 1990), pp. 263–265.

11. Joyce R. Starr, "Water Wars," *Foreign Policy* (Spring 1991), 30; Israeli Foreign Ministry, Multilateral Talks, The Water Working Group, Washington, D.C., September 15–17, 1992, p. 29.

12. John Kolars, "Water in the Middle East: 1990," summary presented to the U.S. House Committee on Foreign Affairs, Sub-Committee on Europe and the Middle East, Washington, D.C., June 26, 1990. Kolars is a professor of geography and Near Eastern studies at the University of Michigan, Ann Arbor.

13. Ibid.

14. Ibid.

15. For the situation in Egypt see Arnon Soffer, *Rivers of Fire. The Conflict of Water in the Middle East* [Hebrew] (Tel Aviv: Am Oved Publishers and Haifa University Press, 1992), p. 64.

16. David Nordell, "The Wet War," *Scopus* (magazine of the Hebrew University of Jerusalem) 41 (1991): 40–45.

17. Joyce R. Starr, press conference, National Press Club, Washington, D.C., October 7, 1991.

18. On the data bank, see Israel Foreign Ministry, The Water Working Group, Washington, D.C., September 15–17, 1992, p. 8; ibid., paper by the American Delegation ("Good Data: The Key to Effective Water Planning"); James W. Moore, "Water-Sharing Regimes in Israel and the Occupied Territories—A Technical Analysis," Ottawa, Dept. of National Defence, Operational Research and Analysis Establishment, Project Report 609, August 1992, p. 12 ("collection of an accurate hydrological data base . . . is one of the first critical tasks.")

19. Water potential per capita is all the known quantity of water resources divided by the number of people in a given area. The results are temporal because of the continuous growth of populations. The results could also be misleading because not all the water resources are actually usable.

20. Naff and Matson, *Water in the Middle East,* p. 53.

21. Ibid., p. 91; Soffer, *Rivers of Fire,* p. 27. The GAP, the Southeastern Anatolia Project, is planned to supply 45 percent of Turkey's hydroelectricity. See also Ali Ihsan Bagis, *GAP: Southeastern Anatolia Project—The Cradle of Civilisation Regenerated*, Istanbul, 1989.

22. Naff and Matson, ibid., p. 148.

23. Ibid., p. 174.

24. Gershon Baskin, "The West Bank and Israel's Water Crisis," in Baskin, ed., *Water: Conflict or Cooperation* [Israel/Palestine Center for Research and Information (I.P.C.R.I.)], 1, no. 2 (May 1992); The Palestinian Delegation, Statement to the Middle East Peace Multilateral Negotiations, Working Group on Water Resources, Vienna, May 13, 1992, p. 5.

25. Haim Gvirtzman, *Ha'aretz*, weekend supplement (January 31, 1992) [Hebrew].

26. Israeli Foreign Ministry, Multilateral Talks, The Water Working Group, Washington, D.C., September 15–17, 1992, pp. 18–20.

27. Starr, "Water Wars," p. 26.

28. Baskin, "The West Bank and Israel's Water Crisis."

29. Yoav Vizel and Lev Fishelzon, eds., *Ecology: Man and His Environment* (Tel Aviv: The University of Tel Aviv, 1982), p. 234 [Hebrew].

30. Ministry of Environment, *Environment Affairs in Israel: Annual Report No. 16, January–December 1989*, Jerusalem, 1990, pp. 366–367 [Hebrew].

31. From 3,265 grams in 1975–1976 to 12 grams per unit in 1984. Ministry of Environment, *Environment Affairs in Israel: Annual Report No. 15, April 1987–December 1988*, Jerusalem, 1989, p. 372 [Hebrew].

32. Ibid.

33. The Israeli daily *Ha'aretz* (July 22, 1993; August 13, 1993; August 24, 1993).

34. Starr, "Water Wars," p. 23.

35. Ibid., pp. 22–23.

36. Elisha Kali, *Water in Peace* (Tel Aviv: Sifriyat Poalim and The University of Tel Aviv, 1989), p. 49 [Hebrew].

37. The Turkish daily *Hurriyet* (June 28, 1990). See also the Turkish daily *Gunash* (September 26, 1990; *Mideast Mirror* (October 8, 1991).

38. Letter of James A. Cran, president, Medusa Corporation Inc., to the Turkish daily *Milliyet* (September 7, 1993). See also George Gruen, "Contribution of Water Imports to Israeli-Palestinian-Jordanian Peace," paper presented at the First Israeli-Palestinian Academic Conference on Water, Zurich, Switzerland, December 10–13, 1992, pp. 10–11. Israel revealed interest in buying 400 million m^3/yr from the Manavgat project. (The river yields 4.7 billion m^3/yr.) The water was to be imported to Israel by supertanker or by the "medusa" balloon bags. The Medusa Corporation calculates that shipping the water by its bags would be only one-eighth the cost of using supertankers ($0.20 for each m^3 of the first 250 million m^3) (letter of Medusa president to *Milliyet*).

39. Kamran Inan, *Gunaydin* (Turkish newspaper) (August 27, 1991).

40. ALARKO, "Manavgat Project Water Report," May 23, 1991. The sale price for a cubic meter of water from the Manavgat River is here estimated at $0.20–0.25.

41. Turkish paper on "Cooperation on Water Resources in the Middle East," The Middle East Multilateral Negotiations Working Group on Water Resources, Vienna, May 13–15, 1992. In Israeli Foreign Ministry, Multilateral Talks, The Water Working Group.

42. The term *Marshall Plan* was first used in regard to Middle East water by the Turkish businessman, Uzier Garih, in a memo to the Israeli Foreign Ministry, May 23, 1991.

43. State of Israel, Water Commission, "Proposals for Development of Water Resources in the Middle East: The Israeli View," Moscow, January 1992.

44. Klaus Wangnick, *1990 IDA [International Desalination Association] Worldwide Desalting Plant Inventory*, Report no. 11, Wangnick Consulting, Gnarrenburg, Germany, 1991, pp. 17, 38.

45. Pinchas Glueckstern, "Cost Estimates of Large RO [Reserve Osmosis] Systems," *Desalination,* 81 (1991): 49–56.

46. Soffer, *Rivers of Fire,* p. 220; *World Media no. 4* and *Ha'aretz* [Hebrew] (July 1992), pp. 45–46.

47. Pinchas Glueckstern, "Desalination: Options and Costs," *Water and Irrigation Review,* 11, no. 4 (February 1992), pp. 13–14.

48. Solar energy works well for desalinating brackish water. For desalinating seawater—much more salty than brackish water—oil-burning energy is needed at temperatures higher than those produced by solar energy.

49. Glueckstern, "Desalination," p. 16.

50. Soffer, *Rivers of Fire,* pp. 221–222.

51. Joyce Starr has written recently that "contrary to popular assumptions, the Middle East and North Africa are not confronting overall water shortages. In fact, water consumption for all uses remains less than available freshwater." And Dan Zaslavsky, formerly the Israeli Water Commissioner, has called the Middle Eastern water crisis "a myth." He added that "There are local and temporary shortages because it's not the highest priority of the countries involved; that's all, nothing else." For Starr, see Joyce R. Starr, "Middle East Water Security Framework: Historic Opportunity for Regional Stability and Sustainable Development," presented for Cooperative Water Management in the Middle East, Washington, D.C., Global Water Summit Initiative, June 17, 1992, p. 6. For Zaslavsky, see Priit J. Vesilind, "Middle East Water Critical Resource," *National Geographic,* 185, no. 5 (May 1993), p. 62.

CHAPTER 11

From Boycott to Limited Scientific and Technological Cooperation

Gil Feiler

Science and technology are two of the most important tools for increasing productivity and exploiting the economic aspects of land and labor.[1] The search for scientific and technological progress is usually undertaken as part of each country's effort to advance its own self-interest. Nevertheless, where international cooperation exists to pursue common aims, this inevitably leads to increased mutual interdependence and therefore a better understanding of one's partners. In the Middle East, personal interactions at both government and private levels will help break down the psychological barriers that separate Arabs and Israelis. The combination of all these factors will, in the long term, lead to increased security.

Two opposing views have considered[2] how states should provide security for themselves. The realist view argues that states should arm themselves to deter wars, if possible, and to fight them, if necessary. The idealists, on the other hand, argue that recurrent warfare reveals the impotence of traditional diplomacy; they reject balance of power politics and advocate forging a comprehensive system of peace based on collective security. One step before the ideal of utopian collective security is the attempt by some to explore more cooperative efforts to provide national security by recognizing that conflicting national interests are often mixed with other more compatible interests and goals that can sustain some form of international cooperation.

States recognize that they often have powerful interests in cooperation and exchange. The search for scientific and technological cooperation advocated in this chapter falls within the category of a less than utopian ideal, but one that with some effort and mutual will is within the grasp of the states of the Middle East.

One of the main issues that must be resolved is the creation of institutions to capture potential gains from cooperation, while minimizing the dangers of deception and nonperformance. In the case of the Middle East these dangers will be minimized by the very real advantages to be gained by mutual cooperation as already proven by the Egyptian example described later, and performance can to a certain extent be guaranteed by the supervision of international bodies and cooperation funds established perhaps by the United States and the United Nations.

Despite these hopes it is clear that the realist element of this neo-liberal view will always have some force: For at least the foreseeable future the security of the states of the region, in terms of building arms and deterrence structures, will have primary importance. The cooperation advocated here can only pave the way for a better understanding in the future which, in the long term, will have an effect on the mutual security relationships of these countries.

Thus, the first steps in cooperation between Israel and its Arab neighbors, at least in the fields of science and technology, can be taken even without the signing of a formal peace treaty, and indeed some such steps have already been taken as will be described later.

This chapter discusses the potential for scientific and technological cooperation between Israel and the Arab states in the postboycott era. Egypt's role in this endeavor is particularly important for two reasons: first, because of Egypt's position as one of the leading economies in the Arab world, and second, because of the already existing framework for cooperation established by the Camp David Accords.

Following a brief review of the boycott, this chapter will consider the potential for scientific and technological cooperation in the Middle East in the light of the changes exemplified by the peace process. The current scientific cooperation that exists between Israel and Egypt is given particular attention.

THE ARAB BOYCOTT

Economic sanctions have been defined as the deliberate, government inspired withdrawal or threat of withdrawal of customary trade or financial relations. Alternatively, sanctions are sometimes regarded as tools used to coerce target governments into particular responses and are premised on the country operating the sanctions as being willing and able to interfere in the internal affairs of the target government.[1]

The Arab boycott of Israel does not quite fit either of these two categories. Historically, the Arab boycott has been motivated by an Arab desire to obstruct the development of Israel and at the same time keep Israel constantly before the Arab people as a unifying issue. No Arab country has ever seriously proposed discontinuing the boycott, although it has operated at different levels of intensity by different countries of the Arab League.[ÅÅ]

Israel's $4 billion annual deficit with the EEC and the low level of investment by European and Japanese financial institutions may be attributed to the boycott, although some analysts have suggested that the boycott has no real effect.[5] On a global level, studies have shown that sanctions will reduce income in the country imposing them but are unlikely to cause maximum economic dislocation in the target country, and indeed most attempts at sanctions—Poland, Panama, and South Africa are a few examples—have had limited effects and even, on occasion, a damaging effect on weak and untargeted communities of the country being sanctioned.[6]

A number of reasons have been given for the failure of sanctions to change the behavior of target countries. Such reasons may include their unifying effect on the target country; that is to say, resulting in popular support for the government and searches for commercial alternatives, or in some cases, the sanctions may result in powerful allies of the target country lending economic support—as happened to some extent between Israel and the United States.[7]

Probably both these reasons have played some part in the failure of the Arab boycott against Israel. Israel's refusal to succumb to such pressure and some measure of support abroad has meant that there is no realistic prospect of the boycott altering Israel's policies in any way, although, as already noted, Israel's economy has suffered serious damage as a result of the boycott.

In the period following the Gulf War, the issue of the boycott has been linked by the Group of Seven (G-7), with the strong support of Egypt, to the settlement issue. This move gave tacit recognition to the legitimacy of the boycott as an economic weapon, and undermined what had previously been acknowledged as the illegality of at least the secondary and tertiary boycott in the eyes of international law. It also eliminated any hope of a unilateral end to the operation of the boycott. The declaration by the G-7 also eased pressure on the Gulf states to cancel the boycott as a gesture of thanks to the United States after the war, and indeed they have openly declared that they will end the embargo only when Israel stops its settlement policy.

Although a broad front of organizations, Jewish and non-Jewish, has been working to end the boycott, little national legislation has been passed making such activity illegal. The United States has enacted comprehensive antiboycott laws and some efforts have been made by a number of West European countries to also legislate antidiscriminatory laws, although without the same enthusiasm or success. Most European and Far East countries however have no such laws on their statute books, with the result that the issue of compliance with the boycott has been left to the discretion of individual persons and companies.

The reluctance of individual European countries to enact antiboycott legislation has also been reflected within the framework of the EEC, which has consistently refused to consider initiating legislation and has preferred to leave any action to the individual member states, although in a recent breakthrough the European Parliament did indeed order the preparation of a detailed report on the boycott issue.

ECONOMIC COOPERATION

The cultural and economic differences between Israel and the Arab states of the Middle East point to the wide range of possibilities for scientific and technological cooperation between these countries. Nevertheless, in the light of traditional enmities in the area and existing political circumstances that preclude the possibility of open collaboration between Israel and the Arab states (with the exception of Egypt—although it should be noted that during the period since the signing of the Camp David Accords with Egypt, there have been a number of instances in which Egypt complied with the boycott), it is generally recognized that the most that can reasonably be anticipated is limited cooperation in areas which will be of obvious mutual benefit to the countries concerned. Examples of less controversial areas of potential cooperation include education, water resources, agriculture, health, energy and environmental sciences.

Following the Camp David Accords numerous plans were drafted for Israeli-Egyptian scientific and technological cooperation, particularly with a view to Israeli scientists providing assistance to their Egyptian counterparts. Israeli scientists have traditionally been willing to expand cooperation both for its scientific advantages and for the symbolic and political gains involved. On the other hand, a number of factors that will be considered later have led Egypt to give a lower priority to bilateral cooperation with Israel, while, clearly, the other Arab states will be willing to openly pursue such ventures only within the framework of a general peace agreement. On a less public level, some Arab countries do engage in economic activities with Israel, as will be discussed.

Since the creation of the Arab League in 1945, a number of pan-Arab conferences have considered the issues of development in the Arab world. A general consensus has been reached in these gatherings on the need for a stable scientific and technological base that will influence economic and social development.[8] This need has been reflected in individual development programs published by most of the countries of the Arab world, although in practice little has been done in most of the Arab states to close the gap between rhetorical declarations of intent and the reality of an underfinanced and underdeveloped industrial base.

Nevertheless, the 1970s did see a significant change in the technology and economy of both the oil producing and non-oil producing Arab states. Income from oil, totaling $1,100 billion in the decade between 1974–1983,[9] enabled the oil producing states to import knowhow, managerial skills, and personnel, on a massive scale, usually on a turnkey basis. Commencing with American engineering assistance and services and followed shortly afterward by West European and Japanese technology, exports from the industrial countries to the 15 Islamic states climbed from $5.5 billion in 1970 to about $100 billion in 1982.[10] In addition, the Arab governments turned their attention to the institutes of higher education and research establishments in an effort to encourage scientific research,[11] with the result that the ratio of scientists and engineers to each 100,000 population has increased sharply since the oil boom and currently stands at 523/100,000, a figure comparable to that found in most of the developing countries.[12]

In recent years Egypt has become increasingly aware of the importance of science in the development and proper exploitation of the country's natural resources. Nevertheless, despite great progress, the Egyptian economy has remained agrarian and unsophisticated, with most scientific activity focusing on agriculture, irrigation and control of the Nile River waters.[13] The agricultural sector employs about 38 percent of the labor force, and its portion of GDP totals about 20 percent.[14]

Egyptian industry, which employs about 14 percent of the labor force, has also failed to expand in spite of government efforts. Industry, like agriculture, is based on cheap, mass labor and suffers from poor investment planning, lack of capital, and backward technology. Industrial production (excluding oil) is concentrated in textiles and food,[15] although the government has succeeded in establishing a number of heavy industries: iron, steel, aluminium and a developing fertilizer industry. However, these industries are still small and the overall industrial successes of Egypt are limited. Egyptian industrial exports totaled $588 million in 1986, compared to Israeli industrial exports of $6.052 billion in the same year.[16]

The Egyptian government succeeded in eradicating illiteracy in large segments of the population and established an extensive university system for the masses. Nevertheless, the rate of illiteracy in Egypt still stands at 50 percent compared to about 7 percent in Israel. At the same time the Egyptian universities produce more graduates than the economy can absorb, and the majority of these graduates specialize in the humanities as opposed to science, biology, or technology. After leaving university, many of the graduates join the ranks of the unemployed or seek work in the Gulf states.[17] Of the science and technology graduates less than 2 percent become involved in research and development, and Egypt spends only about 0.30 percent of her gross national product on R&D. It is interesting to note that the United Nations recommends that each state should devote 1 percent of GNP for R&D.

Scientific and technological activities in Israel are of major importance in advancing her national aims—whether in the fields of medicine, national security, absorption of immigrants, social welfare, or economic development. Despite her small size, Israel is one of the leading countries of the developed world in areas of new technology and progressive scientific thought.

Through to the mid-1980s it has been estimated that Israel allocated about 3 percent of her national product to research and development (including defense)—one of the highest proportions in the world. Calculations made in the years 1988–1990, at the time when Israel was putting intense effort into the development of the Lavi aircraft, outlays on R&D actually rose to 4.2–4.8 percent of the Israeli GNP, of which defense accounted for half. As with most Western states, the industrial sector in Israel (including the defense industry) provides the source of most R&D: 61 percent in industry, 29 percent in universities, and 9 percent in government agencies.[18]

Compared to the Egyptian economy, the Israeli economy is modern, concentrating on industry and services. Although only 6 percent of the labor market works in agriculture, the level of scientific-technological expertise in this area is one of the highest in the world. Approximately 25 percent of the labor force is employed in industry, the most prominent sector of which is complex electronics. Recently, intense efforts have also been directed toward other high-technology industries such as computers and biotechnology. Sluggishness has, however, been felt recently in the agricultural and industrial sectors, attributed in part to a slowdown in scientific research.

Despite the clear cultural, economic and technological difference between Israel and Egypt, some similarities of purpose may be found. Until recently Israel, too, was a developing country; methods used in Israel for providing professional and technical education include components suitable for Egypt. Egypt, too, may offer methods applicable to mutual problems. For example, in the construction industry, a number of problems are endemic to the region, particularly the issue of building in dry climates. In Israel, Jordan, and Egypt, governmental and research institutions deal with housing problems and attempt to encourage fast, mass and cheap housing in what are fundamentally desert conditions.[19] Exchange of information and cooperation in research could be of great practical benefit to each of the participants and at the same time lead to closer relations between the countries. One need only remember in this connection the exchange program for scientists organized by the Weizmann Institute in Israel and the Max-Planck Society in Germany at the end of the 1950s, which paved the way for the institution of diplomatic relations between the two countries five years after the establishment of the program.[20] Another example of scientific cooperation leading to closer ties with a traditionally unfriendly country is provided by the recent establishment of the Israeli academic center in China.

Cooperation between Israel and Egypt within the framework of the Camp David Accords has already achieved results both in practical scientific terms and in the context of building mutual trust between the scientists concerned. These successes have relied to a certain extent on the participation of American universities and American funding (through the United States Agency for International Aid). Initially, at the wish of Egypt, contacts between Israeli and Egypt scientists were conducted through the U.S. Agency of International Development; more recently, contacts have been direct, although out of the public eye.

The first and most successful of the three major joint Israeli-Egyptian projects, which have evolved as a result of the Camp David Accords, relates to research in marine science. Planning of the project commenced in 1978 and the first cooperative agreement was reached in 1980. The program attacked two issues of great importance for both countries: the production of fish and the erosion of the coastline. The purpose of the project is to enhance the supply of nourishment and the coast line management—aspects of the project included lake management, shore protection, and fish nutrition.[21]

The second group of projects concerns the health sciences. Egyptian and Israeli universities are investigating five regional diseases with the objective of preventing these diseases through scientifically based control strategies. More than 200 scientists and graduate students from both countries have worked on various segments of the project, and more than sixty scientific papers have already been written in connection with it.[22]

The third venture consists of joint agricultural projects. One program, the cooperative arid lands agricultural research project (CALAR), was founded in 1981, and combines agricultural and industrial development. The second project is the trinational agricultural technology exchange project, which was founded in 1984. The main object of this project is to increase food production. More than 300 scientists and working technical staff participate in these two programs and both have achieved significant results.[23]

A number of successful cooperative projects have been discussed already, however, political tensions have led the parties to engage in only limited cooperation; Egyptian scientists have displayed reluctance to enter into cooperative ventures with Israel. The cold relations with Israel and Egyptian displeasure with Israel's policies in the administered territories have prevented rapid progress toward scientific cooperation, and indeed the Egyptian government has itself often directed Egyptian scientists to refrain from joint ventures with Israel until complete normalization of relations has taken place.

Apart from the political obstacles, other reasons lie at the back of Egyptian reserve. Some Egyptian scientists believe that Israel has little if anything to offer Egypt. They argue that Egypt has at its command some of the best infrastructure and skilled personnel in the Middle East. Any shortfall lies only in the areas of financing and ways of exporting surplus labor, not in the need for consultation and cooperation with foreign experts from Israel. Some Egyptian scientists have even expressed the fear that cooperation would end with some form of Israeli control of the Egyptian economy. Another section of the Egyptian scientific community thinks that benefit may be derived from cooperation with Israel in areas in which Israel has developed expertise; particularly in the fields of electronics, agriculture, medicine and research of arid zones.[24]

Egyptian sensitivity to Israeli scientific and technological superiority has resulted in a rejectionist attitude, aggravated by Egyptian misinterpretation of the initial Israeli excitement at the possibility of entering into cooperative ventures with Egypt.

Egyptian reservations, particularly toward the end of the 1980s, were also increased by concern at the possibility of damaging relations with the Arab oil states. Despite the severing of political ties between Egypt and the Arab states, which lasted until the end of the 1980s, the Arab world continued to inject money into and import scientific and technological personnel from Egypt. Many Egyptians are employed in the oil states and vast numbers more wished to become so. All of these fear that strengthened ties with Israel will imperil their chances of employment in the lucrative labor markets of the Gulf states.

Therefore, the key questions are these: Why should Egypt be interested in developing cooperative ties with Israel? What can Israel offer Egypt that could not be more easily obtained in the United States and Europe?

A number of problem areas, of special relevance to the region, may be listed in which Israel has displayed particularly good technological ability. The exploitation of water resources and growing produce in arid areas are such examples. Nevertheless, it cannot be said that Israel has exclusive expertise in any field, and none of the areas of interest mentioned previously can be said to be at the top of Egypt priorities. The real motive for cooperation must therefore lie in its political-symbolic value, with the economic motives providing added incentive and support.

Apart from the cooperative ventures with Egypt already mentioned, Israel has also secretly engaged in trade with other Arab states. Israeli high-tech products are being sold in Syria, Libya, Kuwait, and other states officially at war with Israel. To circumvent political barriers between Israel and Arab customers, a firm from a third country often serves as a gobetween. Israeli companies produce special batches of goods that bear no brand names. Such goods, which in part, reflect some of the most superior technology available in the world, include farm and irrigation equipment, plastic products and medical equipment; these are transferred from Israel to Arab countries by land through Jordan and Lebanon or by sea through Cyprus, Greece, Spain, Italy, and France. The secrecy of the deals makes it difficult to estimate the exact volume of trade; some researchers, however, estimate that Israeli annual exports to the Arab world total at least several hundred million dollars and may even be as high as $1 billion. The extent of the hidden trade makes it clear that if the borders were open, making trade between Israel and the Arab states politically acceptable, the amount of potential trade in goods and technology, as well as exchange of services, is vast.

In this connection it should also be noted that much scientific and technological knowhow is transferred from Israel to the Arab states through other channels, particularly through the offices of skilled Palestinian workers who leave Israel to work in the Arab labor market; thus avoiding direct contacts with Israel.

PROPOSALS FOR SCIENTIFIC COOPERATION

Areas of potential cooperation in the Middle East, on an institutional level, include the following:

1. Exchange of information—on matters such as resources, capabilities, research studies, institutions, and scientific programs.
2. Exchange visits, starting with private visits and ranging through student exchanges, exchange visits by researchers and experts in the public sector.
3. Finance of joint projects and development of scientific technological ability. For political reasons such projects may be conducted separately in the participating countries and be funded by a third party.

More specifically, cooperation may be fostered between institutions such as universities or scientific foundations, with coordination controlled by a bilateral council. Such a council would coordinate, initiate, and encourage mutual contacts, determine classes of projects, and assist in deciding the nature, extent, and direction of the bilateral coordination. The council could also design the overall strategy of the cooperative venture, recommend sources of funding, arrange meetings and committees and the like.

Establishment of regional institutions for scientific and technological cooperation is an idea of vital importance, and numerous problems of regional significance could provide suitable material for research—such as desert agriculture, water and energy. Nevertheless, some caution must be exercised in determining the class of projects, because it is precisely these matters of regional concern that would be regarded as sensitive by national and pan-Arab elements.

Indeed, it is questionable whether initially it would not be better to put aside the idea of the creation of new regional cooperative bodies, which would inevitably be the subject of suspicion during the first years, and instead arrange for Israel's acceptance as a member or observer of already existing organizations, such as the Conference of Arab and Other Ministers for the Implementation of Scientific and Technological Developments and ALESCO, despite the negligible success shown by these organizations to date.

From the preceding it would seem that emphasis should be laid upon organizing cooperative ventures between existing establishments in the participating countries. Such contacts might maximize results in the short term, although the benefits of setting up new regional councils—with their symbolic value and practical importance as a source of research material for third party countries, as well as their function as a channel for funding—would be lost.

In any event, at this stage, prior to the establishment of peace between Israel and all its Arab neighbors, it would seem viable to set up a joint Egypt-Israeli research body, which would be open to membership to all interested countries at a later time. To avoid unnecessary difficulties such a body should be located in Egypt and not in Israel.

At this stage it is almost impossible to estimate the cost of any of these options, although it is clear that costs may range from the negligible for exchange visits to millions of dollars for joint projects. As a first step in setting up any joint venture, sources of funds should be sought.

Two options might prove suitable even in the absence of a formal peace agreement:

1. Establishment of a broad regional development fund.
2. Establishment of smaller regional development funds, which would be open to any country, including those outside the region.

There is little doubt that the United States would contribute to such funds, in view of their importance for regional stability. Participation by the member states of the European Community may also be expected; Japan, with its high dependence on Arab oil and interest in the stability of the area, is another potential partner, especially in the context of Japan's interest in taking part in the ongoing peace process.

The United States would have a central role to play in any cooperative venture with Egypt or in the region as a whole.[25] The United States has offered to provide the major part of the funds needed for such a project and, indeed, even today, both Israel and Egypt regard the United States as their most important partner in bilateral treaties on cooperation in scientific and technological matters, with, in each case, structures already in place for coordinated decision making.

A few areas of general importance to the region, which could be the subject of substantive cooperative research, have already been mentioned. In slightly more detail, the list may be categorized under seven main headings:

1. *Agriculture,* including development of the desert, production of crops not vulnerable to saline, studies in halting the spread of the desert, marine farming and irrigation.
2. *Health,* including environmental studies, epidemiology, developing professional skills and health services.
3. *Earth sciences,* including geology, marine geochemistry and limnology, oceanography of the Red Sea, stratography and mapping, gas and oil searches, mining, geophysical searches and ground water studies.
4. *Remote sensing,* for geological and agricultural mapping purposes.
5. *Sea sciences,* with a view to conserving the ecology of the Gulf of Aqaba, as well as pollution and water purifying studies.
6. *Meteorology,* including exchanging data for forecasting purposes, air pollution studies and climatology.
7. *Education,* including exchange of information and students between educational institutions, cooperation with respect to similar educational problems, improvement in teacher training in the fields of science and mathematics, innovations in state curricula, improvements in supplementary education and prevention of a brain drain.

CONCLUSIONS

One of the key questions posed by this chapter has been whether scientific and technological cooperation between Israel and its Arab neighbors is possible in the absence of a formal peace treaty. It has been suggested that the advantages to be gained by cooperation are such as to provide adequate incentives to traditionally hostile parties to temporarily set aside their ideological differences. Because it is easier to achieve scientific and technological cooperation than political cooperation, efforts should be devoted primarily toward that goal.

On the other hand, scientific cooperation need not necessarily warm the political relations between the parties, as the example of the scientific and technological cooperation between Israel and Egypt has shown; and indeed, the hidden trade relations between Israel and the Arab world further support this argument.

There is ample room for increased cooperation between Israel and the Arab world. Although each country is able to conduct research or buy technology without having to deal with its neighbors, there is no doubt that cooperation may be of mutual benefit, by enabling a sharing of expertise and by reducing tension in the region. Clearly caution must be exercised in choosing the subject matter of joint research so as not to aggravate the traditional suspicions that exist on both sides; instead, the aim should be to solve common problems while at the same time ensuring that each country participates equally and each country benefits equally.

This chapter began by considering the motivation behind the Arab boycott of Israel. Against such a background, regional scientific cooperation seems possible on only the most limited scale. The after-effects of the Gulf War have confirmed this assessment. The Arab boycott is still operating on its primary and secondary levels, to Israel's detriment. Despite the recent rush of international companies to Israel and the rapproachment Israel has reached with many Asian and other countries since the Gulf War, the boycott continues to have a chilling effect on the willingness of international businesspeople to trade with, or invest in, Israel. Small and middle-sized companies, in particular, are easily intimidated by Arab suitors.

Since the end of the Gulf War, Arab leaders have made vague commitments to the United States and other Western leaders about dropping, at least, the secondary boycott. But they have also insisted that Israel meet several conditions, such as ending settlement in the territories. Where Israel has complied, Arab leaders have consistently found new reasons for maintaining the boycott. Despite the recent Israeli–PLO agreement (September 1993), Arab leaders now say an end to the boycott can come only after more Israeli territorial withdrawal, resolution of Jerusalem's status, an agreement on water resources, and dismantling of Israel's nuclear capability. Although Kuwait announced that it would no longer apply a blacklist to foreign firms that have ties with Israel (secondary boycott), U.S. Department of Commerce statistics indicate that Kuwait (and Saudi Arabia) remain the countries of origin for the highest number of boycott compliance requests sent to U.S. companies. Ironically, the primary boycott appears to be weakening faster than the blacklist. Although illegal (with the exception of Egypt), Arab-Israel direct trade is developing rapidly; it appears that some Mideast businesses are not waiting for the politicians to come around on the boycott. Although the secondary boycott continues to deter Israeli trade expansion in the West, Israel-Arab trade is growing.

It is to be hoped that Arab recognition of the true needs of the region and the mutual benefits that can be gained by cooperation with Israel will obviate the need for such maneuvering on the international arena and will instead lead to a better understanding between the partners to such cooperation.

NOTES

I would like to express my gratitude to advocate Rahel Rimon for her kind assistance.

1. I. S. Rosing et al., *Science, Technology and Society* (London: Sage Publications, 1977); J. Schmookler, *Invention and Economic Growth*, (Cambridge, Mass.: Harvard University Press, 1966); E. Denison, *Why Growth Rates Differ*, (Washington, D.C.: Brookings Institution, 1967); R. Nelson et al., *Technology, Economic Growth and Public Policy* (Washington, D.C.: Brookings Institution, 1967); Ina Spiegel-Rosing and Derek De Solla Price, eds., *Science, Technology and Society* (London: Sage Publications, 1977); Jack Behrman, *Science and Technology for Development* (Cambridge, Mass.: Oelgeschlager, Gunn and Hain, 1980); Joseph Ben-David, *The Scientist's Role in Society* (Chicago: University of Chicago Press, 1984).

2. See Charles Lipson, "Are Security Regimes Possible? Historical Cases and Modern Issues" in this book.

3. Gary C. Hufbauer and Jeffrey J. Schott, *Economic Sanctions Reconsidered: History and Current Policy, Institute for International Economics*, (Washington, D.C.: Institute for International Economics, 1985), pp. 2, 9–10.

4. Robert W. Macdonald, *The League of Arab States: A Study in the Dynamics of Regional Organization*, (Princeton, N.J.: Princeton University Press, 1965), pp. 119–120.

5. Gil Feiler, "The Boycott: No End in Sight," *Jerusalem Post (JP)* (July 22, 1991); Feiler, "A Missed Opportunity to End the Boycott," *JP* (October 9, 1991).

6. William H. Kaemfer and Anton D. Lowenberg, "The Theory of International Economic Sanctions: A Public Choice Approach," *American Economic Review* 78 (September 1988): 786; Stefanie Ann Lenway,

"Between War and Commerce: Economic Sanctions as a Tool of Statecraft," *International Organizations* 42, no. 2 (1988): 397 (review article); Stanislaw S. Wasowski, "U.S. Sanctions Against Poland," *Washington Quarterly* 9, no. 2 (1986): 167; Charles M. Becker, "The Impact of Sanctions on South Africa and Its Periphery," *African Studies Review* 31, no. 2 (1988): 61; Paul Lansing and Sarosh Kuruvilla, "Business Divestment in South Africa: In Whose Best Interest?" *Journal of Business Ethics* (Netherlands) 7 (August 1988): 561.

7. Hufbauer and Schott, *Economic Sanctions Reconsidered*, pp. 10–12.

8. Ziauddin Sardar, *Science and Technology in the Middle East* (London and New York: Longman, 1982).

9. Gil Feiler, "The Decrease in Oil Prices and Its Effect on the Foreign Labour Force in the Middle East," *Middle East Focus* 9, no. 6 (1987): 13; *Arab Oil and Gas* 13, no. 307 (July 1, 1984): 4.

10. *Technology Transfer to the Middle East*, (Washington, D.C.: U.S. Congress, Office of Technology Assessment, OTA-ISC-173, September 1984), p. 4.

11. US Institute of International Education, *Open Doors* (annual publication, New York), various issues; National Science Foundation, *Science and Engineering Doctorates, 1960–1985*, (Washington, D.C.: Author, 1987).

12. Proceedings of the Roundtable on Science, Technology, and Development in the Arab World (Cambridge, Mass.: MIT, 1985); *Technological Manpower and Expenditure for Research and Experimental Development in Arab Countries* (UNESCO: Sc-76/CASTARAB/I, 1976).

13. A. B. Zahlan, "Planning Science in the Arab World," *Nature* 283 (January 17, 1980), p. 239.

14. International Labor Organization, *Statistical Year Book 1987* (Geneva: ILO, 1987), p. 50; World Bank, *World Development Report 1987* (published for The World Bank by Oxford University Press, 1987), p. 206.

15. World Bank, *World Development Report 1987* (published for The World Bank by Oxford University Press, 1987), p. 20; Arab Republic of Egypt, Central Agency for Public Mobilization and Statistics, *Statistical Year Book 1987* (Cairo: CAPMAS, June 1987), p. 71.

16. World Bank, *World Development Report 1988* (published for The World Bank by Oxford University Press, 1988), pp. 226–227, 248–249.

17. Gil Feiler, *The Number of Egyptian Workers in the Arab Oil Countries, 1974–1983: A Critical Discussion* (Tel Aviv: Tel Aviv University, Dayan Center for Middle Eastern and African Studies, October 1986).

18. Israel, Ministry of Science and Development, *Scientific Research in Israel 1986* (Jerusalem: Ministry of Science and Development, 1986), p. 20; and personal interviews.

19. See Gil Feiler, "Housing Policy in Egypt," *Middle Eastern Studies* 28, no. 2 (April 1992): 295–312.

20. S. Freier, "Science for Development in a Region at Peace," Paper presented at the Middle East Development Conference, Geneva, March 23–26, 1989.

21. *Middle East Regional Cooperation Programs*, hearing before the Subcommittee on Europe and the Middle East of the Committee on Foreign Affairs, House of Representatives, May 6, 1988 (Washington, D.C.: U.S. Government Printing Office, 1988), pp. 14–17; Texas A&M University Research, *Cooperative Marine Technology Program for the Middle East*, Sixth Annual Report, February 1990, 2 vols.

22. *Middle East Regional Cooperation Programs,* ibid., pp. 6–9.

23. A. S. El-Beltagy et al., "CALAR: The Cooperative Arid Lands Agriculture Research Program, Egypt, USA, Israel," *Arid Lands Newsletter*, no. 22 (September 1985), pp. 2–13; Harry R. Albers and Davene L. Gibson, "CALAR in Egypt and Israel," *Grants Magazine* 8, no. 1 (March 1985), pp. 9–16; CALAR Program, *Fodder Production and Utilization by Small Animals in Arid Regions* (Ben-Gurion University, Applied Research Institute, February 1983); Colin Norman, "Scientific Collaboration in the Middle East," *Science* 215 February 5, 1982), p. 639; Middle East Regional Cooperation Programs, hearing before the Subcommittee on Europe and the Middle East of the Committee on Foreign Affairs, House of Representatives, May 6, 1988 (Washington, D.C.: U.S. Government Printing Office, 1988), pp. 18–22, 46–75.

24. Gil Feiler, *Scientific and Technological Cooperation Between Israel and Egypt: Possibilities and Achievements* (Tel Aviv: Tel Aviv University, Armand Hammer Fund for Economic Cooperation in the Middle East, January 1991), p. 4 [Hebrew].

25. For the importance of U.S. institutions see Lieber, in this book.

PART 5

From Deterrence to Security Regimes

CHAPTER 12

The Arab-Israeli Relationship: From Deterrence to Security Regime

Efraim Inbar and Shmuel Sandler

INTRODUCTION

Israel in the 1990s faces a strategic environment characterized by continuing challenges to its security, but also by a political climate that might foster better relations with its neighbors. Despite the sobering effect of the 1991 Gulf War on many Arab states, we doubt whether a "new Middle East" has emerged. The continuities in the patterns of foreign policy behavior in the Middle East provide little hope for the ongoing peace process to result in a relationship such as that between Canada and the United States. It is totally unrealistic to expect the Arab states to have a relationship with Israel that is more cooperative than the current level of inter-Arab relations. The Middle East still exists in a different socio-political time zone than the West. It is an Islamic region undergoing a process of modernization, which releases various social forces including radical forms of Islam, and is beleaguered by internal as well as international instability. The Middle East still remains a region where the use of force is part and parcel of the rules of the game, and its use evokes remarkable popular support even when some of the goals entertained by local political leaders are quite radical.

Although the Middle East is not about to be transformed into what Karl Deutsch called a *security community*,[1] a more modest goal—a security regime between Israel and its neighbors—may be within reach. Such a relationship, as defined by the scholars of international regimes,[2] is less elusive than full peace in the Middle East because currently regional and worldwide changes seem to foster stability. Robert Jervis defined a *security regime* as "those principles, rules and norms that permit nations to be restrained in their behavior in the belief that others will reciprocate. This concept implies . . . a form of cooperation that is more than the following of short-run self-interest."[3] Despite the conceptual difficulties with this notion, it does involve a setting located in between a deterrence relationship, which characterized to a great extent the Arab- Israeli conflict in the past, and a security community, in which the option of war as a mechanism for resolving differences no longer exists.

Past experiences between Israel and its neighbors have not been totally negative concerning cooperation in security matters.[4] Yet, the most important change in the Middle East, from an Israeli perspective, is a greater acceptance by its Arab rivals, as the peace process started in October 1991 at Madrid demonstrates. The more the Arab states move away from revisionist positions and accept the status quo, the better are the chances for erecting politico-military arrangements that would lead to greater stability and to a decrease in the danger of war. If the Arab-Israeli relationship can be transformed into something like the Soviet-U.S. rivalry during the detente period, which was characterized by mutual recognition, diplomatic relations, and open channels of communication, then a security regime is within reach.

At this particular historical juncture, conditions are beginning to ripen for more collaboration than ever before between Israel and its Arab neighbors on security issues. Until now, Israel's strategic preference has been to establish a credible deterrent and the capacity for unilateral military measures. As its environment seems to change, the idea of a security regime constitutes not only an intellectual challenge but also a serious policy option.

This chapter will investigate the chances for greater Israeli interest in reliance on cooperative security arrangements and a transition to security regimes with its neighbors, in light of three considerations: (1) the changes in the international system; (2) the influence of the peace process between Israel and its neighbors on deterrence and on security regimes; and (3) the impact of regional perceptions and politico-military developments on Israel's ability and desire to act unilaterally. The discussion of these issues is preceded by a presentation of Israel's traditional reliance on a deterrence posture in the past and the threats it might face in the near future.

ISRAEL'S RELIANCE ON DETERRENCE

Israel has traditionally always preferred self-reliance and hoped to achieve a measure of security through deterrence. In contrast to its regional revisionist rivals, Israel has basically been from its inception a status quo power.[5] Because the Arab objective was politicide[6] (i.e., the destruction of the Jewish state), the situation approximated a zero-sum game, and little cooperation was expected in the area of security. In addition, the political and military leadership of the Jewish state realized that it could not compel the Arab states to accept its existence through the use of force. Therefore, deterring Arab schemes to destroy the Jewish state became Israel's goal. The expectation was that the Arabs would eventually see the futility of their military efforts and would reconcile themselves to the idea of having a Jewish state in their midst.

Deterrence seems to be a straightforward concept: the use of military threats to prevent an opponent from doing something (generally using force) that it regards as desirable. The threats should extract a cost that outweighs the benefits to be achieved by the presumed planned act. Therefore, an attempt is made to influence the opponent's strategic calculation with regard to its cost without the need for cooperative interaction. Deterrence is thus a unilateral policy, which assumes that the rival is a rational actor capable of calculating costs and benefits and of reading correctly the capability and the intent of the deterrer to implement the threats communicated.[7] Despite the methodological problems concerning deterrence, it is still a useful concept.[8] Furthermore, whatever armchair strategists have to say about deterrence, it has been and still is a central pillar in Israel's strategic thinking.[9] Obviously, it is affected by a complex interaction of factors such as Israel's perceived politico-military power, the regional balance of power, the policy priorities of Israel's rivals, and the role played by extraregional actors.

Despite being on the defensive at the strategic level, the Israel Defense Force (IDF) has been operationally offensive minded for a variety of reasons, including its need to materialize the threats to use force in both denial and punishing modes. The IDF has employed preemptive strikes primarily for denial, whereas retaliation constituted punishment.[10] Furthermore, in case of a major failure of deterrence, Israeli doctrine postulated that only a "decisive victory" (*hachra'a*) extracting considerable cost from the Arab side could restore deterrence. After 1973, this Israeli idiosyncratic term usually meant (1) a rapid penetration of enemy lines; (2) the destruction of a considerable part of the rival's arsenal; (3) the capture of enemy territory for bargaining purposes; and (4) that the first three components be achieved at a reasonable price in terms of personnel and material. A decisive Israeli victory is an imperative and constitutes the counterpart of deterrence in Israel's strategic thinking.

Although it is difficult to prove that deterrence works, it seems very plausible that in many instances Israel has succeeded in influencing the strategic calculations of the Arabs toward inaction.[11] Obviously, foolproof deterrence is not realistic because a highly motivated challenger cannot always be deterred. Indeed, there are instances when deterrence has failed. Terrorist activities have continued unabated. Other events include the 1967 closure of the Tiran Straits and the concentration of large Egyptian forces in the Sinai (both well-known Israeli casi belli); the surprise attack of October 1973; the introduction of Syrian SAMs into Lebanon in April 1981; and Iraqi missile attacks on Israel during the Gulf War. Surprisingly, the missile attacks are not universally accepted as a deterrence failure, though it is very clear that they had been preceded by a series of explicit Israeli threats. Iraqi behavior actually demonstrated that under certain circumstances (not necessarily unique) Israeli threats are ineffective. The failures of deterrence can be explained by either one or a concatenation of the following reasons: the ability of Israel to extract costs outweighing benefits is questioned; the Israeli intention, will power, or its freedom to act is questioned; and the Arabs' willingness to pay costs is higher than expected, primarily when the status quo is politically unbearable.

In the post-1973 period, deterrence was used mainly in the context of preventing a large-scale war, one involving an Arab invasion of Israeli controlled territories. Yet Israel has threatened—publicly or tacitly—to use its force in the case of additional contingencies.[12] It is widely believed that the Israeli nuclear program, in combination with Israel's conventional power, deter any plan to destroy the Jewish state by a large-scale conventional attack. Possibly, Israel's nuclear option has deterred the Iraqis from using chemical weapons against Israel.[13] This could well be true, but other types of military challenges are obviously not influenced by nuclear weapons or conventional preponderance. Although deterrence at the strategic level is in all probability relatively simple, deterrence of conflict at the lower levels of the violence spectrum is highly context dependent and is therefore more problematic.[14]

As a matter of fact, uses of force against Israel short of an all-out attack can have devastating results; for example, a short Syrian advance into Israeli-held territory or a stationary war of attrition, both intent on bleeding Israel. Syria, in contrast to today's Egypt, is dissatisfied with the status quo and retains a high interest in regaining the Golan Heights. Following the 1979 Egyptian-Israeli peace treaty, the chances for a two-front war against Israel drastically decreased and Syria consequently embarked on a significant quantitative and qualitative military build-up in its quest for "strategic parity" with Israel, waiting for the political circumstances that would allow it to achieve its goals by force. Such a political constellation can materialize, particularly if tensions between Israel and the United States were to increase—a possibility discussed in the next section. The Syrian motivation and military capacity for engaging Israel obviously exists, while the political timing still remains an open question.

Additionally, Israel cannot rule out the revival of an "Eastern Front" to include Syria, Jordan, and an expeditionary force from a post-Saddam Iraq. Baghdad ruled by a different general just might be viewed again as a vital barrier against the hegemonic aspirations of Tehran and would then be accepted back into the "family of nations." At the same time, the rather cautious King Hussein might be replaced by a less conservative ruler. Such a coalition probably has no capacity to launch a successful blitzkrieg against Israel, but a strategy of limited war is definitely an available option to Syria, alone or with a coalition of Arab actors.

The political and material costs of such a strategy could be very painful for Israel. Limited Arab action would place Israel in the dilemma of whether to escalate to achieve a decisive victory, which might be very costly, or to limit its reaction to cut its losses, which leaves the challengers of the status quo unpunished. Similarly, a gradual violation of the demilitarization arrangements on the Golan Heights or in the Sinai peninsula could present a most difficult choice for Israel as to whether to respond militarily, as required by its deterrence rationale. Actually, the same political conditions that would permit Syrian aggression could bring about Egyptian action, particularly if a regime change takes place in Cairo.

In a worst-case analysis, the potential continuities in the patterns of Arab states' behavior or reversals to greater hostility toward Israel could pose serious challenges to Israel's security. Therefore, Israel still needs effective deterrence for a variety of actions in the wide spectrum of violence. But Israel is in a transition period, characterized by the potential of serious threats, as well as unprecedented potential for conflict regulation. (A more optimistic evaluation considers conflict resolution as a possible outcome of the peace process.) The main variables for Israel in this transition period that affect the potential for the establishment of security regimes involve the global transformation, the regional setting, and Israel's perceptions.

THE IMPACT OF CHANGES AT THE GLOBAL LEVEL

Upon the creation of Israel, the United States distanced itself from identifying too closely with the Jewish state because of its own interests in the Arab world. Yet Soviet encroachment in the Middle East and the emergence of Arab radical states allied with Moscow brought about a gradual change in the American-Israeli relationship, leading to greater cooperation. Indeed, the change in the American perception of Israel as an useful ally in its competition with the Soviet Union in the Middle East was one of the main factors in the increase of American support for the Jewish state.[15] In contrast to American behavior in 1956, Washington not only supported Jerusalem in its preemptive strike of June 1967, but have also allowed it to keep its territorial gains until the Arabs have shown a willingness to come to terms with Israel. During the War of Attrition (1969–1970), the Nixon administration encouraged Israel to administer heavy blows to the Egyptians, a Soviet client.[16] The changing perception of Israel as an American ally led to a greater understanding for Israeli security policies, which included the use of force to strengthen deterrence, although Washington's strategic calculations vis-à-vis the Soviet Union and its interests in the Arab world remained a constraint on Israeli freedom of action. Therefore on the eve of the 1973 War, Israel refrained from a preemptive strike because of American warnings resulting from the Nixon-Kissinger global policy of detente. Later, toward the end of the war, American pressure prevented the destruction of the encircled Egyptian Third Army.

Although considering American desires has been a constant feature of Israeli national strategy, the most feared scenario was an American-Soviet understanding on the Middle East that could have facilitated the implementation of an imposed settlement. Superpower cooperation in the Middle East has always been viewed with concern in Jerusalem. In contrast to the years of detente, there was greater tolerance for Israeli use of force during the renewed Cold War rhetoric of the Reagan years, which saw the June 1981 air strike against the Iraqi nuclear reactor and the 1982 invasion of Lebanon. The pronounced bipolar perspective to international affairs of the Reagan years increased the value of Israel and intensified the strategic cooperation between the United States and Israel.

The thaw in relations between the superpowers in the mid-1980s and the ensuing collapse of the Soviet empire put an end to the competition between the superpowers. The loosening of the bipolar system is sometimes heralded as having positive effects on stability and peace. Yet, the effects of the systemic changes on the Middle East are definitely mixed. It is true that Israel's rivals have lost the Soviet umbrella, which was a restraining factor for Israel. Yet it is not at all clear that Soviet disengagement has a negative effect on their capabilities, as Moscow's desperate need for hard currency leads it to continue to sell the latest weapons in its arsenal. The Czechs and the Poles are also in the arms business with less interference from Moscow than before. In addition, the breakup of the Soviet empire makes specialists in arms manufacturing available to the highest bidder. Some of this personnel might find employment in the burgeoning Arab weapons industry. At the same time, the loosening of the Middle East subsystem portends greater freedom of action for actors such as Syria, Egypt and Iraq. Once constrained by the superpower patron's fear of uncontrolled escalation, the regional actors can now pursue their own interests with less need to pay attention to the global implications of their aggressive actions.

Most important is a decline in the general perception of Israel's value as an American ally. In the past, an attack on Israel was seen by the Arabs as also challenging the United States.[17] An important component in Israel's deterrence was therefore its alliance with the United States. This amounted to a form of extended deterrence, an attempt to prevent an attack against a third party.[18]

The 1990–1991 Gulf crisis and the war against Iraq clearly demonstrated the problematic status of Israel as an ally. Washington welcomed the low-profile policy of Jerusalem and was particularly eager to prevent an Israeli military response to the Iraqi missile attacks on Israeli cities. The messages coming from Washington constituted the most important input in Israel's decision not to retaliate despite previous explicit threats to do so. The American Patriot crews sent to Israel were indeed primarily intended to restrain Jerusalem[19] and also to enhance American extended deterrence. They failed, however, to intercept the incoming missiles attacking Israel.

Israel's main source of leverage during the Gulf crisis and the ensuing Operation Desert Storm was not its status as a strategic asset to the United States, as Israelis would like to believe, but its nuisance value. Israeli "intransigence" in the American-initiated peace process could well lead to limited Arab military action, which could be viewed in Washington as understandable. Under certain circumstances, a Syrian stationary war of attrition or a limited incursion on the Golan Heights (like Egypt's attack in 1973) would not necessarily be regarded as an affront to the United States. Indeed, the changing international system could result in increased tensions between Israel and the United States and growing diplomatic difficulties for Israel.[20] The Arabs, as well as the Jews, understand well that Israel is unable to maintain its military superiority for long without the support of an extraregional power because of the huge asymmetry in resources when compared with the Arab world. Presently, Israeli fears about a gradual elimination of U.S. economic assistance are not unfounded. In a loosened international system foreign aid is under increasing criticism in the United States, and Israel is less of an asset. Furthermore, although Israel might have theoretically greater freedom of action in the new international era, Washington's level of tolerance for Israeli military action may decline. The need to preserve good relations with the United States would still keep Israel on a short leash.

On the other hand, the changes in the global system that have left the United States the only superpower could augur well for the creation and enforcing of cooperative security arrangements in the Arab-Israeli region. The structure of the international system is an important factor in the erection of security regimes,[21] for the main problems faced by security regimes are detection of violations or defections, that is, strategic surprise. Washington has played an important stabilizing role in securing and maintaining the post-1973 security arrangements between Egypt and Israel. As it has done in the past, it can provide financial inducements for participating in a security regime and assurances to minimize the risks taken by the parties in the conflict.[22] Actually, nowadays its hegemonical position allows the United States to impose sanctions for defection. Indeed, all participants in the ongoing peace negotiations hesitate to obstruct the process in order not to invoke American wrath. Similarly, Arab states reluctantly joined the U.N.-imposed sanctions against Libya in 1992.

Arms control is another area where the new American global status might have a positive impact. A not yet evident U.S. determination to curtail its own arms transfers to the Middle East and erect a suppliers' regime could prevent a destabilized arms race in the region. Though conventional weapons pose serious threats to regional stability, the United States is involved primarily in attempts to control the spread of nonconventional weapons and missile technology.

The United States can also perform the role of information provider to the parties of a security regime. It has done so in the past for the parties to the Arab-Israeli conflict. This is an important function in fostering cooperation among states.[23]

Yet the American role should not be overestimated, as the United States has neither the political will nor the imperial political culture to impose a pax Americana on the region. As a matter of fact, regional actors have shown remarkable resilience and great ability to maneuver extraregional powers according to their interests. A reduction in tensions and stability will come to the region only when the regional actors are ripe for it. Nevertheless, the systemic changes have had a negative impact on Israeli deterrence and its ability to act unilaterally, while seeming to provide a more conducive environment for the erection of collaborative security arrangements.

THE PEACE PROCESS IN THE REGION AND SECURITY REGIMES

Regional developments seem to reinforce these new trends that make it more difficult to exercise deterrence while encouraging cooperation in the area of security. Beginning in September 1975, a process of tension reduction was initiated in the second Sinai withdrawal agreement signed by Israel and Egypt. This agreement constituted a security regime on the road to the 1979 Peace Treaty. The resilience of the Egyptian-Israeli peace treaty, and particularly its military clauses, indicates to many Israelis that demilitarization and some arms control measures are worth pursuing. Similarly, Israeli-Jordanian coexistence seems to constitute an interesting security arrangement.[24] Israel has even achieved satisfactory security arrangements with Syria on the Golan Heights since 1974. The peace process has clearly enhanced Israel's security as it significantly lowered the military threat emanating from Egypt, the largest Arab state. We are presently witnessing in the Arab world a historic process of grudgingly accepting Israel as a fait accompli, although it is too early to conclude that this is an irreversible trend.

The emerging threat of Islamic fundamentalism could possibly serve as a common interest necessary for erecting a security regime. Similarly, the decline in the appeal of pan-Arab ideology could augur well for the Arab-Israeli conflict, which was often manipulated by Arab actors to score points in inter-Arab struggles. If the main Arab actors indeed move away from competition for hegemony in the Arab world and show greater inclination to pursue their statist goals, this might increase the possibilities for discovering common interests and mutual aversions, as individual egoistic behavior allows for greater cooperation than does competitive behavior.[25]

Yet the very process of expanding the number of Arab nations having better relations with Israel may also make it more difficult for Israel to exercise its traditional deterrence policy. There is an inherent tension between a deterrent posture and a conciliatory policy designed to lower tensions and eventually to achieve peace between neighbors.[26] To be sure, a strong Israel is a sine qua non for Arab acceptance of it as an unchallengeable fact, but Israeli military prowess and its occasional use of force could elicit in the Arab world traditional fears of Israeli militarism and expansionism. The problem is that restraint meant to reassure the Arabs of Israeli moderation could be misunderstood as weakness or lack of resolution. Israel has actually employed a strategy of reassurance to signal that the use of diplomacy could be more productive than the use of force.[27] Yet the Israeli desire to project an image of moderation in order to encourage those elements in the Arab world interested in a modus vivendi with Israel and its willingness to accept cooperative security arrangements can also be construed as feebleness. Moreover, acceptance of Syrian territorial demands, for example, could further narrow Israel's margin of security.

In addition, the peace process has hampered Israel's ability to militarily punish challengers of the status quo in order to enhance deterrence. Having paid dearly in territorial currency for the Peace Treaty with Egypt, even a Likud government (generally considered more hawkish than Labor) would have to consider the Egyptian reaction to any Israeli use of force against other Arab countries. Such calculations indeed restrained Israel from an all-out military response against the Palestinians after the outbreak of the intifada. Similarly, Israeli cabinet members voiced the hope that Israel's restraint during Operation Desert Storm would encourage Saudi Arabia and the oil sheikdoms to join the peace process. Such considerations are more prominent within Labor and dovish circles outside it, where it is argued that the use of force is counterproductive to Israel's desire to lower tensions in the area and to make progress in the political process. Laborites were critical of the Lebanon war on this account. Former Israeli Defense Minister Ezer Weizman opposed the air strikes on the Iraqi nuclear reactor (June 1981) and on PLO headquarters in Tunis (October 1985) because he feared these might hamper relations with Egypt. In 1985 he also claimed that such actions could interfere with the attempt to involve Jordan more actively in the political process. Despite the rather broad consensus for fighting terrorism with all possible means, Weizman, Yitzhak Navon, and Shimon Peres (all cabinet members) did not support the elimination of Abu Jihad in April 1988. This was partly because of the identity of the target, a PLO leader. Their greater willingness to talk to the PLO lessened their incentive to hit it.[28]

The contradictions between strengthening both deterrence and reconciliation in the Arab-Israeli context are amplified by the multilateral and multifaceted structure of the relationship that has evolved over the last two decades. Although most of the Arab world is formally at war with Israel, it has a peace treaty with Egypt and with Hashemite Jordan; it signed a declaration of principles with the PLO; it is committed to a well-kept disengagement agreement with Syria on the Golan; it holds on to a security zone in southern Lebanon; and it is occasionally engaged in a friendly or hostile dialogue with more distant Arab actors such as Iraq or Morocco. Israeli use of force is thus presently tied to a more complex matrix of costs and benefits than when there had been unanimity in the Arab world about conducting politicide, the destruction of Israel.

Despite the inherent tensions between reassurance and deterrence, it seems that a peace process in the Middle East requires an Israel that projects both of those elements. Only an Israel that is perceived as strong but not threatening has a chance to become an accepted part of the region. Furthermore, the peace process influences positively the chances for building a security regime in several specific ways. First, the unprecedented intensity of the direct dialogue between Israelis and Arabs and the broad scope of issues addressed sensitize both sides to the security concerns of each other.

Second, the peace process allows more reliance on regional frameworks and a lesser role for extraregional actors. In the area of arms control, for example, Israel has always preferred a regional approach rather than of involving international agencies.[29] Israel also regards such explicit regional arrangements as measures confirming its acceptance and legitimacy in the region.

Third, the peace process could facilitate the emergence of effective verification procedures. As noted, verification (sometimes called *detection*) is one of the main problems involved in the erection and maintenance of security regimes.

Fourth, when taking into consideration Israel's limited leeway in meeting the territorial demands of the Arabs, Israel might prove more flexible in negotiating the various elements required for a security regime. As a matter of fact, interim arrangements on Israel's eastern border are the most realistic goal for the present process. The peace process is important not because it offers peace—which it does not—but because it entails possibilities for the establishment of security regimes to stabilize or manage the conflict.

Another contributing factor in the search for collaborative security measures between Arabs and Israelis, one usually unmentioned, is the increased weariness of the protracted conflict found among all parties. It is, of course, not easy to prove weariness, but it is our conviction that this was one of the main reasons for the resolution of the differences between Egypt and Israel. Weariness in a protracted conflict leads the actors to redefine their goals. Pan-Arab energies seem to have dwindled, just as the ethos of Greater Israel is increasingly under criticism in Israel. In many instances, protracted conflict became susceptible to conflict management because the protagonists were worn out by their dispute. Quite possibly, the Arab-Israeli conflict has reached this point.

THE EROSION IN DETERRENCE AND INCENTIVES FOR SECURITY REGIMES

Finally, Israel may have to rely more on collaborative security arrangements because an erosion in its conventional deterrence may have taken place and because of the diminishing returns of its deterrence policies over the last two decades. The main factors behind a plausible erosion in Israeli deterrence have been discussed by the authors in detail elsewhere and are briefly noted here.[30] Several of those factors serve as incentives for complementing Israel's diminished deterrent power with cooperative security arrangements.

First, as noted, Israel's deterrence posture relies on its ability to achieve a decisive victory that would be very painful for the Arabs. Yet the Arabs do not necessarily regard Israel as able to decisively win a military encounter as previously. On the modern battlefield, victories similar to those of 1956 or 1967, characterized by a quick rout of Arab armies with few losses to Israel, are no longer expected. It is certainly plausible for the Arabs to conclude from their past performance that they can prevent a decisive Israeli victory.[31] Syria did just that in 1973;[32] and in 1982, despite its astounding losses in the air battle, Syria succeeded in preventing the IDF from reaching the Beirut- Damascus highway (its strategic goal) in the central and eastern sectors of the front.[33]

Actually, since the 1973 war, Israel has become militarily assailable in the Arab mind as the Arab world savored destroying the "myth of Israeli invincibility." Indeed, the Arab literature on the conflict with Israel shows that despite its defeats in the past, an Arab victory in a future encounter is believed by some to be within reach if certain lessons are drawn.[34]

Nor does the Iraqi defeat in 1991 necessarily indicate an Israeli ability to win easily against Arab opponents. Israel cannot employ its air force to soften resistance to a ground attack as did the United States. Past military engagements clearly indicate that a political clock is set in motion when hostilities begin, and a cease fire is imposed usually within a matter of weeks, not months, particularly if the Arabs are losing. Furthermore, an interpretation that the 1991 American victory was primarily the result of superior technology, which could augur well for the IDF with its clear technological edge over the Arab armies, is simplistic. The American victory was basically the consequence of a flawed Iraqi politico-military strategy, rather than the result of technological disparity.[35]

Second, after 1973, it became clear that Israeli military successes could not be easily translated into political gains. Even if Israel has the ability to win decisively, this could be irrelevant to ensuing diplomatic developments. In 1973, an *Egyptian military defeat* was followed by *Israeli withdrawals*. Post facto, the agreements reached in 1974 and 1975 can be regarded as the beginning of a process that led to a peace treaty. Yet, Israeli territorial concessions were then viewed by all to be motivated by American pressure. Similarly, military preponderance had little corresponding political value in 1982. The Israeli attempt to restore Christian hegemony in Lebanon, to limit Syrian influence there, and to compel Lebanon to sign a peace treaty failed. Since the 1973 war, the Arabs have recognized that losing a war does not necessarily mean a political disaster. Arab power was not great enough to defeat Israel militarily, but it could be employed to change the status quo and create more favorable political conditions to further Arab political and military interests.[36]

Third, as noted, deterrence is based upon the ability of the deterrer to heavily punish the challenger. It seems that the Arab countries have a vast ability to sustain punishment and their sensitivity to cost is lower than expected. The destruction of Arab military forces following an annihilatory Israeli strike is only a temporary setback. In the past, the Arab states have rebuilt their military machines with the help of the Soviet Union or the oil-rich Arab countries in a rather short period of time. In fact, the rebuilding of the Arab armies involved not only quantitative growth but also qualitative improvement. They were able to learn from their mistakes and plan operations taking into consideration their shortcomings.

The Arab states, like others, have shown great willingness to bear heavy costs to achieve goals deemed very important. Therefore, it is not clear that Israeli countervalue threats have much impact, particularly if the tolerance thresholds of Arab authoritarian or competing fundamentalist elites are rather high.[37]

Fourth, the appearance of long-range ballistic missiles in the Arab arsenals, some armed with chemical warheads, has somewhat balanced the tacit Israeli threat to strike with nonconventional warheads at population centers in the Arab world. Furthermore, the Arab ability to launch missiles against targets in Israel negates the IDF ability to prevent an air attack on Israeli targets.

The vulnerability of the home front is not a new phenomenon in the Arab-Israeli arena. Nevertheless, the period of Israeli control over escalation dominance[38] with respect to strikes against civilian targets was brought to an end in the mid-1980s with the introduction of missiles capable of hitting Israeli centers of population. The Iraqi missiles fired at Israel clearly demonstrated the effectiveness of limited missile attacks. The number of casualties was rather small, although the damage to property was considerable, but the country was practically paralyzed for almost a month, causing significant economic and psychological damage.

The emerging symmetry in the capacity of Israel and the Arabs to inflict considerable damage on each other's population centers allows greater Arab freedom of action because Israel might hesitate to escalate. A Middle East balance of terror—a questionable proposition in itself—could possibly eliminate the threat of a large-scale invasion of Israel, but threats of massive Israeli retaliation have little deterrent value against threats of attack at the lower levels of violence.

Fifth, maintaining a reputation for using force as threatened is extremely important for maintaining deterrence. Deterrence is supposed to work when the intention of the deterrer to use force when challenged is not in doubt.[39] In the Israeli case, since the 1973 war there has been a clear trend at the leadership and the public level toward greater hesitancy in using force against the Arabs. This trend began in the aftermath of the 1973 war, but it became more pronounced after the 1982 war in Lebanon. For example, elements within the Likud-led government and all of

Labor, then in opposition, opposed the air strike on the Iraqi nuclear reactor.[40] The debate around the concept of a "war by choice" generated by the events in Lebanon indicated that a large part of the current Israeli political elite refrains from supporting preemptive and preventive strikes.[41] The Labor party platforms since 1984 carry an article on the need for consensus when the IDF is employed, which clearly signals greater reluctance to use force. Yitzhak Rabin and Mordechai Gur (a former chief of staff and currently deputy defense minister) both preferred to threaten great destruction in the case of Arab chemical attacks rather than to suggest preemptive attacks.[42] This was typical of Israel's strategic thinking after 1973. With the exception of the 1981–1982 period when Ariel Sharon was defense minister, Israel has refrained from emphasizing preemptive strikes and has actually enhanced its defensive posture.[43]

The intifada, the Palestinian uprising that erupted in 1987, was not eradicated even after the establishment of a right-wing government in June 1990.[44] This government also refrained from using force on other occasions, such as in response to the 1991 Iraqi missile attacks and in reaction to the Syrian disregard of Israeli "red lines" in Lebanon, specifically the use of Syrian air power against the Aoun regime in October 1990.

The reduced emphasis on military force at the elite level is partly the result of a new perception concerning the nature of national power. It was argued by Shimon Peres, for example, that economic and technological progress are more important elements in a nation's might than military prowess. Also new is the greater attention paid by Israeli political leaders to the negative side effects of being at war.[45]

If the Arabs detect a declining Israeli willingness to use force, they might begin to question Israeli resolution to make good on their threats. The Israeli resolve to repel an invasion or to respond in kind to a war of attrition is quite clear. Less clear is whether Israel will decide to preempt, to fight to take back lost territory, or to escalate to punish the aggressors heavily in case of a limited war. The greater Israeli aversion to using force hampers deterrence, but enhances its readiness to enter a security regime.

Sixth, the latter part of the 1980s was characterized by a decrease in defense expenditures in almost all the states of the region. In the four-year period 1985–1988, several indicators such as total defense expenditures, defense expenditures per capita, and percentage of government spending and percentage of the GNP devoted to defense exhibit this trend.[46]

This trend of decreased defense expenditures leveled off in 1989 and 1990 and was reversed following the August 1990 Iraqi invasion of Kuwait. The events in the Gulf precipitated an arms race in the region. Obviously, Israel has difficulty sustaining an arms race and preserving a reasonable quantitative ratio. The need to absorb Soviet immigrants further reduces Israel's ability to divert financial resources to the growth of the IDF. As a result, Israel has a clear incentive for some kind of arms control regime for the region, particularly in respect to conventional capabilities. Indeed, Israel seems ready more than ever to consider ways to erect a meaningful arms control regime.[47]

Seventh, another reason for Israel's greater willingness to engage in security regimes is the distinct increase in the level of threat perception. In light of the peace process, a greater apprehension of hostile Arab actions seems to be paradoxical but it is not. Despite a perceived decline in overall Arab hostility, there is a marked increase in the capacity of Arab actors to damage the Jewish state. Israelis focus their attention on the advent of long-range missiles and have greater fears concerning the use of chemical weapons. The aversion to war constitutes a powerful incentive for engaging in collaborative security arrangements. If similar apprehensions about war develop in Arab countries—something not yet evident—it would facilitate the creation of a security regime.[48]

Eighth, it is not only increased threat perception that can lead Israel to a greater interest in collaborative security arrangements, but also the realization that some of the impending threats cannot be dealt with unilaterally. In 1981 Israel eliminated the Iraqi nuclear threat for some time. It is quite clear that Israel cannot repeat such a feat singlehandedly. As the Americans have learned in Iraq, it is difficult to destroy the entire nuclear infrastructure of a country. There are significant operational difficulties and probably the greatest barrier is a lack of sufficient intelligence.

Skepticism about establishing unilateral defense measures, such as an active defense against incoming missiles, is widespread in Israel, despite the present attempts to develop the Arrow anti-ballistic missile system. The technological uncertainty surrounding such a program and the traditional Israeli reluctance to rely on one-mission weapons amplify such concerns. Therefore, unilateral measures are perceived as increasingly difficult to implement.

All these factors lead to an uneasy feeling in Israel that unilateral techno-military responses are less available, and to a greater openness to explore alternative cooperative security arrangements. As noted, the U.S. hegemonic role in world politics and the peace process strengthens this search in several ways.

FROM DETERRENCE TO SECURITY REGIMES

The Arab-Israeli conflict is in a state of flux. It is moving toward reconciliation, though what we see is not necessarily an irreversible process. Although the parties to the conflict still consider resorting to force to realize their interests, the costs of war are climbing and its benefits seem to be in decline. Therefore, although the rationale of deterrence still has some validity, it is less satisfactory for meeting the security needs of Israel and its rivals. Indeed, several international and regional developments seem to lead to a plausible inference that Israel's ability to deter limited wars, in particular, has been hampered. The perceived reduced value of Israel as an American ally; the Arab perceptions concerning Israel's war-waging capability and its political utility; the renewed regional arms race; the increased Arab capacity to inflict damage on Israeli population centers; the growing doubts about Israeli resolve to use force; the constraints on Israel's freedom of action as a result of the peace process and its desire to maintain good relations with the United States—all indicate that Israel's traditional emphasis on deterrence has become less dependable. Effective unilateral military action has become more difficult because of political, economic, operational and intelligence constraints. The costly nature of the future battlefield has become a disincentive for military action, in particular for Israel. Concomitantly, the peace process entails promises for enhanced conflict management and the establishment of security regimes between Israel and its neighbors.

Although the region is not yet ripe for becoming a security community, where the use of force is irrelevant, the utility of military coercion is diminishing. The adoption of a mutually agreed-upon security regime with a strong U.S. role in it might be a promising venue for further reduction of tensions in the region.

The need for revision of Israeli policy is clear, but the direction and content of Arab policies is fraught with uncertainty. Whereas the changes in the global arena and the promises of peace require a more conciliatory approach on the part of Israel, with less emphasis on the use of force, the seeming erosion in its deterrence indicates a need for a more confrontational policy emphasizing threats and the actual use of force. Moreover, a security regime will probably be limited to only part of the Middle Eastern actors; others such as Libya and Iran will not join it. Fears of defection from a security regime could also discourage a more cooperative approach.

As the Middle East is still a region where the employment of military force is an acceptable tool of policy, abandonment of deterrence is not wise. Its enhancement is problematic, however, in light of Israel's quest for acceptance in the region. This tension has to be recognized by Israeli decision makers, as well as by the Arab states. A policy of Dr. Jekyll and Mr. Hyde may serve the Israeli need to be both feared and liked.[49] Such a policy contains many contradictions and can be misinterpreted. Yet, small and embattled states, situated in unstable regions, may not have the luxury of being able to choose fully coherent policies.

Deterrence requires the capability to extract costs and the maintenance of a reputation for using force. Therefore, Israel has to preserve a large offensive-oriented force capable of defeating an Arab coalition. This will not achieve the moderate image Israel is seeking, however. To do so requires the adoption of a purely defensive posture, which is problematic because it clearly undermines deterrence. Even if the IDF is successful in denying an Arab breakthrough on the ground, it cannot prevent the Arabs from bleeding Israel. Actually, it is impossible to organize a defense that will be entirely nonprovocative.[50] A dual defensive-offensive capability reduces the need to preempt, which is politically problematic, while it retains the option of being able to administer heavy punishment on the aggressor.

A posture intended only to enhance deterrence obviously will not convince Israel's neighbors of its good intentions. As noted, deterrence can be complemented by occasional conciliatory steps, though not without certain risks. Israel, for obvious reasons, must pursue a policy of tension reduction in the region. A position projecting a bona fide desire to reach agreement with its Arab neighbors through the American-sponsored peace process is helpful in this endeavor, though it might lead to pressures on Israel to further compromise its narrow margins of security by making dangerous concessions. A gradual approach emphasizing "confidence building measures" (CBMs) could be useful here in managing the conflict.[51]

Israel's national security is dependent upon the preservation of good relations with the United States. With the collapse of the Soviet empire, the region is now more than ever under the influence of Washington, around whom any effective security regime must be based. Under these circumstances, Arab violations of their commitments within an American-sponsored security regime become more difficult. American behavior is an extremely important factor in future Arab-Israeli relations, because the perception of a strong U.S. commitment to Israel's survival is the greatest incentive for the Arabs to accept Israel. As the American-sponsored peace process continues it remains to be seen whether the Arab-Israeli relationship will be able to move toward a stable security regime.

NOTES

The research for this article was supported by the BESA Center for Strategic Studies at Bar-Ilan University.

1. This term denotes the disposition of a group of neighboring states to resolve their disputes without recourse to arms. See his discussion of this term in Karl W. Deutsch et al., *Political Community and the North Atlantic Area* (Princeton, N.J.: Princeton University Press, 1957), pp. 5–7.

2. For a review of the literature see Charles Lipson's contribution to this book; the best-known work is Robert Jervis, "Security Regimes," *International Organization* 36 (Spring 1982): 357–378; for other aspects of international regimes, see Stephen Krasner, ed., *International Regimes* (Ithaca, N.Y.: Cornell University Press, 1983); for a discussion of security regimes and the application of this notion to the Arab-Israeli arena, see Janice Gross Stein, "Detection and Defection: Security 'Regimes' and the Management of International Conflict," *International Journal* 40 (Autumn 1985): 599–627; for a review of the literature on international cooperation, see Helen Milner, "International Theories of Cooperation Among Nations: Strengths and Weaknesses," *World Politics* 44 (April 1992): 466–496.

3. Jervis, "Security Regimes," p. 357.

4. Stein, "Detection and Defection," pp. 615–627.

5. The conquest of territories in 1967 was not a goal of the war, but a consequence of Israel's attempt to curb aggression and restore deterrence.

6. This term was coined by Yehoshafat Harkabi. See his *Fedayeen Action and Arab Strategy*, Adelphi Paper No. 53 (London: IISS, 1969), p. 1.

7. The concept of deterrence is methodologically problematic because ascertaining why the challenger does not commit the act that the deterrer tries to prevent is difficult. We are certain only when a failure of deterrence occurs, and even then it is not always clear why it happened. Furthermore, the perceived benefits of the use of force are the result of a subjective process of choosing priorities. Similarly, the willingness to pay the price for challenging the deterrer is related to the subjective evaluation of the intended result. Indeed, we have recently witnessed a comprehensive debate over deterrence and about the empirical evidence supporting this concept. See, inter alia, the special issue dedicated to The Rational Deterrence Debate: A Symposium, in *World Politics* 42 (January 1989); Frank C. Zagara, "Rationality and Deterrence," *World Politics* 42 (January 1990): 238–260; Richard Ned Lebow and Janice Gross Stein, "Deterrence: The Elusive Dependent Variable," *World Politics* 42 (April 1990): 336–369; and Paul Huth and Bruce M. Russett, "Testing Deterrence Theory: Rigor Makes a Difference," *World Politics* 42 (July 1990): 441–465. For a review of the earlier debates in the literature of deterrence, see Barry Buzan, *Introduction to Strategic Studies* (London: Macmillan, 1989), Part 3.

8. For an argument belittling the differences between the two sides of the debate, see George Downs, "The Rational Deterrence Debate," *World Politics* 42 (January 1989): 225–237.

9. For a recent reformulation, see Yitzhak Rabin, "Israeli Strategic Thinking After Desert Storm," in *Thoughts on the Concept of National Security* [Hebrew] (Ramat Gan: Bar-Ilan Center for Strategic Studies, August 1991). For works analyzing Israeli deterrence, see Yoav Ben-Horin and Barry Posen, *Israel's Strategic Doctrine*, R-2845-NA (Santa Monica, Calif.: Rand Corporation, September 1981); Shai Feldman, *Israeli Nuclear Deterrence: A Strategy for the 1990s* (New York: Columbia University Press, 1982); Efraim Inbar, "Israeli Strategic Thinking After 1973," *Journal of Strategic Studies* 6 (June 1983): 36–59; John J. Mearsheimer, *Conventional Deterrence* (Ithaca, N.Y.: Cornell University Press, 1983), pp. 134–164; Jonathan Shimshoni, *Israel and Conventional Deterrence. Border Warfare from 1953 to 1970* (Ithaca, N.Y.: Cornell University Press, 1988); Avner Yaniv, *Deterrence Without the Bomb* (Lexington, Mass.: Lexington Books, 1987).

10. For the distinction between deterrence by denial and deterrence by punishment, see Glenn H. Snyder, Deterrence and Defense (Princeton,

N.J.: Princeton University Press, 1960), pp. 13–14; for a review of the Israeli use of force see Stuart A. Cohen and Efraim Inbar, "A Taxonomy of Israel's Use of Military Force," *Comparative Strategy* 10 (April 1991): 121–138.

11. Yaniv, *Deterrence Without the Bomb*, p. 56.

12. The scenarios include preventing the capture of small pieces of Israeli-controlled territory, a stationary war of attrition, forestalling attempts to concentrate large military forces in proximity to its borders for long periods of time, preventing violations of demilitarization arrangements, and retaliating for attacks on Israeli targets within Israel and abroad by terrorists, artillery fire, or missiles.

13. See Shai Feldman, "Israeli Deterrence," in *War in the Gulf—Implications for Israel* [Hebrew] (Tel Aviv: Papyrus, 1991), pp. 170–189. For a view that Israel's nuclear potential was of little relevance, see Aharon Levran, "The Strategic Lessons from the Second Gulf War," in *The New Strategic Map* [Hebrew] (Ramat Gan: BESA Center for Strategic Studies, Bar-Ilan University 1992).

14. For the complexity of conventional deterrence, see Snyder, *Deterrence and Defense*, pp. 44–45; Alexander George, *Presidential Decision Making in Foreign Policy* (Boulder, Colo.: Westview Press, 1980), pp. 249–250.

15. A. F. K. Organski, *The $36 Billion Bargain: Strategy and Politics in U.S. Assistance to Israel* (New York: Columbia University Press, 1990).

16. Yitzhak Rabin, *Memoirs* [Hebrew] (Tel Aviv: Maariv, 1978), pp. 253–254.

17. Gabriel Ben-Dor, "Arab Rationality and Deterrence," in Aharon Klieman and Ariel Levite, *Deterrence in the Middle East,* JESS Study No. 22 (Boulder, Colo.: Westview Press, 1993), pp. 87–96.

18. For a sober analysis of extended deterrence in the Middle East see Janice Gross Stein, "Extended Deterrence in the Middle East: American Strategy Reconsidered," *World Politics* 39 (April 1987): 326–352.

19. In the alliance literature such an act is termed a *pactum de contrahendo,* i.e., an alliance to limit the freedom of action of the ally rather then to enhance his security. See Paul Schroder, "Alliances," in Klaus E. Knorr, ed., *Historical Dimensions of National Security Problems* (Lawrence: University of Kansas Press, 1976), pp. 227–262.

20. For the importance of systemic factors in isolating states and for the strategic implications of isolation for Israel, see Efraim Inbar, *Outcast Countries in the World Community*, Monograph Series in World Affairs (Denver: University of Denver Press, 1985).

21. Jervis, "Security Regimes," pp. 369–371.

22. Stein,"Detection and Defection," pp. 622–623.

23. Milner, "International Theories of Cooperation Among Nations," pp. 476–477.

24. See Aharon Klieman in this book; see also Adam Garfinkle, *Israel and Jordan in the Shadow of War* (New York: St. Martin, 1992).

25. See Stein, "Detection and Defection," p. 669. For the decline in Arab nationalism following the 1990–1991 events in the Gulf, see Fouad Ajami, "The End of Arab Nationalism," *The New Republic* (August 12, 1991).

26. For a general argument that deterrence could lead to fears and escalation, see Alexander George and Richard Smoke, *Deterrence in American Foreign Policy* (New York: Columbia University Press, 1974); Robert Jervis, *Perception and Misperception in International Relations* (Princeton, N.J.: Princeton University Press, 1976), Chap. 3; Ned Lebow, "The Deterrence Deadlock," *Political Psychology* 4 (April 1983).

27. For an analysis of such strategies, see Janice Gross Stein, "Reassurance in International Conflict Management," *Political Science Quarterly* 106 (Fall 1991): 431–451.

28. Efraim Inbar, *War and Peace in Israeli Politics. Labor Party Positions on National Security* (Boulder, Colo.: Lynne Rienner, 1991), pp. 135–137.

29. See Efraim Inbar, "Israel and Arms Control," *Arms Control* 13 (September 1992): 217; Gerald M. Steinberg, "Arms Control in the Middle East," in Richard D. Burns, ed., *The Encyclopedia of Arms Control and Disarmament* (New York: Charles Scribners' Sons, 1993).

30. Efraim Inbar and Shmuel Sandler, "Israeli Deterrence Revisited," *Security Studies* 3 (Winter 1993).

31. For a similar conclusion, see Yair Evron, *War and Intervention in Lebanon* (London: Croom Helm, 1987), pp. 186–187, 194.

32. See Hanoch Bartov, *Daddo: Forty-eight Years and Twenty More Days* [Hebrew] (Tel Aviv: Maariv, 1981), vol. 2, pp. 189–190, 195, 198–199, 209, 212.

33. On the war in Lebanon, see Avner Yaniv, *Dilemmas of Security Politics, Strategy, and the Israeli Experience in Lebanon* (New York: Oxford University Press, 1987).

34. See Muhamed Feisal Abd al Manam, "The Arab Deterrence and the Shattering of Israeli Strategy," in Emmanuel Sivan, ed., *The Arab Lessons from the October War* [Hebrew] (Tel Aviv: Am Oved, 1974), pp. 25–27; Shmuel Bar, *The Yom Kippur War in the Eyes of the Arabs* [Hebrew] (Tel Aviv: Maarachot, 1986), pp. 70–77; Avi Kober, ed.,*The Iraqi Army in the Yom Kippur War* (Tel Aviv: Maarachot, 1986) (this is a translated and annotated volume of a book published by the Iraqi Army); Mustafa Tlas, ed., *The Israeli Invasion of Lebanon* [Hebrew] (Tel Aviv: Maarachot, 1988).

35. Lawrence Freedman and Efraim Karsh, "How Kuwait Was Won: Strategy in the Gulf War," *International Security*, 16 (Fall 1991): 36. For a sober analysis of the technological and organizational dimensions of the Gulf War, see Gene I. Rochlin and Chris C. Demchak, "The Gulf War: Technological and Organizational Implications," *Survival* 33 (May–June 1991): 260–273; the Pentagon's Gulf War study indicates that the impact of smart weapons had been exaggerated and the reduction in Iraqi combat capability was the result of the tremendous tonnage of conventional bombs dropped on Iraqi positions. (*Washington Post* [April 11, 1992], p. A–12).

36. See Shimon Shamir, "Arab Military Lessons from the October War," in Louis Williams, ed., *Military Aspects of the Israeli-Arab Conflict* (Tel Aviv: University Publishing Projects, 1975), p. 175; Bernard Lewis, "Settling the Arab-Israeli Conflict," *Commentary*, 63 (June 1977), p. 53.

37. Ben-Dor, "Arab Rationality and Deterrence."

38. For this term, see Herman Kahn, *On Escalation: Metaphors and Scenarios* (Baltimore: Penguin Books, 1968), p. 290.

39. For a discussion of establishing reputations, see Thomas C. Schelling, *Arms and Influence* (New Haven, Conn.: Yale University Press, 1966), pp. 55–59.

40. See Shlomo Nakdimon, *Tammuz in Flames* [Hebrew] (Tel Aviv: Eidanim, 1986).

41. Efraim Inbar, "The 'No Choice War' Debate in Israel," *Journal of Strategic Studies* 12 (March 1989): 22–37.

42. Inbar, *War and Peace in Israeli Politics*, pp. 125, 132.

43. Inbar, "Israeli Strategic Thinking After 1973."

44. Efraim Inbar, "Israel's Small War: Its Military Reaction to the Intifada," *Armed Forces and Society* 18 (Fall 1991): 29–51.

45. See Efraim Inbar, "Attitudes Toward War in the Israeli Political Elite," *Middle East Journal* 44 (Summer 1990): 431–445.

46. See "Comparisons of Defense Expenditures and Military Manpower 1985–1988," in *The Military Balance 1989–1990* (London: IISS, 1990), p. 209.

47. Inbar, "Israel and Arms Control."

48. One of the conditions for erecting such a regime, according to Jervis, is the perception that war is too costly (see his "Security Regimes," pp. 361–362). For the role of common aversions to collaboration, see Arthur Stein, "Coordination and Collaboration: Regimes in an Anarchic World," *International Organization* 36 (Spring 1982): 304–311.

49. This concept was coined by Yehezkel Dror, *A Grand Strategy for Israel* (Jerusalem: Akademon, 1989), p. 131 [Hebrew].

50. Gideon Y. Akavia, "Defensive Defense and the Nature of Armed Conflict," *Journal of Strategic Studies* 14 (March 1991): 27–48. For a discussion of offensive vs. defensive postures for Israel, see Ariel Levite, *Offense and Defense in Israeli Military Doctrine* (Jerusalem: Jerusalem Post, 1988). He proposes a defensive-offensive posture.

51. For a discussion of such measures, see David B. Dewitt, "Confidence- and Security-Building Measures in the Middle East: Is there a Role?" in Gabriel Ben-Dor and David B. Dewitt, eds., *Conflict Management in the Middle East* (Lexington, Mass.: Lexington Books, 1987), pp. 241–259.

CONTRIBUTORS

Yaacov Bar-Siman-Tov is chair of the Department of International Relations of the Hebrew University of Jerusalem. He is the author of four books on the Middle East and the Arab-Israeli conflict, of which the most recent is *Israel and the Peace Process 1977–1982: In Search of Legitimacy for Peace* (forthcoming).

Avi Beker is executive director of the World Jewish Congress in Israel and the Israel Council of Foreign Relations. He has written *Disarmament Without Order: The Politics of Disarmament at the United Nations* and *The United Nations and Israel* and lectures on international security and foreign policy at Bar-Ilan University.

Gil Feiler is senior lecturer in Middle Eastern economics at Bar-Ilan University and a senior researcher at the BESA Center for Strategic Studies. He is also a consultant to Info-Prod Research, Ltd., which provides investment advice to firms dealing in the Middle East, including the West Bank and Gaza Strip.

Adam Garfinkle is a resident scholar at the Foreign Policy Research Institute in Philadelphia and a contributing editor to the institute's journal, *Orbis*. His most recent books are *Israel and Jordan in the Shadow of War* and *The Devil and Uncle Sam: A User's Guide to the Friendly Tyrants Problem.*

Efraim Inbar is associate professor of political science in the Department of Political Studies at Bar-Ilan University and director of the university's BESA Center for Strategic Studies. He has written extensively on Israeli foreign affairs and national security issues and is the author of *Outcast Countries in the World Community* and *War and Peace in Israeli Politics*.

Aharon Klieman is professor of international relations and former chair of the Department of Political Science at Tel Aviv University and a senior research associate at the BESA Center for Strategic Studies. Presently at the University of Chicago during the 1994–

95 academic year, he is the author of *Israel's Global Reach: Arms Sales as Diplomacy,* and *Israel and the World after Forty Years,* as well as co-author of *Rearming Israel: Defense Procurement Through the 1990s,* and *The Gulf Crisis and Its Global Aftermath.*

Joseph Kostiner is a senior research associate at the Moshe Dayan Center for Middle Eastern and African Studies at Tel Aviv University and a senior lecturer in the university's Department of Middle Eastern and African History. Having written widely on the modern history of Arabia and the Gulf, his two most recent books are *South Yemen's Revolutionary Strategy* and *The Making of Saudi Arabia from Chieftaincy to Monarchical State 1916–1936.*

Charles Lipson is an associate professor of political science at the University of Chicago, chair of the Committee on International Relations, and founding director of PIPES, the University of Chicago's Program on International Politics, Economics and Security. His publications include *Standing Guard: Protecting Foreign Capital in the Nineteenth and Twentieth Centuries.*

Robert J. Leiber is professor and chair of the Department of Government at Georgetown University. He is the author of six books, including *No Common Power: Understanding International Relations*, *The Oil Decade* and *Eagle in a New World: American Grand Strategy in the Post-Cold War Era*, his latest book, of which he is co-editor with Kenneth Oye and Donald Rothchild.

Bruce Maddy-Weitzman is a senior research associate at the Moshe Dayan Center for Middle Eastern and African Studies at Tel Aviv University. He is the author of *The Crystallization of the Arab State System 1945–54*, and has contributed articles on inter-Arab politics and North African Affairs to *Orbis*, *Middle Eastern Studies* and *Middle Eastern Contemporary Survey.*

Amikam Nachmani is a senior lecturer in the Department of Political Studies at Bar-Ilan University. His published works include *Great Power Discord in Palestine: The Anglo-American Committee of Inquiry into the Problem of European Jewry in Palestine, 1945–46*, *Israel, Turkey and Greece: Uneasy Relations in the East Mediterranean* and *International Intervention in the Greek Civil War: The United Nations Special Committee in the Balkans, 1947–52.*

Shmuel Sandler is associate professor of political science in the Department of Political Studies at Bar-Ilan University and heads the university's Center for International Communications and Policy. He is author of *State of Israel, the Land of Israel—Statist and Ethnonational Dimensions of Foreign Policy.*

Gerald M. Steinberg is senior lecturer in political science in the Department of Political Studies at Bar-Ilan University and a member of the university's BESA Center for Strategic Studies. Among his numerous articles on arms control are "Arms Control and Regional Security in the Middle East: A Realistic Approach," in *Survival*, and "Israeli Responses to the Iraqi Chemical Threat," in *Armed Forces in Society.*

Eyal Zisser is a research fellow at the Moshe Dayan Center for Middle Eastern and African Studies and a lecturer in the university's Department of Middle Eastern and African History. His articles on Syria and Lebanon have appeared in various journals including *Middle Eastern Contemporary Survey*, *Middle Eastern Studies* and *Orient*.

INDEX